Crosses & Comforts

D1500751

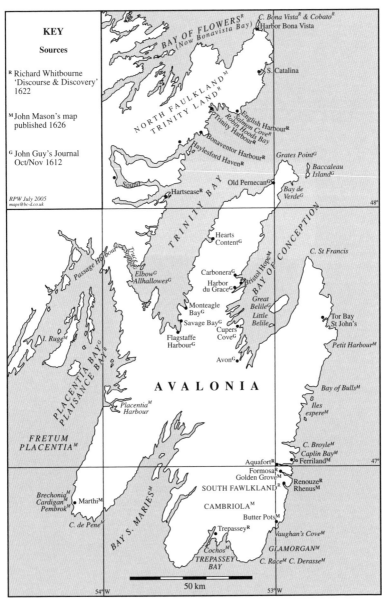

BAY OF FLOWERS[R]
(Now Bonavista Bay)

C. Bona Vista[R] & Cobato[R]
Harbor Bona Vista[R]

S. Catalina

NORTH FAULKLAND[M]
TRINITY LAND[R]

English Harbour[R]
Salmon Cove[R]
Robin Hoods Bay
Trinity Harbour[R]
Bonaventor Harbour[R]
Haylesford Haven[R]

Grates Point[G]

Baccaleau
Island[G]

Sound

Hartsease[R]

Old Pernecan[G]

Bay de
Verde[G]

48°

TRINITY BAY

Hearts
Content[G]

C. St Francis

Passage Harbour[R]

Trinity[R]

Elbow[G]
Allhallowes[G]

Carbonera[G]

Harbor
du Grace[G]

BAY OF CONCEPTION

Bristol Hope[M]

Great
Belile[G]

Monteagle
Bay[G]

Savage Bay[G]

Little
Belile[G]

Tor Bay
St John's

I. Ruge[M]

Flagstaffe
Harbour[G]

Cupers
Cove[G]

Petit Harbour[M]

Avon[G]

A V A L O N I A

PLACENTIA BAY[G]
PLAISANCE BAY[R]

Bay of Bulls[M]

Iles
espere[M]

Placentia[M]
Harbour

**FRETUM
PLACENTIA[M]**

C. Broyle[M]
Caplin Bay[M]
Ferriland[M]

Aquafort[R]

47°

Formosa[R]
Golden Grove[R]

Renouze[R]
Rhenus[M]

Brechonia[M]
Cardigan[M]
Pembrok[M]

Marthi[M]

SOUTH FAWLKLAND[R]

CAMBRIOLA[M]

Butter Pots[M]

C. de Pene

BAY S. MARIES[M]

Vaughan's Cove[M]

Trepassey[R]

GLAMORGAN[M]

Cochos[M]
**TREPASSEY
BAY**

C. Race[M] C. Derasse[M]

54° W

50 km

53° W

*Map of Avalon Peninsular and Trinity Bay, Newfoundland
with Early Stuart place names*

Crosses & Comforts

being
The Life and Times of

Captain Sir Richard Whitbourne
(1561-1635)
of Exmouth in Devonshire

by
Richard Whidborne

GREAT AUK BOOKS – St John's, Newfoundland

First published in 2005 Great Britain by
Great Auk Books

© Richard Whidborne 2005

The right of Richard Whidborne to be identified as the author of
this work has been asserted by him in accordance with the
Copyright, Designs and Patents Act 1988.

ISBN 0 -9549655-0-7

Printed in Great Britain by
Short Run Press Ltd, Exeter, Devon.

This book is dedicated to my wife,
Jean

'Truth has as many coats as an onion and each one of them hollow when you peel it off.'

Helen Wadell in 'Peter Abelard'.

Contents

Illustrations and Texts

Preface

'I may well say that my life hath beene a mixture of crosses and comforts, wherein neverthelesse they have not been so equally ballanced, but that the one hath ouerweighted the other.'

Richard Whitbourne – His Preface

Like Topsy, this book just grew, with a gestation period of several decades. It was never intended to be either a biography or a history. For one thing, too little is known for certain about Richard Whitbourne's personal life, his wife, children or his home: for the other, I leave that to historians, for I trained as a civil engineer and I have but slight knowledge of the times – Richard was born in 1561 and died in 1635 – or of the places – East Devon and Newfoundland – needed for such scholarly study.

Over the years I have fossicked around in libraries and local study centres, dipped into books and trod some of the ground that Richard knew. I have uncovered many surprising and curious incidents derived from Richard's life and his book, "A Discourse and Discovery of New-found-land." From the moment of conception, the coin of his luck would land either way – like us all. Did the outrageously disastrous really outweigh the good fortune? You, the reader, may judge. What I have found most fascinating is the outcome of these accidents of time and place and their consequences and their influences on Richard.

I first became interested in my ancestral namesake in 1954. On completing a three year contract with the Fiji Public Works Department, I took 'a gap year', thumbing my way around New Zealand and Australia before crossing the Pacific by ship to arrive in

Vancouver in May. I worked for three months as a 'roustabout' for a cousin who ran a skiing-cum-fishing lodge, 'Forbidden Plateau', in the pristine, remote wilderness inland from Courtney, Vancouver Island. Then for four weeks I washed dishes at the Banff Springs Hotel, with plenty of time to explore the surrounding Rockies. When the hotel closed for the winter I took the Trans-Canadian railroad, with several stops en route, arriving at the end of the line at North Sydney, Nova Scotia early on the morning of Monday 30 October 1954.

Leaden skies, sombre streets, closed shops and long faces greeted me on leaving the station. It seemed that the well beloved, popular but lamented, mayor was to be buried that afternoon. My plan had been to take the nightly ferry to Port-aux-Basques at the south-west tip of Newfoundland, and then the train to St John's, where I should arrive mid-day on Wednesday. On enquiring at the tourist centre, I was shattered to learn that there would be no ferry that night, this being the day the winter timetable started. It meant that I would have barely twenty four hours in St John's before leaving for my Trans-Atlantic flight home from Gander. The prospect of an extra day in North Sydney was not a happy one. With only $42 in my pocket I went to the Airways office. Yes! – there was a plane that afternoon, ticket priced $39, but no! – the flight was fully booked. I had hardly left the building, resigned to my fate, when the attendant hurried after me to say that he had just had a cancellation for the two o'clock plane. I paid cash for the ticket there and then.

In those post-war days, there was no way to get funds from England. Although only $3 was left in my pocket, I was not worried since a college friend, David, had promised me a bed in St John's. I went without lunch, hitched seven miles to the airfield. On checking in, my luggage was found to be overweight. I had to don my heavy boots and shed some junk. As we became airborne, the weather closed in and it was murky and very wet when, an hour later, we touched down at Tor Bay airport, five miles out of St John's. By the time I had searched for my mislaid baggage ticket and tried, fruitlessly, to phone David, I was down to seventy one cents. All the taxis had gone. So I approached the first car about to leave the forecourt. It was a very posh limousine. The driver agreed to drop me in town, explaining that he was chauffeur to 'Joey' – the Hon. Joseph R Smallwood – Newfoundland's Premier, who had just departed for Halifax on the same plane that I had come on. 'What an appropriate arrival,' I thought, 'for the namesake and descendant of Captain Sir Richard Whitbourne., one of the island's first governors, and the author of a book on Newfoundland published by the authority of King James the First.' A minor 'Worthy of Devon', he had been in St John's to witness the birth of the British Empire when Sir Humphrey Gilbert planted the English flag here in 1583.

I had no difficulty in finding David and his new wife, Joanne, and they cared for me until the Saturday – having missed my Super Constellation aircraft when it decided to fly before its appointed time and I was put on the following day's flight. It was time enough in which to discover how warm-hearted and welcoming the Newfoundlander is, and of the considerable respect there is there still for my Richard. There was even a railway junction named after him, but since the track was pulled up many years ago, the railway station now serves as a museum.

The next day, David had to go to the Memorial University College. I went with him and there met Agnes O'Dea, a library assistant who waxed enthusiastically when she learnt who I was. She showed me the University's copy of Richard's book, amongst other treasures, and after work took me on a tour round the town. I met the President of the Historical Society, Robert Furlong, a very pleasant and knowledgeable lawyer. Through him it was arranged that I should make a short broadcast on the local radio station, which he kindly introduced. I also enjoyed the local food – in which cod fish was prominent, the piece de resistance being cod's tongues. I was given a short tour out of town visiting Portugal Cove, where the traditional cod drying stages were still in use. It was all together too short a stay and I vowed to return at sometimes in the future.

Back in England, I had time on my hands while job hunting. I visited the British Museum and spent some happy hours in the famed circular Reading Room. I learnt much about what records and books were available there to help in researching Richard's life and times. I found the original draft manuscript for his book written in his well-formed and legible handwriting – unlike so many others of his day. I visited the Public Records Office in Chancery Lane to follow up several leads. I also visited Exeter where I found a treasury of local records that held the promise of hidden gems.

After ten weeks endeavour, I had failed to find any satisfactory employment, so opted to fly to Johannesburg where my sister was about to be married. After that I went with my parents to neighbouring Southern Rhodesia, now known as Zimbabwe. I liked what I saw and a feeling of optimism around at that time caused by the newly formed Federation of the Rhodesias and Nyasaland. I found work and thought to stay three or four years – an idea that was abandoned on getting married to Jean Brunton and starting a family. There was no opportunity to continue my researches from such a distance and it was only twenty five years later, after moving to Guernsey, that I thought again about old Sir Richard.

There were two very good libraries on the island, the Guille-Allez, a lending library with a substantial reference section and the Priaulx Library, with a fine collection of interesting titles from Caxton's time onwards. In the 1980s I resumed my studies both there and on occasional visits to London and the West Country. I found few personal references to Richard, and that only half a dozen of his letters had survived. There was very little about his family or his private life. But in his book trails begged exploration. For instance he claimed to have served under the Lord High Admiral during the Armada campaign, yet there was nothing in the official records to show any ship of his being present nor any record of his being paid off. It was a fascinating paper-chase. What I found out is told in Chapter 5, but there remains much room for conjecture.

Although Richard readily admitted to many blessings – his comforts – he felt them to be overweighed by the crosses fate piled upon him. Most of these were by the hand of a succession of pirates. First it was Peter Easton, a colourful and successful corsair who gets Chapter 9 to himself. There are many references to Easton, but many questions remain unanswered – about his background, how he came to be a pirate, the muddle over his pardon, and what happened once he retired to Savoy. Four more times Richard fell foul of nefarious ne'er-do-well pirates – two English, one French and one 'Turkish'. They have to share Chapter 11, where I just hope they wont start fighting amongst themselves.

Richard's claim to be the first Englishman to hold an English court in the North America cannot be substantiated by any official record. He was never compensated for his time and expenses, which might explain why no records have been found. The government, ever wanting in its search for ready money, tried to get the whole country to give towards his expenses for this, and for other services rendered, including the cost of writing his book, by way of a 'Royal Brief.' I believe it to be unique in the annals of governmental largess and no doubt went some ways to salving the Royal conscience (if it ever had one) but did little to help the by then impoverished Richard. (Chapters 10 and 14)

His story of an encounter with a mermaid led to a long quest for information on these alluring creatures from the dawn of history right up to the middle of the last century when sightings appear to have ceased.

Richard's life was dominated by fishing for cod, but I make no apology for persuing a fish of a different kind and hue in Chapter 13. His chance encounter on the streets of Lisbon in 1619 led to the unfolding of the remarkable story of the Nuns of Syon Abbey that stretches over a period of six hundred years. Richard's intervention added in a small way to a real life drama six years later – a drama about a scandalous play which was a nine days wonder in London – until halted by order of the king James himself. Essentially, this encounter also led to his audience with the king and the writing of his book.

I returned to Newfoundland for the first half of October 2001, three weeks after the 'nine-eleven' terrorist strike. The mass of stranded airliners had just flown out, with many thousands of passengers full of praise and gratitude for the help and hospitality give them by the Islanders. I spent much time in the Centre for Newfoundland Studies where Joan Ritcey and her staff were unstinting with their help. Jim Winter, of Portugal Bay, drove me to Ferrilands, where Jim Tuck showed me round the site of his impressive 'dig' of Calvert's settlement. Jim Winter also took me to Trinity where the late David White took me round 'his' treasure of a township, full of history and interest.

Jean and I spent all of June 2003 exploring the long coastline of Avalon Peninsular where Richard had spent so much of his working life. We soaked up the feel and ambiance of the shores and cliffs, harbours and settlements We made many friends and found everywhere unstinted help and kindness.

I have many people to thank for their help over the years including the late Nigel Walker and Brian Whitburn Brassett, who spent many hours researching the Whitbourne back-ground. The staff of many libraries and museums for their unfailing courtesy and patience in unravelling knotty queries. and besides Joan Ritcey, Margaret Rowe of the Devon Records Office was particularly helpful. Tim Earl did the copy-proofing and Catherine Stansfield the indexing, without whose help and advice I doubt that I would have ever finished. Malcolm Chambers read the drafts and gave both suggestions and encouragement. John Mitchell helped with his extensive knowledge on Easton and there were many others, too numerous to mention by name – excepting, as always, my ever supportive, long suffering and lovely wife Jean, to whom this book is dedicated

It has all been such fun and fascination – but not without frustration. I hope you will find what follows worth the reading.

1

Fair Child of Devon

'EXMOUTH. Near this castle, Ex taketh his last tribute, with a wider channel and curled waves, shedding itself into the sea, thereof called *Exmouth*, anciently *Exanmouth*, where, for the inhabitants' more ease, is a chapel erected within the parish of Littleham. Here (as Holingshed hath it) was sometime a castle, but now the place hath no other defence than a barred haven, and the inhabitants' valour. At this place was born Sir Richard Whitebourne, knight, whose adventurous voyages in discovering the commodities of Newfoundland and endeavours for the plantations and profitable fishing there, hath merited a general commendation of his country, and received honour of the king.'

Tristram Risdon – Survey of the County of Devon.

I grew up in the belief that Richard was an ancestor of mine and that he was born in Exmouth. It was many years before I discovered that I had been misled on both counts. Even the reliable Dictionary of National Biography accepted Tristram Risdon's unsubstantiated word for Richard's birthplace.[1]

Risdon amassed a fund of knowledge on Devon, its people and history. He was born in about 1580 at Winscot near Great Torrington, North Devon, and educated at Oxford. Risdon lived the life of a well-heeled country gentleman, travelling extensively throughout the county. He was a contemporary of Richard's and may have known him. On his death in 1636 he left a large and scholarly manuscript of his life's work entitled: The Chorographical Description, or Survey of the County of Devon with the City and County of Exeter: Containing Matter of History, Antiquity, Chronology, the

IMMEDIATE FAMILY OF JOHN WHIDBORNE (c.1535 –1597[B/WT])*.
Yeoman of Coombe Farm, Bishopsteighton

BY FIRST MARRIAGE TO: (?) AGNES ? (? –1570[B])

RICHARD of Exmouth.(1561[B] – 1635[WT])
Kt: Merchant: Ships Captain, Author:
Inherited House in E Teighnnmouth:
House Exsome in Dawlish: Residue
of estate: (Sole Executor)
M: (?) JOANE (? –1620[L])

— ? —— **DOROTHY [Whidbourn]**(? - ?)
M: (1606[L]) JOHN CROOT (? - ?)

— **KATHERINE** (? - ?)
M. (1613[B]) WILLIAM HELE, (? - ?),
Vicar of Bishopsteignton

WILLIAM (1563[B]-1563[B])

JOANE.1. (1565[B]– ?1626)
Inherited Kingsdown & Haywood Park
dwelling in Bishopsteignton: I heifer:
pewter dishes, etc.
M: (1583[BC]) THOMAS CORNELIUS (? - ?)

— **2 SONS.**
— *Each inherited 1 sheep*

JOHN 1. (1570[B] – 1570[B])
Died at birth

BY SECOND MARRIAGE TO: (1571[SF]) RICHARDE SAYRE (? –1597[B/WT]) of Stoke Fleming

THOMAS (c1572-1625[+])of Ashcombe
Inherited Dawlishwater & Dawlish Ford farms, pound
Etc: Goods & chattels;3 heifers: 10 sheep;bay mare; etc
M: (1598[SSG]) FRANCES PERRYMAN (1581[SSG] - ?)

— **WILLMOTTE** (c1599-1670[A])
— **THOMAS** of Mamhead (c1601-1629[M])**
— **JOHN** of Holcombe(c16??-1667[A]}
— **JOHANNE** (1609- ?)

MARRIAN (c 15??- 1637[WT])
Inherited £30
M: (pre 1597) RICHARD BRICKNELL (? - ?)

— **THOMAS** (pre 1597 - ?)
Inherited 1 sheep
— **AGNES** (? - ?)
M. (1634 [WT]) NICHOLAS EMBLING.

JOHN.2. (c1573- ?) ? of Exmouth, Mariner
Inherited 2 heifers, 6 sheep mare colt, goods &
chattels.
M: (? - ?) ? ? (.? - ?)

— **GILBERT** (pre 1597-1612[L])
Inherited 1 sheep
— ? —— **ANN [Whitborne]**
M. (1613[L]) HUGH PARSONS

JOANE.2 (? - ?.)
Inherited 1 heifer, 2 pewter dishes.
M: (pre 1597) JOHN TOWILL (? - ?)

— **3 SONS.**
— *Each inherited 1 sheep*

WILLIAM.2 Away in 1597
To inherit £100 on return

KEY – DEVON PARISH RECORDS.
A – Ashcombe
B – Bishopsteignton
BC –   ditto -(Combe)
L – Littleham (Exmouth)

M – Mamhead
SF – Stoke Fleming
SSG – Shillingford St. George
WT – West Teighnmouth

*Ref: John's will. PCC 1597
PROB 11/90 (107 Cobham)
[+]PM Inquis. 22nd of James
**From whom the author
   Richard Whidborne descends

Nature of the Country, Commodities and Government thereof; with sundry other Things Worthy of Observation.

During the next 60 years, Risdon's manuscript was handed around the intelligentsia of the county. A number of copies of it were made and circulated among sundry gentlemen of Devon. Inevitably many errors occurred in the transcriptions and it seems that the original may have disappeared altogether. Unfortunately, the first version to be published, in 1714, was by a 'noted piratical bookseller' named Curll. He was careless in his transcription and in parts edited the work for his own purposes so that it bore little relation to the original. Consequently, blunders committed by the printer were wrongly attributed to Risdon, whose reputation suffered.

John Prince (1643–1723), another notable antiquarian of Devon, in discussing Risdon's work in 1693, had reason to censure some he knew 'who either to boast their own skill, which is not much, or to vent their malice, which is more, carp and cavil at this worthy person's performance herein'. After moralizing at length Prince ends by quoting the Latin poet Horace to the effect that critics should: 'kindly impart, if you know better things. If not, then use those which the author brings.' It was not until 1810 that new and accurate editions of Risdon's 'Survey' and Prince's 'Worthies' were published.[2]

That Richard had a house in Exmouth in which he lived for most of his adult life there can be no doubt. He was a churchwarden for the parish of Littleham with Edmond Day in 1589[3] and he was still living there in February 1626. However, surviving parish records start only in 1603. They give four relevant entries:

John Croot & Dorothy Whidbourne	married 1 Jul 1606
Hugh Parson & Ann Whitborne	married 8 Oct 1613
Gilbert Whidbourne	buried 30 Jul 1612
Joane wife of Richard Whitborne	buried 4 Sep 1620

Gilbert was the son of John, Richard's younger half brother, but it is impossible to identify either Dorothy or Ann with certainty. There is nothing to indicate that Richard himself was born either in this parish or in the other Exmouth parish of Withycombe Raleigh. There are several other kinds of records that help to establish where the Whitbournes originated, but Exmouth does not feature.

Today the clan is widely spread, except that there is no one listed for Scotland, Ulster or North-east England. Thus there seems to be no connection to places named "Whitburn", one situated between Edinburgh and Glasgow and another on the coast a few miles north of Sunderland, nor to a hamlet of Whitbourne in Herefordshire

Instead it is more pleasing to think that the name derives from the Old English, HWIT + BEARN, which means FAIR + CHILD.

With such an uncommon surname, tracing ancestors has not been too difficult – at least back to 1559. That year, in article X of the Queen's Injunctions, it was required that: 'the parson, vicar or curate, and the parishioners of every parish within this realm shall in their churches and chapels keep one book of register, wherein they shall write the day and year of every wedding, christening and burial made within their parish, and also therein write every person's name that shall be so wedded, christened and buried[4] . . .'

All budding family historians who seek details of their ancestry, should daily offer a prayer of thanksgiving for Good Queen Bess and her immense foresight. It did, however, take many years before all parishes obeyed this injunction nor have all the early records survived.

There are scattered records of Whitbournes before then, nearly all from the West Country including some from Exeter. Henry VIII raised taxes to fight the Scots in about 1524 and again in 1544. Details of those liable to be taxed survive in the Devon Subsidy Rolls. In the first roll John Whytborn, husbandman, of Bishopsteignton, (a parish on the northern slopes of the river Teign, adjoining the port of Teignmouth) was rated as G6 with an income of £40 to £60 a year, with Thomas Whytburne, presumably John's son, rated as W1 – the lowest category. John Whytborn would have either leased his farm, known as Ashill, from the lord of Radway Manor, who was the Bishop of Exeter; or he would have been his steward. Twenty years later, Thomas Whidborn was in possession, with his sons John and Robert. By this time the Reformation had taken place, when the church was dispossessed of much of its land countrywide, including, in 1549, the little used, near ruinous, Bishops Palace, a quarter of a mile above Ashill – together with the rest of Bishopsteignton. At that time it was a small village of about 600 inhabitants within a largish parish of more than 4,000 acres. It was not until 1612 that the family was able to buy title to Ashill farm from the then owner, Robert, Earl of Salisbury, the Lord High Treasurer of England. It remained in Whitbourne hands until sold to the Comyns family in 1696.

By good fortune, the vicar of Bishopsteignton church started his register quite promptly, following Elizabeth's Injunction. One of the first entries was:

Richard Whitborne – baptised 20 June, 1561.

In the same parish Joane Whitborne was born in April 1565 and married at Coombe in 1584. This Coombe refers to Coombe farm that lay a mile and a half due east of Ashill. It is not to be confused with Coombe-in-Teignhead where, according to the 1544 Subsidy Roll, a John Whitborne lived.

From his book 'Discourse and Discovery of New-found-land' it is clear that Richard must have been born in 1560 – or shortly after. For a long time I assumed that this first Richard was indeed my hero.

It was not until 1998 that I found, in the London Family History Centre, a copy of the will of another John Whidborne, a yeoman farmer of the parish of 'Byshoppe Tainton'. Dated 22 September, 1597, it dispelled lingering doubts and difficulties, while at the same time creating new ones. John bequeathed "my soule to Almightie God, my heavenlie father" – and his body to be buried in the southern aisle of West Teignmouth (St James). He made four bequests to charity, fourteen to named relatives and ten to servants or friends. Apart from gleaning many details about his life and possessions it has been possible to draw up a quite comprehensive family tree for John, his children and grandchildren, and to establish beyond all doubt that his first son by his first wife Agnes, was indeed the Richard mentioned by Tristram Risdon. The precise relationship of John to the Ashill Whitbournes cannot be established on the available evidence – probably a younger brother, or a cousin. In the latter case, his father was likely to have been John of Coombe-in-Teignhead.

Seven months after the death of Agnes, John married again. His bride was Richarde Sayre, who came from Stoke Fleming, a small village perched on the cliff tops south of Dartmouth, and about 20 miles by sea from Teignmouth. The village has no harbour, but there is a landing bay – Blackpool Sands – a short way to the west. The wedding took place in the high-towered parish church of St Peter's. Apart from being a place to watch out to sea for marauders, the tower also acted as a landmark for ships making for the Dart estuary. This five mile long estuary was a considerable obstacle to anyone travelling along the coast from the east. Almost certainly, John would have met Richarde before Agnes died. This adds strength to the view that John was not only a farmer but also had a boat that he used for fishing and, perhaps, for coastal trading, so making it easy for him to visit the many hamlets and havens along the coast, both to the east and west, and including Stoke Fleming.

There is no record of the birth of the five children of the second marriage who were alive when John died in 1597. He and Richarde were buried on the same day in West Teignmouth, and it is likely that they both died of the plague. It may be that John started a new home for Richarde, possibly in Dawlish where he bought several properties as is known from his will.

Although their eldest son, Thomas, born about 1572, was to inherit the Dawlish properties, it seems he was then already established in the neighbouring parish of Ashcombe, where he died in 1623. Besides two girls, Marrian and Joane (2), John and Richarde had two more sons, John and William. William was absent from home when his father died.

Richard, as the heir and sole executor of his father's will, inherited Coombe Farm, a house called Estdon in Dawlish parish, and the residue of the estate once the other beneficiaries had been satisfied. From this detailed will it is possible to build up a picture of the sort of childhood that Richard might have had.

Coombe Farm was situated close to what is now Lower Coombe House, the Goal-post Bar of the Teignmouth Football Club[5]. Coombeway, then a track, led straight from Ashill for about a mile and a quarter to Coombe. It went on down Coombe Valley to the parish church of St James', West Teignmouth, and to the Old Quay – a distance of less than a mile. Coombe was originally in Bishopsteignton parish, but, due to the town's expansion, West Teignmouth has poached it in recent years.

The remains of Sir Richard were interred in St James' graveyard in August 1635, further evidence of his roots. In his youth Coombe Farm consisted of ten enclosed meadows, parks, and orchards, totalling forty acres, along with higher unenclosed 'common pastures' on Maudlyn Hill and Black Down where sheep would have grazed[6]. John bequeathed eighteen animals to six different beneficiaries, indicating that sheep were the mainstay of the farm with a flock of about eighty ewes. The lane that leads upwards from the homestead by Headway

Cross to what is now known as Little Haldon Hill, is still called Shepherds Lane.

Life at Coombe was dictated by the changing seasons and varying weather. Over winter the sheep would be pastured on lower fields near the homestead. Sheep not in lamb were returned to the higher common pastures with the return of warmer weather. Lambing took place in the second half of February and March – a busy and anxious time for John and his shepherd, especially if the weather turned cold and wet. Shearing would be in late May followed by haymaking in June.

Judging by the first tithe maps, produced in 1840, that described two-thirds of the farm as arable land, it is likely that crops were grown by John on the exceptionally red clay soil. Oats probably dominated the crops, with wheat, barley, or rye whenever there was a demand. These would be rotated with peas and beans followed by a year with the field lying fallow.

A cow and three heifers featured in John's will, so a small dairy herd was probably kept to make butter and cheese for those living on the farm and any neighbours who cared to come and collect from the dairy. Hay was needed for the livestock and although pigs were not mentioned in the will, it is likely that a breeding sow was kept and the young porkers sold at market – except for the one or two which provided bacon, pork and sausages during the winter months. There would be poultry, a duck pond, and a vegetable garden. There would have been one or two working horses and the young bay mare that Thomas inherited, to plough, draw the work-cart and for use as pack animals. After harvest, there were the apples to collect and take over to the cider press at Ashill. Then there was firewood to cut and store, and hedges to be trimmed or laid, usually before Christmas.

Richard's practical education started from the age of about five with simple tasks, such as feeding the hens and collecting their eggs, weeding the vegetable patch and, on occasions, looking after his sister, four years his junior. A year or two later he would have the responsibility of minding the flock on the common pasture whenever the shepherd was needed for other work. With only the sheepdog for company he would be alone with the flock and the sky on the wild moors of Black Down and Maudlyn, seven hundred feet above the sea.

He would go round checking that all of the flock were present.

Coombe farm seems not to have used the normal method of 'signing' the sheep, as it was called in Devon. Instead of marking the coat with redle (red lead) Richard wrote that the animals were **'sined in the eares with severall markes, as is used in England on Sheepes, and other beasts'**. He would also check to see that there were any wounded or sickly animals. 'Liver rot' was greatly feared for it could soon spread through a flock and the so-called cures to be found for this and other ailments in the Almanacks and Prognostications of the times, seldom proved reliable.[7]

In fine weather he might have sat amid the gorse and heather gazing out to sea and at the entire Devon – Dorset coastline, visible as far as Portland Bill fully 50 miles due east. But when the skies darkened and the wind rose to a storm he huddled under the nearest shelter with his flock close by and watched the cloudbursts sweep across the moor. Then he would be reminded of a bogeyman, the wicked monk of Lidwell who was said to have lured travellers from the moor to a chapel not two hundred yards over the brow of Haldon Hill. There he murdered them, taking all they had before throwing their bodies down the well set in the middle of the chapel.[8]

At his young age Richard would be unsure whether to believe this gruesome tale and his stepmother's threat that, if he did not mind the flock closely, the wicked monk would come after him.

Sugar grown in the Portuguese Atlantic islands first made a sporadic appearance on the tables of the rich at about this time. For ordinary country folk there was only honey. One imagines that many hives were kept in Devon, if only because the moors, meadows and orchards were filled with nectar that the bees gathered so busily. Hives – known as skeps – were either woven from willow and hazel or else from rope-like strands of bound straw, coiled into a dome shape. Neither kind was weatherproof. A plaster coat of mud and cow's dung, known as 'clooning', or a conical hat of straw, offered some protection.

In Devon, 'bee-boles' were sometimes used, particularly where walls were made of cob. This is a form of adobe using stiff clay reinforced with chopped straw, in which dung, lime ash or pebbles were mixed as available. Walls, roughly three foot thick, were built up without a framework. A few hollow, arched, 'boles', each big enough to house a skep, were often formed as building proceeded, as also were "pigeon holes". (See the photo of Ashill Farmstead). Oddly, there has been little written, either then or later, about honey's place in diet or economy, nor does it appear in the surviving household accounts, as one might expect.[9]

On the farm there would nearly always be something of interest going on to keep Richard out of mischief, besides never-ending chores. Doubtless he occasionally took time off to go bird nesting or to fish in brook or pond. He would accompany his father to market which was held in Teignmouth every Sunday until forbidden in the time of Henry III. According to Risdon, 'the Sheriff of the shire was commanded to raise the posse comitatus to suppress the same' but he does not say if the market continued on some other day. There was a much-frequented fair every Michaelmas, however. In good years at least this was the occasion to celebrate the harvest home with cider or ale and to make merry.

The family would be required to attend John the Baptist parish church in Bishopsteignton every Sunday. When the Coombeway track became impassably muddy in winter, they might have attended the much closer St James' of West Teighmouth. The family was content just to obey the Church's requirements like the god-fearing folk that they were, for John and Agnes were never likely to forget the dreaded days when Mary reigned and Protestants became charred martyrs with sickening regularity. Just three years before Richard's birth, Mary died and was succeeded by the young Elizabeth. Religious fervour abated and bible-lessons in church were at last read in English. If John could read, and a man in his position surely would, the first book he owned must have been the bible. Richard would have learned all the familiar bible stories from his parents. He may have attended a small local 'dame school' when not required to help on the farm but his formal education would have been scanty. It is more likely that his parents taught him basic reading, writing and arithmetic.

So it seems that as he grew older Richard's knowledge and farming skills increased steadily, fitting him to take over from his father. But things did not turn out that way and perhaps here is a case of the child being father to the man. Perhaps when John took him out fishing on the boat Richard's imagination and enthusiasm were fired by the sea, its beauty, power and ever changing moods, the salty wind on his small face, and the challenge of pulling fish from below its turbulent surface. He soon learned to handle the single-sailed boat, judge the tides and currents, know where danger lurked and how to find navigation-marks. Meanwhile, on the quaysides, the talk was not of the price of wethers and wool, but of fish and the fortunes to be made by voyaging further afield, not least to the 'new-found-land' which lay two thousand leagues beyond the western horizon.

Ashill Farm, Bishopsteignton – A Devonshire Long House

The house is thought to have been built around 1400 AD. The thick walls are made of 'cob', a stiff mixture of clay and chopped straw. The thatched roof is supported on elm rafters, some still in good condition after six hundred years. Originally, there was no chimney and the ground floor was open to the roof. During renovations thirty years ago, smoke blackened thatch was uncovered. Note the two 'pigeon holes' built into the wall to the right.

Until mid 16th century the left end of the house was used to stable the farm animals, that to the right of the portch by the farmers' family. The Whitbournes occupied the house continuously for close on two hundred years, until 1696. They added the first floor, built in chimneys and stair-cases and partitioned the house into rooms. The work was probably spread over many years of the mid 16th century. Again, the timber used was mostly elm and the building stone came from the quarry, six hundred yards up the hill, close by the ruined Bishop's palace – or, maybe, it was lifted from the palace itself, part of one of whose walls is still visible; so too are the initials RW, carved up-side-down on a fireplace stone and JW, branded on a door.

Included in the farmland, were two enclosures, Pease Park (two acres) and Peace Park (one acre). Traditionally it is thought that, shortly before the end of the first millennium, marauding Danes, pillaging along the Teign river, met here with the local 'thynes' (fore-runners of the land owning barons) to negotiate the price of 'danegelt' needed to persuade the Danes to depart in peace.

Ashill long house is at present a guest house run under the name of 'Whidborne Manor'.

2

Learning a Trade

'And first for mine own poore estate and condition it is well knowne
that my breeding & course of life hath beene such, as I have spent
most of my daies in travel, in marchandizing & sea voyages, . . .'
Richard Whitbourne – Draft Preface

These were some of the first words written by Richard when, in his
fifty-ninth year, he started the draft of his book 'The Discourse and
Discovery of the New Found Land'. Reading his book and letters
today certain things stand out as unusual. He wrote with a cursive
script typical of merchants and secretaries at that time. His spelling is
surprisingly good and consistent, better than some who had been to
one of the two universities; nor are there obscure Latin quotations.
The grammar is good but the style, which at times becomes con-
voluted and muddled, can also entertain with delightful turns of
phrase. He could 'cast' accounts and had a good grasp of business
accounting as it was then practised.

At the time Richard was born, the yeomen of Devon, most of
whom were farmers, could just about sustain themselves and their
families by dint of hard work and frugal living. Forty years on, John
Hooker, long time Chamberlain for Exeter and assiduous chronicler
of the county, wrote of the yeomanry: 'and now of late they have
entered into the trade of usury buying of clothes and purchasing and
merchantises climbing up daily to the degree of gentleman and do
bring up their children accordingly.'[1]

Other contemporary commentators, such as Tristram Risdon,
Thomas Westcote and Adam Moore[2], were full of praise for the way
these yeoman farmers were willing to try out new ideas resulting in a

marked improvement to their land, its products and yields. 'A marvelose metamorphes' was how Hooker put it. Land holdings in general were not large, so when the already substantial trade in wool and cloth continued to expand, the growth of the flocks was limited. Many yeomen-farmers enlarged their income by cottage industry. Hooker found that 'wheresoever any man doth travel you shall find at the hall door . . . the wife, their children and their servants at their turn spinning or at their cards carding.'

One of the first acts passed by Elizabeth's government was to exempt fresh fish from the customs duty known as 'poundage'. The intention was twofold: to encourage people to eat a readily available nourishing food and to ensure a supply of experienced sailors for the navy in time of war.[3]

Devon, with its long coastlines and expanding population, where fishing had long been an important industry, benefited hugely. Coombe Farm was ideally placed for John Whitbourne to advance himself by fishing commercially. A mile to the south, down the gently sloping Bitten Valley, lay Teignmouth harbour. Tucked just inside the Teign estuary, and well protected from sea and storm by a long sandy spit, it was an ideal base for boats and small ships. Vessels up to 40 tons continued to use it safely despite Walter Raleigh's warning to parliament that it had become greatly decayed due to the silting of its mouth.

Twelve miles due north of the homestead lay Exeter, the largest town after Bristol in south-west England. With two markets a week plus several yearly fairs that attracted many London merchants, it serviced a large catchment area with all manner of necessaries in exchange for farm and sea products. It had a thriving and expanding fish trade. Fish would come from a stretch of the south coast one hundred miles long – almost as far as Plymouth. Some was shipped abroad, the rest distributed far and wide. Even merchants from Salisbury ninety miles to the east came to buy their fish here.

The straight track from Coombe followed high ground over Little Haldon Hill, crossed a saddle by Ashcombe, up and along the Haldon Hills to join the ancient Roman road to Exeter. Four miles short of Exeter lay Kennford, which today is a tiny village but was then a borough at a key junction and river crossing on the way into the city from the west. Fish dealers, known then as 'regraters', had long been doing good business buying up the fish as it came through Kennford, selling on either locally or in the Exeter market. But the freemen of

Exeter considered that it was their right to put a toll on all fish traded within a wide arc of the city and made regulations accordingly. There were many cases over the years of Kennford dealers being prosecuted in the Mayor's court, although to little effect.

Assuming he fished seriously, John could land his catch and have it in Kennford within four hours most of the year round. As the track followed high ground he could use the farm horse and cart except after the wettest weather; then he could use his horse as a pack animal. If the fishing took him east of Dawlish he might sail his boat up the Exe estuary, even to Exeter, or sell his catch at any of the many landing places along the way.

Evidence points to the eight-mile stretch of coast between the Teign and the Exe as the best fishing ground off all Devonshire during John's manhood. Pilchards had for long been a major catch around Plymouth. A warm period had set in and fish – pilchards in particular – gathered there in large numbers. They were caught using seine nets and the cured fish sold to France and Spain. John Hooker recorded the nets licensed for the year 1566. Of a total of 105 listed for South Devon, 37 were for the nine-mile length of coast between Dawlish Warren and St Marychurch.

A little later Risdon wrote of Teignmouth: 'their greatest benefit is the abundance of sea fish there taken, whereof the county is from there plentifully supplied'. At much the same time Thomas Westcote said of nearby Dawlish: 'here is plenty of fish taken which is the greatest benefit it has'. Some idea of the size of catches is given by the example of five fishermen of Hope near Salford further west along the coast. It was claimed that in 1583 they caught 900,000 pilchards in the one year.

The scenario that can be constructed for John, joined by one or two other boats – one often being his brother from Ashill Farm – was of fishing with seine nets, usually for pilchards, just off the coast. At other times, he line-fished for sole and plaice, or tried for salmon in the estuary. On returning to Teignmouth harbour, the catch was divided between the boats, John taking his share to the farm where it was gutted and cleaned, wrapped in wet cloths and packed into panniers. In this way it would keep fresh for several days. When he had a goodly load, he took it to Kennford, there selling it to such of the 'regraters' that he trusted to give him a fair price. He was certain to be back home within eight hours.[4]

Work on the farm was slackest from New Year till lambing time in March. It was normally just before Lent when the pilchards arrived off the coast in large numbers. With meat forbidden for the next forty days, the Ash Wednesday Fair in Exeter saw a huge quantity of fish traded and much money went into John's pocket. His expenses were minimal – scarcely any extra labour to be paid and not much by way of overheads. The main costs were in replacing nets, ropes and sails, and maintaining the boat. Often Richard might be one of the crew of three or four and would go with his father to Kennford, if not required for other work on the farm.

The last two paragraphs are conjecture with little real evidence in support. Yet they could explain how Richard came to be apprenticed to John Crooke, a shipping magnate of Southampton. The hypothesis could also explain how John was sufficiently well off by 1575 to make the considerable down payment for Richard's apprenticeship and to employ an extra farmhand during his absence. Why Southampton? Perhaps because it was the principal out-port for London and far larger than Exeter with bigger ships and more varied trade. Southampton was generally more cosmopolitan and up to date.

That there was a lively trade between Southampton and the West Country is shown by the following table of trade:

YEAR	1565	1573	1578	1588
Voyages inward to Southampton	13	17	8	10
Tons inward	193	275	107	196
Voyages outward	35	26	12	15
Tons outward	446	445	276	249

Nothing but tin and fish (undoubtedly cured) was brought in, while beer, salt, canvas, pitch, malt and wood were among the goods sent out to ten of the main ports between Exeter and Penzance.[5]

Few of these trips are to be found in the port records of the time as coastal traffic was not subject to customs. There are just two entries for Southampton ships in the Exeter Port books:- In April 1581 *Phenix* (Master – Jacobus Lophill) paid duty on eight cases of sugar belonging to John Croke; and in April 1588, the *Perill* (Master Johes Cormynge) arrived with a mixed cargo from St Malo. *Perill* was more accurately known as the 'Pearl', with a laden weight of 80 to 100 tons. It appears in the Southampton Port books between 1575 and 1582 as belonging to John Crooke and was employed in the French and Spanish trade. M*ynyon* of Topsham arrived from Southampton with three crates of sugar belonging to John Crook in January 1583.

Originally from Poole, John Crooke moved to Southampton soon after 1560 and quickly made his mark. Admitted as a burgess in 1565, he was Mayor in 1568 and again in 1581. He was one of the town's most prominent ships' merchants. Besides *Pearl*, he owned, at one time or another, the *Ayde*, *John Evangelist*, *Marigold* and *Michael*. He traded extensively with France and Spain and also as far afield as Danzig. When hostilities against Spain started to restrict trade in 1586, he engaged with others in privateering but without great success. He ended by arguing with Lord Admiral Howard over contraband and in 1591 was reported as 'having been a merchant of good wealth and trade and now decayed by losses at seas and other ways'. By this time he was constantly in trouble with the Leet and other courts, usually for 'encroachment' or not maintaining his ditches[6].

So it is quite likely that in 1573, when Richard was just twelve years old, John Crooke and John Whitbourne were more than passing acquaintances and made an agreement, sealed by an indenture, for Richard to serve a seven- or eight-year apprenticeship. No such indenture or other record has survived so we do not know what fee was involved but it certainly proved a good investment for all parties. Records of apprenticeships in Southampton do not exist before 1608, while those which may have been registered with Trinity House were destroyed by a series of fires in after years. Without doubt, Crooke exercised many of 'the mysteries and crafts of a merchant trafficking into parts beyond the sea' as described in the act of 1563 that regulated artificers, labourers, servants of husbandry and apprentices. There was at that time no sort of livery company to which Richard could gain admittance at the end of his apprenticeship but that was of no consequence in the raw West Country world of the 16th century.

Richard lived as a member of John Crooke's household, as was the usual practice for apprentices, and was cared for by John's wife Margery whom John had married in 1570 when she was the young widow of a John Caplin. They owned a farm 'beyond the Bar' on the Winchester Road called Holyrood, but doubtless had a town house as well. Crooke appears to have had two children by a former wife:

Michael was about Richard's age, and in 1585 master of his father's ship *Gabriel,* and a daughter. She married Edmund Caplin, who may have been her step-mother's son.

Richard was kept busy. Crooke had a chief clerk who would have given Richard his good grounding in writing, accounting and commerce. He would have learnt about a whole range of trade goods, their markets and prices, the weighing or measuring, and the legal requirements and pitfalls when striking a bargain. He learnt all about ships, their construction and maintenance, and their equipment, rigging and sails; how they were steered and trimmed, and how cargoes were loaded and stowed. He also learnt about taking soundings with the lead, keeping the log and working out the tides from Boussac's nautical almanac. There was a rope-walk in Southampton so he would have learnt to make up ropes and to cut and stitch canvas into sails.

When Richard was seeking employment many years later he wrote a petition (a sort of *curriculum vitae*) to the Duke of Buckingham in which he claimed he was '**a man fitt to undertake anie such charge upon him as it should so please your Grace to impose. Either concerning the overseeing of the orderly saltings and preserving of victualle, or the well baking of biskett bread and the tymelie and well brewinge of beere as also the fitting of sweet cask for the same, in which kind of imployment your Grace's supplicant hath had much and long experience**'.[m7] It is known from court records that Crooke was involved in brewing beer. Biscuits, along with salted meat, peas and beer (or cider for the West Countrymen) were the staples for long sea voyages.

In his Preface Richard wrote: '**I have been often in France, Spaine, Italy, Portugall, Savoy, Denmarke, Norway, Spruceland [Poland], the Canaries and Soris Ilands [Azores]: and for the New-found-land, it is almost so farmiliarly knowne to me as my owne countrey.**'[7] Only during his apprenticeship would he have gone to Denmark, Norway and Poland. Timber is recorded as coming from Denmark, cod and herring from Norway, with salt, pins, needles, hose and some cloth going to that country.

On these voyages Richard would first learn the duties of an ordinary seaman and later understudy the helmsman, captain and the 'factor'. The latter's job was to act for the owner, making all necessary arrangements with the foreign port officials, supervising the delivery or sale of the outward goods, and finding a cargo for the return journey.

When Richard was nearing the end of his apprenticeship in 1579 at the age of eighteen, he joined '**a worthy ship of the burthen of 300 tunnes set forth by one Master Cotton of Southhampton; wee were bound for the grand Bay . . .**'[8] that is, the Gulf of St Lawrence up towards Belle Island where the Basque had been whaling and sealing for 80 years or even longer.

The ship was almost certainly *Edward Cotton* which was lost off the coast of Guinea when bound for the River Plate four years later. Her owner was a successful merchant who was profitably engaged as the Collector of Customs for Southampton from 1575 to 1580. Later on, he was involved in acts of privateering, described as little short of piracy.

How thrilled young Richard must have been with the prospect of a voyage in such a large vessel, bound to a region of Terra Nova that was quite 'incognito' to the English. As an apprentice, he had no status within the ship's company, employed understudying the professional pilot who was probably a Portuguese of considerable experience undoubtedly hired for the voyage. The art of oceanic navigation was developed mostly by the Portuguese during the previous hundred years while exploring out towards India, China and elsewhere. The English frequently employed their pilots at that time.

Richard would have learnt about the sun, moon and stars, how to measure their altitudes and the part they played in fixing latitude. He probably kept the ship's log working out the estimated course for every half hour of the voyage at sea from the helmsman's report of speed and bearing. Because of ignorance concerning currents and magnetic variation of the compass (both of which could be considerable off the North American coast), navigation was still more an art than a science. Rapid progress was, however, being made in every department, other than for calculating longitude which had to wait nearly two hundred years until accurate chronometers had been developed. Richard would also have picked up a working knowledge of Portuguese, a further valuable asset.

Richard's is the only account of this voyage. In the preface to his 1623 edition he says that the purpose of the voyage was to trade with savage people living along the Labrador coast: '**for whom we carried sundry commodities, and to kill whales, and to make trayne oil, as the**

Biscaines doe there yeerely in great abundance. But this our intended Voyage was overthrown by the indiscretion of our Captaine and the faint-heartednesse of some Gentlemen of our Company, who loved soft featherbeds better than hard cabins, and longed rather to sit by a taverne fire, than to have the cold weather blasts of those seas blow on their faces. Whereupon we set sail from thence, and bare with *Trinity Harbour* in New-found-land; where we killed great store of Fish, Deere, Bears, Beavers, Seales, Otters, and such like, with abundance of Sea-fowles: and so returning for England, we arrived safely at South-hampton.'[8] Richard's apprenticeship closed when he gained his masters ticket – implicitly in those days rather than explicitly – soon after this.

3

Beginnings of Empire

'In a voyage to that Countrey about 36 yeeres since, I had then the command of a worthy Ship of 220 Tun, set forth by one Master *Crooke* of *South-hampton*:: At that time Sir Humfrey Gilbert, a Devonshire Knight, came thither with two good Ships and a Pinnace, and brought with him a large Patent, from the late most renowned Queene Elizabeth, and in her name tooke possession of that Countrey, in the Harbour of S. Iohns, whereof I was an eye-witnesse.'
Richard Whitbourne – Preface.

Sailing the ocean blue under the Spanish flag in 1492, Columbus discovered the New World (which, he remained convinced for the rest of his life, was close to China). Within a year, Spain had established a settlement on Hispaniola, the large West Indian island now shared by Haiti and the Dominican Republic. Henceforth Spain, in the name of the Holy Church of Rome, adopted a policy of explore, exploit and expunge. In the next forty years she conquered Mexico and Peru and all the land between them that bordered the sea. Any threat to her interests from the indigenous races was ruthlessly eliminated.

At the same time Portugal was opening up the sea route round Africa to India, reached in 1498 by Vasco da Gama. Malacca and Indonesia followed in 1509 and China in 1516. She established many trading settlements in the process. Portugal kept a stranglehold on this trade route for more than one hundred years. The Spanish Pope, Alexander VI, buttoned up the Iberian monopoly with the Treaty of Tordesillas as early as 1494. The globe was divided down the longitude of approximately 42°W, with Portugal having all new lands to the east and Spain those to the west. This did not leave much room for exploitation by the other European countries who, generally speaking, were less well organised and more involved in squabbles between themselves.

There was, however, a Venetian, John Cabot, an archetypal lateral thinker. In the mistaken belief that trade in silks and spices originated from northern Asia, he realised that the nearer the poles one sailed westward – or eastward for that matter – the shorter the distance to China would be. After failing to get backing for his ideas from the Crowns of Spain and Portugal ,he petitioned Henry VII, who granted him a patent to sail under the English flag 'East, West or North . . . and to set up our banner on any new-found-land . . .'

After a false start in 1496, John Cabot set sail the following year from Bristol in the fifty-ton *Matthew* with a crew of eighteen. Heading more or less due west he made landfall, in all probability, at Cape Bonavista, Newfoundland, where he took possession in the name of King Henry. He encountered no natives. After exploring the coast for several weeks he returned to England passing over the Grand Bank. His crew reported that fish, notably cod, were encountered in such abundance that: 'A very great trade in the fish they call stock fish from that country' could supplant the Icelandic fishing business of that time.

Well satisfied, King Henry granted him a handsome pension of £20 a year but Cabot did not live long to enjoy it. Setting sail next year with five ships he disappeared unto the blue and his fate has remained a mystery ever since.

Bristol merchants were exploring the western seas even before Cabot's appearance, searching for the Island of Brasilissa. They continued after his disappearance with expeditions in 1501, 1503, 1504 and 1505. They soon realised that cod, there in abundance for the taking, were just as valuable as all the gold from Spanish colonies. They were not alone and from those times Newfoundland's waters and the Grand Bank were profitable fishing grounds for mainly Bretons, Spaniards and Portuguese, while the Basques went in large numbers hunting whales in the Gulf of St Lawrence for their 'traine oil.'[1] Although most of the more outstanding English voyages of exploration were collected and published by Richard Hakluyt, records of fishing trips before 1570 are scant and only gradually did the fishing boats from the West Country switch from Icelandic to Newfoundland waters.

It was in the latter part of the 16th century that the English started to consider the idea of planting colonies in the wide empty spaces of the West. England's population was growing and prosperity increasing – but so was idleness, vagrancy and crime. Why not send the ne'er-do-wells off to the farthest regions, out of sight and mind?

Others saw the opportunities for trading with native tribes – at the same time saving them from the Devil by baptism into Christianity. It was a time when England was trying to expand her realm by force to settle large tracts of land in Ireland with Scottish and English immigrants. Although the Irish were largely able to thwart these attempts, natives of North America were thought to be more malleable.

Humphrey Gilbert, born probably in 1537, was one of those hoping to profit from such schemes. He was the second son of Otho Gilbert, a well-to-do Devonshire landowner, and his wife Katherine Champernoun of Kent. Said to have been a precocious child, it is believed that Humphrey attended Eton and Oxford. He then entered the service of Princess Elizabeth whose governess was Katherine Ashley, his aunt.

Elizabeth took a liking to the lad. When she became queen she employed him occasionally in a military role in Ireland and on the continent. He lived in London and at Court between commissions, becoming interested in geography, voyages of discovery, alchemy and education. He was astute in his marriage in 1570 to Anne Ager, an heiress from Kent. They lived quietly (one report says) in Limehouse with their six children.

One project in which Gilbert showed the keenest interest was a voyage to discover a northwest passage to Cataia (China) continuing where Columbus and Cabot had failed. He submitted a petition for a privilege to the queen in 1566. She was not in favour and sent him back to Ireland the following year. He revised his plans in a 'Discourse of a Discovery for a New Passage to Cataia' eight years later. Elizabeth was again unmoved although Gilbert's paper did help Martin Frobisher to get a licence. Several more proposals were placed before the queen and in 1578 he obtained from her long-coveted letters patent for the discovery and 'planting' of a colony of which he would be governor. Where the colony was to be founded was left quite vague.

Assisted by his young stepbrother, Sir Walter Raleigh, Gilbert set out in September 1578, with a fleet of six ships and provisions for a year. The enterprise was a disaster. Several ships deserted or were scattered by storms. The Spaniards were privy to his plans and laid a trap for him on his arrival at Cape Verde. Badly beaten, he made for Ireland only to have his licence revoked when he arrived the following spring. The queen had received complaints from the Spanish at a time when she was trying to placate them.

Gilbert was ruined financially and it took four years before he could gather enough backers to make a second attempt. Five ships left Plymouth on 11 June, 1583. Gilbert sailed in the 120-ton *Delight* (Master: William Winter) and Walter Raleigh in the 200-ton *Raleigh*. Edward Hayes, who wrote the well-known account of the voyage, was captain and owner of *Golden Hind* (40 tons) and Maurice Browne captained *Swallow* (also 40 tons). The 10-ton frigate *Squirrel* completed the fleet. It did not stay complete for long. Raleigh turned back after five days, his crew reportedly stricken by a contagious disease. Since it was late in the season, Gilbert decided to sail first to Newfoundland and then go south to explore the coast of North America.

The account that Hayes relates of Gilbert's expedition which 'began, continued and ended adversely' is long and detailed. It first appeared in Richard Haklyut's monumental 'Principal Navigations' in 1589. It is a good read and full of interest but here we shall hurry over much of the journey to concentrate on what happens when Gilbert arrived in Newfoundland.

They were beset by strong gales, much fog and contrary winds from the start. They did not make landfall until 30 July, probably in Notre Dame Bay, taking twice as long as normal by which time the fleet had split up. *Delight* and *Golden Hind* turned south following the coast until they reached Baccaleu Island where they met *Swallow* to discover that her crew had been indulging in a spot of piracy against the orders of their captain. On arrival at the entrance to St John's harbour, they were re-united with *Squirrel* which had been refused entry by the fishing merchants within the harbour. Gilbert sent a boat on ahead with news that he came in peace and with a commission for his voyage from the queen.

There followed an incident that doubtless drew some wry smiles from the hardy fishermen watching from within the harbour. Hayes puts it like this: 'and immediately we followed with a slack gale, and

ST JOHN'S HARBOUR, NEWFOUNDLAND

Illustration from 'The Naval History of Great Britain' by Edward Pelham Brenton. Published by C. Rise, London 1823. (Vol. I, opposite page 476).

Brenton wrote: 'The entrance of St John's harbour is only one hundred and sixty yards across, defended by strong batteries, one of which, called the Chain Rock, is but a few feet above the level of the sea: and as ships running in with a strong gale from the eastward are generally taken aback or becalmed in the narrows between the high hills, they become at once exposed to Fort Amherst on their right, the Queen's battery over their heads on the left, and the forts above the town with the Chain Rock battery in front of or a-head of them.'

Brenton records that, in August 1796 during the Napoleonic Wars, the French Admiral Richery, with seven ships of the line and three frigates, escaped from the blockaded port of Cadiz and cross the Atlantic. He was minded to attack the Newfoundland's capital, where Rear-Admiral Sir James Walker was commander-in-chief, but with only a single ship, *Venus*, under command. Her crew were ordered to man the guns guarding the harbour entrance, while *Venus* was moored across the narrows to support the boom and the forts.

Richery stood close in, and realised that if he once entered the harbour he would have to either conquer or submit. Instead he ran to the south, attacking and burning any defenceless settlement he came across.

in the very entrance (which is but narrow, not above two butts' length) the admiral fell upon a rock on the larboard side by great oversight, in that the weather was fair, the rock much above water fast by the shore, where neither went any sea-gate'.

With the wind in certain quarters, a ship entering St John's could suddenly find 'a slack gale' as it rounded the corner and entered the lee of high cliffs. An experienced crew was prepared for this but Gilbert's men were green and ill disciplined, as future events were to prove. Theirs was not the first – nor last – ship to suffer this indignity. There were 36 ships in harbour at the time – Portuguese as well as English. Whatever such a critical audience may have thought, they lent a ready hand and soon a number of boats arrived to tow the ship clear of danger.

Gilbert's fleet entered the spacious harbour on 4 August and dropped anchor in the roadstead. A party of captains and owners came aboard and learnt the purpose of the visit. Richard, captain of one of the largest ships, was probably among the group. The needs of Gilbert's vessels were discussed and orderly arrangements to supply these were worked out. The supplies were distributed equitably between all the ships present in St John's and neighbouring harbours, foreigners and English alike. Most of the foreigners appear to have been Portuguese, possibly assembling in convoy for their homeward journey. Hayes emphasises their willingness, indeed generosity, in supplying 'wines, marmalades, most fine rusk or biscuit, sweet oils, and sundry delicacies', in addition to those items specified.

The king of Portugal had died two years earlier without leaving an heir. Philip II of Spain was a legitimate contender for the crown but the Portuguese had no wish to become a vassal of their powerful neighbour. Philip had to occupy the country by force despite England backing the rival claims of Don Antonio, the illegitimate son of the Portuguese Royal House. Portugal and England had long been allies and it is noteworthy that English ships, when venturing into unknown waters, were often accompanied by a Portuguese pilot.

Gilbert set up his tent on the foreshore on Monday 6 August. In a ceremony reflecting ancient English custom, he took possession of Newfoundland in the name of Queen Elizabeth, along with all other unoccupied lands within a 200-league radius; had a rod and turf presented to him; promulgated three laws; gave title of land (of dubious worth) to several merchants, and erected a plaque. This last event seems to have appealed to the locals – Gilbert initiated a lively practice Newfoundlanders still have for erecting plaques to commemorate every conceivable historic happening.

Hayes mentions numbers of merchants in St John's at that time. He also says that the Admiral of the port, who was appointed to keep law and the peace, changed weekly. The English custom elsewhere on the island was that the first ship to arrive in a port became Admiral for the whole fishing season. It seems clear that not all of the thirty-six ships in St John's were using it as a fishing base. A considerable number of larger ships, including Richard's, must have been 'sack ships' which had come over late in the year to purchase 'dry' fish. This they would sell at a considerable profit in ports around the Iberian Peninsular and the north coast of the Mediterranean.

St John's commodious and safe harbour was an ideal rendezvous for fishing ships from the scattered ports around the coast of Avalon. In a good season, these ships would have caught and dried more fish than they could possibly carry. They could fish on for another month once a successful sale had been made. There would not be enough sun or time to dry this late catch which would be shipped as 'wet' fish packed in salt.

It is also clear that Gilbert's captains and crews were given the sort of welcoming hospitality for which latter-day Newfoundlanders are still noted. Even so, after two weeks in port, some of the baser crews concluded that there would be no joy whatsoever in continuing the voyage. Many stole away into the woods hoping to pick up a passage home on one of the fishing boats that departed the coast daily. One group high-jacked a ship laden with fish leaving the poor crew stranded. When a plot to take over another ship was discovered, Gilbert transferred the many sick and other malcontents to *Swallow* and sent her home under the command of William Winter.

The little fleet, now reduced to three ships, left on 20 August and after rounding Cape Race set sail for Cape Sablon, 400 miles to the southwest. Gilbert transferred to the tiny *Squirrel*, whose master had also shipped home. It was not long before ill fortune struck again. Early on Thursday 28 August, the rising south-by-east wind brought with it rain and thick mist. Visibility was just a cable length. The ships were driven unawares over shallows and sand banks.

Master Cox in *Golden Hind* signalled desperately to the leading ship *Delight* to go about but it was too late. Drawing more water than her smaller sister ships she struck hard on a bank. In no time at all she started to break up. Her horrified companions watched helplessly as the crew drowned before their eyes. Of the compliment of about one hundred men only fourteen managed to escape in the ship's boat. For six long days the sea and wind drove them back to Newfoundland where the twelve survivors were rescued by Frenchmen.

The loss of their chief ship was a heavy and grievous blow. The weather continued thick and blustery until all courage had ebbed away. Everyone agreed that they should abandon the voyage and head for England. Within two days they were back at Cape Race and in due course the Azores lay to stern. Gilbert must have been shattered by the events which he probably felt could have been avoided by better leadership on his part. However, he put on a brave face and vowed that the following year he would persuade the queen to lend him £10,000 to fit out two new fleets to complete his mission, one for the north and one for the south. He insisted on remaining aboard *Squirrel*. But on 9 September the little craft was nearly swamped by a wave and later that night her lantern suddenly went out and she was seen no more. Humphrey Gilbert's luckless, futile and ill-lead expedition had ended in tragedy with nothing achieved – or so it must have seemed at the time.

But chance ordained Gilbert's half brother Walter Raleigh to be the brilliant rising celestial body in the firmament of Elizabeth's court at that time. Raleigh and the queen soon appeared bound together in mutual adoration like closely orbiting double stars. Elizabeth heaped honour and benefits on Walter so that in no time at all his income was comparable with the richest men in the land. Gilbert's patent was transferred to Raleigh who set about planning his colony with care and enthusiasm. He enlisted the help of some of the best and most appropriate talent in England. Elizabeth gave him Durham House, a huge dank mausoleum by the riverside in Whitehall. Here, he assembled a staff of experts that included mariners, geographers, mathematicians and a host of others.

Two ships under Philip Amadas and Arthur Barlowe sailed the following spring to reconnoitre a suitable site for a colony on the mainland of America, far enough north to be unnoticed by the Spaniards, yet well south of the bleak winters found in New-foundland. They returned with glowing reports of the area south of Chesapeake Bay. An outer bank would protect the colony from prying

Spanish eyes, the natives seemed friendly and the land fertile. They brought back two of the savages 'being lusty men whose names were Wanchese and Manteo'.

Thomas Harriott, a man of rare and inquiring intellect, was given the difficult task of learning their language, essential if the proposed colony was to survive peacefully amid the local tribes. The Hakluyts – uncle and nephew – who were noted geographers, wrote a prospectus of the plan with lists of many requirements. It gained the queen's blessing. She lent a ship and gave her title – Virginia – to the enterprise, but was careful to commit none of her wealth.

Raleigh, forbidden by Elizabeth to go himself, sent out a well-organised expedition to establish the first settlement in April 1585. Richard Grenville led its five vessels. Ralph Lane, a military man, was the designated governor of the settlement. He had with him John White as artist, Harriott as recorder, the two Indians and a hundred settlers. A colony was established on Roanoke Island after many and varied adventures. The last ship sailed home in mid September, missing the arrival of supply ships, expected at about that time.

Bernard Drake, the eldest son of Sir John Drake of Ashe House, near Axminster, East Devon, was Richard Grenville's nephew. With Walter's brother Carew Raleigh, he was to have led the back-up supply ships later that summer. His plans were upset shortly before he was due to depart, by the arrival in London of *Primrose*, a merchant ship from the Spanish Basque port of Bilboa.[2]

The Escape of the Primrose

When the Primrose docked below London on 8th June 1585, her Master had this story to tell:

'We anchored in the bay of Bilboa on 24th May, and started to unload our cargo. Two days later a Spanish pinnace came along side with the Corrigador of Biscay. He asked to come aboard. I knew him as a man of great importance with command over a hundred towns. With him were six others, dressed like merchants. Making them welcome, I invited them to my cabin where I was presented with gifts. I made ready a banquet, although we could only offer our usual fare of biscuits and beef – but of the best quality. Things were going most pleasantly when the Corrigador and three of the merchants suddenly left for Bilboa. While maintaining appearances, I secretly let my crew know that I suspected treachery.

When the Corrigador returned, a party of 70 Spaniards – all dressed like merchants accompanied him. Since they were so many. I invited aboard only four men with the Corrigador. I ask that the others should stay in their boat, since there were so many of them. This was agreed, but when an officer bearing a white stick called upon me to yield unto the King of Spain, they all started to swarm aboard, producing rapiers and other weapons from under their robes – and occupied the deck, cabins and lower deck. I cried out: 'We are betrayed' – with which they set upon me most ferociously and held me pinned with a dagger to my throat. I feared for my life, not knowing then that they only intended to make us all captive.

Meanwhile, my crew were mostly huddled brelow decks deciding what best to do. They all feared that if taken prisoner they would taste of the sharp torments in the Holyhouse of the dreaded Inquisition. If they resisted, they felt sure I would be killed – and themselves as well. Then the most manly and bold amongst them grabbed whatever weapons were to hand – javelins, lances, bore spears, anything. There were five caliveres, ready charged, which was little enough against so many, but they were positioned below gratings where they could be fired upwards into the enemy on the deck above. Fired all together, the Spaniards were greatly surprised, not knowing whence the attack came – nor what more to expect. Then the others of my crew rushed at them with great courage, dismaying two or three Spaniards with every blow struck.

With that the Corrigador called on me to stop my men's onslaught; but I replied that such was the English courage, it would only result in them being killed – and me besides. Soon there was blood everywhere, much from those killed where the shot, entering between their legs, had issued forth from their breasts. Many were sore wounded from cuts and thrusting blows. Soon, greatly afeared, they ran to both sides of the ship and so tumbling into the sea, many drowning. Then we did take pity on them, and pulled aboard four who were clutching to the ship's side, including the Corrigador. Our surgeon dressed their wounds and six of my crew. We lost but one man killed – John Tristram.

After his valiant enterprise, wherein 28 of my men vanquished more than 70 Spaniards, we made haste to set sail and depart Bilboa. By God's providence, we avoided all dangers, and bought home our ship, and what remained of her cargo, with all expedition. I did demand of the Corrugators why we had been attacked. Then he did pluck from his soaking hose his wordy Commission from the King of Spain, showing reasons for the embargo and the means whereby it was to be executed. It was dated Barcelona, 29th May.'

4

Rumblings of War

'In another Voyage I made thither, about 34. Yeeres past, wherein I
had command of a good Ship partly mine owne, at that time one
Sir Bernard Drake, of *Devonshire*, Knight, came thither with a
commission, and having divers good Ships under his command, hee
there tooke many *Portugall* Ships, laden with fish, and traine oil, and
brought them into *England* as prizes.'

Richard Whitbourne – His Preface

In the thirtieth year of his reign, 1585, Philip II of Spain acted in a way
that made war with England inevitable. Some argue that this had been
obvious ever since the death of his wife, Queen Mary, and the
accession of Elizabeth to the throne of England in 1558. Under Mary,
England had reverted to Roman Catholicism and Philip had exercised
considerable influence over English policy. Thinking to regain his
influence, he proposed to the new queen, but Elizabeth would have
none of it. Young and politically inexperienced, she was at first careful
not to provoke Philip, while at the same time steering England back to
Protestantism. Philip, on the other hand, was a staunch supporter of
Rome. Philip believed it was God's will that he should bring the
English once more into the Catholic fold. To this end any means, even
war and regicide, were justified.

Unlike France, Spain had never been a traditional enemy of
England and a considerable trade based primarily on wool but also
with a great many other commodities had grown up. This trade did
not extend to Spain's large and rich American possessions. As early as
1494, the Pope had issued a Bull dividing the uninhabited world down
a line of latitude running through the Atlantic, some miles to the west

of the Cape Verde islands. All new lands to the west were to be Spanish, those to the east for Portugal and it was 'hands off' for all other nations. Both countries preserved their 'right' with jealous assiduity.

This was not to the liking of some of the more adventurous entrepreneurs who were beginning to flex their muscles in an England that, at last recovered from the devastation of the War of the Roses, was enjoying increasing prosperity. John Hawkins of Plymouth, followed the lead of his father William who had made three trading voyages to Brazil between 1530 and 1532. John attempted to elbow his way into the markets of Mexico and the Caribbean by making three more voyages between 1562 and 1568. He traded West African slaves for sugar, hides and the like. He was careful to pay all required dues to the Spanish authorities and to keep on good terms with their colonial governors. All was going well until, in September, 1568, his ships were damaged by a storm off the Mexican coast.

He asked and was granted permission to use the port of San Juan de Ulua for their repair. But a newly appointed governor for Mexico arrived with a large fleet two days later. Grudgingly agreeing to allow Hawkins to complete his repairs, he entered the harbour and tied up alongside the English ships.

The governor regarded Hawkins as little better than a pirate and launched a surprise attack. It was half-expected and the English fought fiercely, but in vain. Hawkins was heavily out-numbered and his flag ship, *Jesus*, was overwhelmed. He managed to escape in his second ship, *Minion*, together with his other ship commanded by a young kinsman, Francis Drake. Overcrowded and with starving crews, both ships struggled back to Plymouth. Hawkins and Drake were implacable enemies of Spain from that time on with Hawkins rebuilding and modernising the Queen's navy and Drake causing mayhem and devastation to the Spanish on land and sea wherever he went.[1]

When the King of Portugal died in 1580, Philip was the main contender for the vacant throne. By force of arms he overcame all opposition, principally from Don Antonio, a rival but illegitimate claimant. England's relations with Portugal had long been friendly but within a year Philip controlled Portugal and most of her huge overseas territories making him the most powerful ruler since the days of Imperial Rome. England reacted, becoming more openly aggressive, aiding and abetting Don Antonio who still had considerable support in the Azores.

Philip had inherited the Low Countries through his Hapsburg connections. The Protestant Dutch had been in open rebellion since 1567 with fortunes swinging back and forth. Elizabeth supported the Dutch right to self-government and assisted the Dutch whenever they seemed to be losing, hoping to keep the Spanish tied down by debilitating campaigns.

She also encouraged attacks on Spanish ships by her privateering mariners whenever the opportunity arose, while officially condemning any hostile action against Spain. The line between privateers and pirates was finely drawn and the English sea dogs were content to attack first and hope that the Admiralty Courts would not check up later. On the Spanish side, Philip was covertly involved in a succession of plots against Elizabeth's life, which were sanctioned by the Counter-Reformation. Francis Walsingham, Elizabeth's master spy catcher, was forever un-masking assassination suspects, extracting confessions under torture, and dispensing the ultimate penalty. The queen's throne was no cushy armchair.

London merchants whose trade with mainland Spain had grown considerably during the queen's reign, were unhappy with this mounting hostility. Many factors and other employees of the London merchants were in all the Spanish ports, carrying out trade on the spot. Philip, growing old and ill, increasingly isolated himself from his courtiers and advisers within the vastness of his newly built El Escorial palace. He saw these merchants as likely targets for revenge and encouraged the English to supply grain in unusually large amounts when the Spanish crops failed in1584, while guaranteeing their safety. There were a great number of English ships in the Spanish ports by the following May and Philip clapped an embargo on them all, seizing their cargoes and ordering their crews to be thrown into prison. Only one English ship escaped detention, the London-based *Primrose*.

One can picture the consternation, closely followed by determination, in the City and Whitehall, when news of the seizures and *Primrose's* escape broke. The hitherto dovish merchants clamoured for revenge. Elizabeth, her ministers and council soon realised that war was now a certainty and that it would be won or lost at sea. Indecision was set aside and action swiftly taken.

The Lord Admiral set about issuing 'letters of marque,' to those merchants and ship owners whose vessels had been impounded. These were licences to attack Spanish ships as opportunity arose and seize goods as compensation for their losses. In practice these letters became an excuse to plunder any foreign shipping that was encountered.

Sir Frances Drake was ordered to assemble a large force of ships and soldiers to go to the Spanish ports and attempt to rescue the imprisoned crews. This took some time and with the queen's customary vacillations his fleet did not sail until mid September.

War appeared certain. It was vital to warn the Newfoundland fishing fleet of their danger. With Walter Raleigh's consent, a small squadron ready to set out for Roanoke with urgently needed supplies, was diverted. On 20 June the queen signed a commission to Bernard Drake. She had – 'been given to understand . . . that others of our subjects that do employ themselves in the fishing at the new found land are determined after they have finished their said fishing to repair into Spain with intent to make sale of their fish there' – where a better price could be had than in England. So for 'the safety and weal of our subjects [she is sending] our trustie and well beloved servant Barnard Drake Esquire . . . not only to advertise our said subjects [so that] they may avoid the peril and danger that might otherwise ensue'. Her express wish and commandment was that all those with whom Bernard made contact 'should join him so that together they might seize all ships that they find appertaining to Spain'[2].

All such ships captured were to be brought into one of the western ports of England to remain there without dispersing any part of their cargoes until the Queen's wishes were made known. As for ships of other nationalities they were to be treated in a constant and friendly manner. Sailing orders followed a week later and the squadron left early in July.

West Country squire Bernard Drake, a cousin of Richard Grenville, was only distantly related to Sir Francis. Francis' family came from near Plymouth, whereas Bernard's had lived in Exmouth for at least five generations prior to 1535. About that time, Bernard's father John, took possession of Ashe House (Musbury) near Axminster, following a long running legal dispute. John married Amy Grenville and Bernard was born about 1537. Bernard inherited Ashe house when he was nearly forty and married Gertrude Fortescue, by whom he had six children. Most of these would be grown-up by 1585.

Bernard served with Walter Raleigh on Humphrey Gilbert's first abortive voyage in 1582 but usually Bernard acted as a Justice of the Peace, a job that kept him occupied when not looking after his estate or relaxing at Court. Prince wrote about him as one of Devonshire's 'Worthies . . . a gentleman of rare and excellent accomplishments, and as well qualified for a soldier as a courtier: he was in great favour with that illustrious princess of immortal memory Queen Elizabeth, and of high esteem in her court'. There was no more senior commander available that could be placed over him and, in the event, he acquitted himself with distinction, although he had little experience at sea.

Bernard's voyage is not well documented. He sailed with Amyas Preston as his second in command in *Golden Royale*, Raleigh's heavily armed 800-ton flagship and one of the most powerful ships of the time. With him went *Job* (70 tons), also owned by Raleigh, under Captain Andrew Fulford, and 'divers good ships'. It was too late in the year to attempt the direct crossing, so they sailed towards the Azores where they encountered and captured a rich sugar-laden Portuguese 'Brazilman'. Preston escorted her back to Exmouth while the rest of the fleet continued to Newfoundland where they probably gathered at St John's early in August. Bernard knew from Hayes' experience in 1583 that ships of all nations, but especially the Portuguese, would be assembling in St John's prior to their return journey. He would have learnt at which of the many harbours the rest of the fishing fleet was to be found and would have dispatched others to help execute his commission.

After securing captives in St John's Bernard sailed south, rounding Cape Race, and entered Bull's Bay [probably Bull Cove] one hundred miles further west. There he encountered the 100-ton *Red Lion* of Chichester, under command of George Raymond. She had been part of Grenville's fleet to Virginia but became detached. Dumping his colonists off at Croatoan on the Carolina Outer Banks in June, Raymond did not wait for Grenville but made for Newfoundland hoping, no doubt, to pick up an Iberian prize on the way home. He joined forces with *Golden Royale*.

Bernard returned by way of the Azores after arranging for all the captured fishing vessels to be escorted home. Fortune again smiled in the form of a Spaniard with wine and ivory aboard and three more Portuguese 'Brazilmen' laden with sugar. The enterprise then struck foul weather. Some of the captive fishing boats were sunk while *Job* and the captive 180-ton *Lion of Viana*, with Thomas Raynsford as captain of her prize crew, were forced to seek shelter in a Breton port where they were held captive.

The operation was an outstanding success, despite these setbacks; the fishing boats had been warned away from Spain – although they would not have come to harm since Philip had second thoughts and raised the embargo. The Iberian fishing fleet had been reduced significantly – at least sixteen were captured with about six hundred Portuguese seamen. The six prizes seized were hugely valuable. One estimate put the overall total value at £70,000. Portugal, an unwilling vassal of Spain, was the unfair victim of this episode and her Newfoundland fishing fleet never fully recovered.

The prized boats were brought to various western and south-coast ports. The queen knighted Bernard at Greenwich on 9 January the next year but he did not live long enough to enjoy either his title or his new found wealth. It appears that he kept many of the prisoners in Exeter gaol over winter. They starved, despite the fact that the government allowed 3d daily per head to feed the captives. Thirty eight of them were up on charges, presumably for mutiny against the English prize crew that brought them to England. All seriously ill, they were arraigned before the Exeter assizes which opened on 14 March. Sergent Flowerday with eight Justices of the Peace sat on the bench with twelve good men and true in the jury box. When the prisoners were brought in 'there arose such a noisom smell from the bar that a great number of people there present were therewith infected'.

They were suffering from the dreaded gaol fever typhus of which Francis Bacon wrote: 'The most pernicious infection next the plague, is the smell of the gaol, when prisoners have been long, and close, and nastily kept where of we have had in our time experienced twice or thrice.' Bacon wrote that: 'They are not those stinks which the nostrils straight abhor and expel that are the most pernicious but such airs as have similitude with man's body, and so insinuate themselves, and betray the spirit.' Modern medical wisdom might well agree with him.

The upshot was that eleven of the jurymen, Judge Flowerday, all eight JPs, including Sir John Chichester, Sir Arthur Bassett and Sir Bernard himself, and 'divers other persons,' (court officials) all caught the fever. As no record of the trial has come down, the court recorder is likely to have been another victim.[3]

One last mystery remains involving Bernard. The Dictionary of National Biography says: 'Sir Bernard Drake, when he fell ill, struggled as far as Crediton on his way home but died there on 10 April, 1586, and was buried two days later.' Crediton lies nine miles northwest of Exeter, his home in Musbury 25 miles to the east. The Crediton register states that he was buried on 26th April 1586. A possible explanation is that Bernard was too ill to travel home and went to the closer Crediton, where his son, John, was living.[4]

Meanwhile Francis Drake's fleet, having sailed in September 1585, made straight for the north-west coast where he confronted the authorities holding the English crews captive. The merchantmen were released and there was no fighting, only a fair amount of looting by the English. Drake was then free to follow his own course. He crossed the Atlantic via the Canary and Cape Verde islands to Dominica, most easterly of the Caribbean islands. He captured San Domingo, Hispaniola's first city, in a daring attack on New Year's day. Looting and desecration followed. Cartagena on the Spanish Main was the next place captured following a fierce assault. The fleet remained there until mid April, the time that Bernard Drake was buried.

The fleet sailed to Cuba where they ran short of water. By this time crews were sick and weak. Everyone wanted to return home but they received word that the Spanish in St Augustine, Florida, were planning an assault on Raleigh's Roanoke colony. On arrival in St Augustine, they took the fort and later the town without difficulty. Anxious to be home, for it was now June, the fleet soon left, sailing up the coast until they found the Roanoke colony.

It was in poor shape, having missed out on supplies that should have been delivered by Bernard Drake the previous autumn. After a vicious storm which damaged the fleet gravely, agreement was reached to abandon the colony and for all to return home with Drake. There, once all the booty had been counted, it was found insufficient to repay more than a 75% return to the investors. Although the first English colony in America had failed for the time being, Sir Francis Drake's exploits were a great morale booster for the English nation.[5]

5

Against the Spanish Armada

'In the year 1588, I served under the then Lord Admirall, as Captain in a ship of my Owne, set forth at my charge against the Spanish Armada: and after such time as that service was ended, taking my leave of his Honour, I had his favourable Letters to one Sir Robert Denis, in the County of Devon, Knight; whereby there might bee some course taken, that the charge, as well of my owne Ship, as also of two other, and a Pinnace, with the victuals, and men therein imployed, should not be any way burthensome to me. Wherein there was such order given by the then right Honourable Lords of the privie Councell, that the same was well satisfied; which service is to be seene recorded in the Booke at White-Hall'

Richard Whitbourne – His Preface

Spain and England embarked on a collision course a few years after Elizabeth succeeded Mary as queen. Once Elizabeth spurned King Philip's offers of marriage, a conflict became a matter not of if but when. Following Philip's embargo on English shipping in May 1585 and Sir Bernard Drake's retaliatory foray to Newfoundland, the king decided that crunch-time had come. He set in train preparations for the invasion of England. It turned out to be a lengthy process for several reasons: rank bad organisation; Sir Francis Drake's attack on the fleet as it lay in Cadiz harbour in April, 1587; the death of the Marquis of Santa Cruz, appointed to command the Armada early in 1588, and bad weather at crucial times.

The Armada eventually set sail from Lisbon on 23 May, 1588. It was met by severe storms and was scattered. Its ships limped back into Corunna to repair, reform and await favourable wind and weather.

But the weather that summer was dreadful. It was cold and sunless while gale followed gale after gale. The Spanish Armada – 140 ships totalling 62,000 tons, manned by 7,500 seamen and carrying 18,500 soldiers – finally sailed on 12 July. It was sighted off the Isles of Scilly a week later.

The English navy at that time consisted of thirty six royal ships totalling, perhaps, just 13,000 tons. In normal times the queen's finances would not allow more than a few of these to be in commission at any one time although at least twenty four could be brought into active service within a fortnight. England relied on privately owned merchantmen to augment the fleet. Some were well armed, having been engaged in privateering – a form of legalised piracy – but most carried only enough cannon to ward off pirates.

The Privy Council wrote to all the country's main ports at the end of March, 1588, requiring them to furnish a total of forty nine ships of sixty or more tons, also twenty pinnaces, usually about twenty to thirty tons. They were to 'repair' to Sir Francis Drake at Plymouth by 25 April, where the main fleet was gathering under the command of the Lord Admiral, Lord Charles Howard of Effingham.[1]

Exeter with Apsham (now Topsham) was required to supply three ships and a pinnace. Like most other ports Exeter was quick to raise objections and difficulties with the Privy Council but, nevertheless, went ahead commandeering whatever ships they could and making them ready for sea. The ships, which eventually served, were:

No.137 *Bartholomew*	130 tons	70 men. Capt. Nicholas Wright.
No 138 *Rose*	110 tons	50 men. Capt. Thomas Sandye.
No 139 *Gyfte of God*	25 tons	
No.186 *Grace*	100 tons	50 men. Capt. Walter Edney.[2]

All four ships were from Topsham, but *Grace* was a 'voluntary' ship belonging to Edney and did not come under Exeter's control at all. She cleared the Exe estuary on 13 June bound for 'Rame', that is Rame Head that guards Plymouth Sound. The others, although ready by the end of April, did not sail for Plymouth until 9 July, arriving on the 16th, to serve with the fleet until 9 September.[3]

Drake had been fretting time away at Plymouth, waiting for the queen's permission to sail for the Spanish coast where he might, with luck, catch the Armada while it was still in port – as he had done with such success at Cadiz the year before. The queen worried, as always, about raising the money to pay her sailors, dithered for two months. At last, on 7 July, Drake and Howard were permitted to leave, a northeast wind speeding their journey.

They were already two thirds of the way to Spain two days later when the wind swung right round and blew a gale from the south. Due to the great difficulties that arose from trying to keep this large, remotely sited navy supplied for several months and with sea routes constantly disrupted by bad weather, they were short of food. Fearful of missing the Armada, the fleet had no choice but to sail with the wind for Plymouth where they arrived on the 12th. They immediately set about replacing sick crewmen, repairing damage and replenishing stores. The same day the Duke of Medina Sidonia led the Armada out of Corunna and headed for England.

And what of Richard? As with so many other parts of this story the supporting evidence of his share in these stirring events is meagre. He was owner, or at least part owner at the time, of the 50-ton *Gyfte of God* of Exmouth, which first appears in the Port of Exeter records in 1583. Richard was probably connected with her from that time. She returned home from a voyage to Nantes on 17 May, 1588, and left again on 6 July, bound for La Rochelle, Richard being named as master. However, she turned up in Plymouth a few days later. It is possible that the southerly gales that forced Drake to turn back also persuaded Richard to make for the shelter of Plymouth – or he may have already decided to go there after chatting to the crews of the Exeter contingent who were waiting for sailing orders in the Exe estuary.

Richard's arrival in Plymouth Sound probably coincided with that of the returning English fleet on 12 July, a few days ahead of the Exeter contingent. This timing might explain why Lord Howard decided to place these ships under Richard's command. Otherwise it is difficult to understand why he, as an unknown and relatively young and inexperienced sea-captain, was given such responsibility. Captains Wright and Sandy, who were probably naval men with no connection to Exeter, would have been assigned to *Bartholomew* and *Rose* at a later date.

The great drama was now about to unfold. The story of the

Armada fight has been retold countless times, but a brief summary here may be helpful.

It was some time in the afternoon of 19 July that Captain Thomas Fleming of *Golden Hind* arrived in Plymouth with the news that the Armada had been sighted off the Isles of Scilly. Tradition has it that Drake was playing bowls on Plymouth Hoe with his captains and there was time to finish their game before the tide started to ebb. Only then could the fleet warp itself clear of Plymouth Sound, a protracted operation. The following dawn found the English squadrons at sea and to windward of the tight crescent formation of the Spanish fleet as it began its ponderous journey up the Channel. All that day Howard engaged the Spaniards with much expenditure of cannonball, musket-shot and powder.

The last great sea battle before this had been at Lepanto in 1571. There the Turkish and Christian ships had grappled one with another and the issue had been decided by hand-fighting. On this occasion the English kept their distance. A totally different strategy and form of naval engagement was being developed – naval gun duelling. The English proved their superiority both in fire-power and manoeuvrability but inflicted singularly little damage on the enemy. Two Spanish ships, *Rosario* and *San Salvador*, were disabled but that by accident rather than enemy action. As night fell they were abandoned by the Armada to be captured the next day by Drake and John Hawkins respectively.

For six more days the Spaniards continued their slow progress up the Channel before anchoring off Calais. If Armada Commander the Duke of Medina Sidonia entertained any thoughts of landing on English soil the close attention of Drake's squadrons persuaded him otherwise. Keeping at long range, the English harassed the enemy with cannon-shot whenever possible, intending to 'pluck their feathers little by little'. Major actions took place off Portland Bill and the Isle of Wight. These about exhausted the fleet's stock of ammunition.

The English fleet was short of powder and shot even before battle was joined. This has been blamed on the parsimony and anxiety of Elizabeth to contain costs. At the outset of the battle there were on average no more than thirty rounds per cannon, which, according to Drake at the time 'is but for one and a half days' service . . . which I judge to be just a third of that which is needful.'[4] The situation was critical and on 24 July Howard sent his auxiliaries, barks and pinnaces, to scour the nearby ports, forts and arsenals for all possible shot and powder to replenish the fighting ships. Stocks captured from *Rosario* and *San Salvador* were of considerable help. With the great variety of cannon-bores in both fleets it must have taken a lot of luck to get the right size shot to each vessel. Howard now husbanded his reserves and scarcely a shot was fired between the Isle of Wight and Calais.

Then came the famous attack with fire ships as the Armada lay at anchor off Calais causing the Spanish captains to panic, cut their anchors and flee up the coast of Holland. The final battle took place the following day off Graveline. The Spaniards having failed to link up with the Duke of Parma, whose ground-forces were to have been escorted across to England, gave up the endeavour, fleeing northwards around Scotland. The English shadowed them as far as the Firth of Forth but, bereft of ammunition, could do no more. Untimely and fierce storms off the Scottish and Irish coasts then wrought damage where English fire-power had failed. More than thirty ships were wrecked on these coasts while those that finally made it back to Spain were in a sorry state.

What part did Richard play during his time with the fleet? He wrote: '**And after the service was ended the right honourable Lordes of the privie Councell were so truly satisfied by the said Lord Admiral of my goode services in that action and also from the Lord Lieutenant of ye countie of Devon of my endevor used whereby to furnish the said Lord Admiral with some especiall necessarie as I knew his Lordship and some other shippes of the navie then greatly wanted.'**[m7]

Richard was writing in a long letter to the Duke of Buckingham seeking employment, thirty eight years later. As no official record of Richard or his ship has survived, reliance must be put on his writings. The first difficulty is that there is no mention of the Exmouth ship *Gift* in Laughton's detailed list of vessels that formed part of the English fleet. Nor is there any record of 'book at Whitehall'. That may have been lost in the fire on 12 January, 1619, which destroyed the great banqueting hall in Whitehall together with the offices of the Signet Privy Seal beneath it and most of the writings and papers stored there. (See page 44)

Of the 197 ships in Laughton's list, there is only one possible candidate. It is No. 192, recorded as an unnamed 60-ton fly-boat with a crew of forty. No port of registration is given and neither the captain nor master named. It is included in the list of 23 'voluntary ships that came unto the fleet after the coming of the Spanish forces upon our coasts and were paid for by Her Majesty for the time they served'. It is also possible that confusion occurred in drawing up the list because of the presence of two ships each called *Gift* and both from Exe-estuary ports.

We know that the Exeter contingent was paid off for two months service from 16 July to 9 September; also, that the 18-ton *Gift of God*, of Exon, left the Exe for St Malo on 8 September and the 40-ton *Gifte*, of Exmouth, left the following day for Barbarie.[3] This seems a most unlikely destination for that time. Perhaps, Richard undertook some clandestine government mission. We shall never know.

Naval historian Michael Oppenheim, writing about the Armada battle at the beginning of the 20th century, said: 'Like all the other armed merchantmen, those from Devon did no more during the historic week up Channel than hamper the movements of the men-of-war and hover round in the hope of picking up a winged bird.' He gives no authority for this assertion and certainly knew nothing of Richard's exploits.

Clearly the most likely 'especialle necessarie' would be ammunition.[4] Richard may well have known where available powder and shot were to be had in Southampton as he served his apprenticeship there. Could he have collected and delivered the same to a grateful Howard with the help of the three ships under his command? Howard was more than willing to write a favourable letter to the Lord Lieutenant of Devon.[5] It is unlikely that further details of this event will ever be uncovered to settle this question.

In the same letter to Buckingham, Richard wrote at length that he was ready to reveal to Buckingham, when convenient, some observations he had noted in 1588 and '**partly shew in what way**' each of the king's ships could be equipped with '**fit stratagems**' that could be employed to protect them from any danger and desperate assault attempted by enemy forces; likewise these stratagems could be used offensively against such enemy, putting them in '**great and sudden danger**' and so distract them that, very probably, they will run away from the king's navy as they did in 1588.

Richard was writing to one of the most powerful figures in the land, craving his favours for employment. He clearly thought that the Duke would be more impressed by verbosity than substance, and he certainly had no intention of giving away any of his ideas at this early stage. We can but guess what he had in mind.

If he had witnessed all the action up the Channel and at Calais and Graveline he would know that only once were the Spaniards put into great and sudden danger and totally distracted. That was at Calais when the fire-ships evaded the grappling efforts of the Spanish pinnaces. The Armada captains, losing first their heads and then their anchors, fled. Although their orders were to move back to their stations and drop anchor once the fire-ships were past, all but five fled unceremoniously.

In those days an outbreak of fire at sea was an ever-present fear. Fire had to be available at all times for lighting, cooking and fighting. But the risk of accidents was real and considerable. If a sure way of setting fire to the enemy could be found without risk to oneself, such a stratagem would put them in a great and sudden danger.

One can picture Richard during long night vigils on the way to Newfoundland when the threat of icebergs forbade sleep. Ever watchful, he would turn his mind to ideas for setting light to the enemy's ships. We can only guess what they were: perhaps involving hot-shot or chain-shot, or lobbing some fiery incendiary device into the opponent's rigging. Whatever he dreamt up, Richard was a practical man, convinced it would work. But he needed trials which were beyond his time and means to undertake. So he could only claim to show 'partly' how his ideas would work in practice. Without proper tests, he could never be certain that the user might not be 'hoisted with his own petard'.

Book Feared Lost in Whitehall Blaze

London, January 16, 1619
We have had here a great mischance by fire at Whitehall, which, beginning in the banqueting house, hath quite consumed it, and put the rest in great danger, but that there was so much help at hand, besides that which was sent out of London on all sides, and so good order taken, by the presence of the lord chancellor, the Duke [of Lennox,] and the Earl of Arundel, that all passed with as much quiet as was possible in such a confusion; and the fire, although it was exceeding furious, kept from spreading further than the limits of that building, saving only, that the vehemency of the heat burnt down one of the rotten terraces or galleries adjoining, and took hold of the pulpit-place, which was soon quenched. One of the greatest losses spoken of, is the burning of all, or most of the writings and papers belonging to the offices of the Signet, Privy Seal, and Council Chamber, which were under it. And, in such a mishap, it fell out happily to be in the day time, about eleven o'clock, on Tuesday, the 12th of this month. For if it had happened at night, the whole house, and all in it, had been in great danger; for, though it were at high noon, yet there was much embezzling, and much spoil, though there was as much provision made against it as the shortness of time could permit, and divers taken with the manner, and committed. There is much speech of divers miscarried; but we hear yet no certainty, only some are hurt and maimed; and the fire is not yet so thoroughly quenched, that they can search any corner. You can guess the fury of it, when it lasted not in any strength above an hour

  John Chamberlain Esq to Sir Dudley Carleton.

Cause of Blaze Revealed

London, January 19th, 1619
The unhappy accident that chanced at Whitehall, last week, by fire, you cannot but have heard of but haply not the manner how, which was this. A joiner was appointed to mend some things that were out of order in the device of the masque, which the king meant to have repeated at Shrovetide, who, having kindled a fire upon a false hearth, to heat his glue-pot, the force thereof pierced soon, it seems, the single brick, and, in a short time that he absented himself upon some occasion, fastened upon the basis, which was of dry deal board, underneath; which suddenly conceived flame, gave fire to the device of the masque, all of oiled paper, and dry fir, &c. And so, in a moment, disposed itself among the rest of that combustible matter, that it was past any man's approach, before it was almost discovered. Two hours begun and ended that woeful sight. All the loss was bounded in the banqueting house, and in the offices underneath. All the records of the Signet office utterly perished, one chest of writings excepted

  Rev Thomas Larkin to Sir Thomas Puckering

6

Crossing The Pond

'. . . I have spent most of my dayes in travell, especially in merchandising and sea-voyages. I have beene in France, Spaine, Italy, Portugall, Savoy, Denmarke, Norway, Poland, the Canaries and Seris Islands: and for New-found-land, I may truely say it is almost as familiar to mee as mine owne Countrie.'

Richard Whitbourne – Draft Preface

These days, we are accustomed to seeing television pictures and reading of long, often solo, voyages in small sea-craft. The skill, endurance and courage of those who undertake such ventures is remarkable even when we remember the high quality technology at their command. Constantly in touch with land base, position known to within a few metres, aided by reliable weather forecasts and detailed charts of approaching land-falls, they sail craft of the very latest design, construction and comfort.

It was an entirely different matter for sailors in the tiny fishing boats of four and five hundred years ago, who regularly crossed the 'Pond', as the North Atlantic is often called. The yearly crossings by hundreds of small boats had been going on for nearly sixty years by 1560 when significant numbers of West of England fishermen began to join the Basque, Portuguese and Breton fishing boats on the Grand Bank and around Newfoundland.

They were no pleasure cruises. Space was at a premium – it was unlikely that even the master would have a cabin. Hammocks were not yet in use so the crew would be hard pressed to find space to sleep with shelter from the elements. Of sixty-one recordings of ships from the Exe Estuary between 1570 and 1600, the average size (or burden) was thirty seven tons, with only four ships over sixty tonnes. The origin of this measurement of hold-size came from the long established wine trade with Bordeaux. Each tonne was equivalent to one cask holding 252 gallons of claret wine. Master shipwright Matthew Baker coined 'Baker's Old Rule' in 1582. This stated that the tonnage was the product of the hold height, the beam and the length of the keel – all measured in English feet and divided by 100. Thus a 37-tonner might be six feet between decks, have a 17-ft beam and 37-ft keel. The overall length of this ship might be sixty feet. This rule, no doubt, saved many a maiden voyage to Bordeaux for an on-the-spot verification of the ship's burden.

These tiny ships had to carry a multitude of stores and spares and be entirely self-sufficient for up to two months. Included would be spars and sails, hawsers and ropes, several spare anchors, planks, nails, vital pump leathers, pitch and tar to plug leaks, many and varied tools – and much else besides. Then there were the 'victuals' – food and drink – for both the crew and the additional fishermen aboard. Fishing gear would include nets and even new boats.[1] Distances were large – over 2,000 sea miles in ships driven only by uncertain winds and currents. Then, after three or four months isolated in Newfoundland they made the return journey with a full cargo which, even when cured and salted, smelt decidedly fishy and must not on any account be allowed to get wet.

Space was at a premium. There was room for only a main deck apart from the one in the hold just above the bilge and permanent ballast. There would be a forecastle and a stern-castle built over the main deck, separated by the 'well' amidships. Here the ship's boat would be stowed. Perhaps it would be turned up-side-down to allow shelter for the crew when not on watch. The stern-castle housed the tiller and its attendant tackle, bunks and space for the captain and/or master, and mate. There was no galley just a fire-box in the forecastle, probably brick-lined on a bed of sand. Near-by would be a lock-up 'bread cupboard', and the many barrels and casks of 'victuals' – all securely lashed down. Each man had his own sea-chest. There was no room for latrines or ablutions and certainly no fresh water for washing. When needs must, every man jack had to stick his back-side over the ship's side and hold on grimly – which in rough weather meant 'for dear life'.

When James I came to the throne in 1603 one of his first acts was to make peace with Spain. The result was an increase in overseas trade and fishing, which in turn led to a shipbuilding boom. The Duke of Buckingham's 1619 'Survey of Ships and Mariners of South Devon' lists 187 ships with their names, size and age (and a further fifty where age is not given.) Of these, 118 were commissioned in the eleven years between 1603 and 1613.[2] A fair number may have come from Holland and elsewhere but at least a dozen must have been built yearly along the south Devon coast. The average size of these new ships had roughly doubled.

Not one wreck of any such ship has been found. Neither designs nor drawings have come to light and there is little written record of where and how they were built. Much that follows is surmised. It is reasonable to assume that ships were built along the south Devon coast for several centuries before 1600 using the same time-honoured methods as were hundreds of thousands of timber ships throughout much of the world up till the last world war. One major change in technique occurred in the first half of the 15th century when clinker-built ships (where hull strength was achieved by overlapping and cleating together the edges of the plank sheathing) gave way to 'carvel' type vessels for which a skeletal framework was sheathed with planks the edges of which butted. With few exceptions, small ships were built on the sloping foreshore of sea or estuary on a skid just above high tide mark. When the hull was built it was not difficult to slide it into the water and complete the work while afloat.

Ships were built and maintained by highly skilled shipwrights. A list of names by location was included in the Duke of Buckingham's survey. When work ashore was scarce the craftsmen would often sail as ships' carpenters. The survey lists 168 shipwrights, seventy from the Dartmouth area, thirty-three from around Plymouth but only nine from the Exe estuary. Others were scattered along the coast, except for twenty-six from Otterton and nearby Colaton Raleigh about seven miles east of the Exe estuary.

There has never been a harbour at the mouth of the river Otter. Somewhere along its banks would have been a thriving shipyard for boats and small ships but with the exception of a few rusty nails, shipbuilding leaves little archaeological evidence. The 1619 list for Otterton shows 55-year-old John Bayley and three probable sons – John (34), William (30) and Robert (29). John Bayley is known to have built at least five ships of between 130 and 250 tons burden.[3]

Judging by present day silting of the river mouth, it seems unlikely that the larger ships could have been launched from the banks of the Otter. These ships were for Exeter (including *Resolution*, 130 tons, built in 1626) Dartmouth and Plymouth. I think that the Bayleys were a mobile family of ship builders who set up their yard at the most suitable site for each commission, which would largely depend on the source and ease of timber supply.

I have had to look to Fowey in Cornwall to find details of any West Country ship built in Richard's lifetime. John Rashleigh, a member of a well established ship-owning family of those parts (featured in Daphne du Maurier's novel 'The King's General'), traded fish – mainly pilchards – tin and lead, to Spain, Portugal and Italy in return for wine, fruit, salt, alum and pig iron. He started trading, if not actually fishing, in Newfoundland in 1585. Rashleigh grew rich, probably aided by some privateering and smuggling, and acquired substantial properties. He seems to have built several ships including, a 60-ton successor to his 40-ton *Success* in 1606. Some of John's meticulously kept notebooks have survived. Not intended as a full record of the building of each boat but more as personal 'aid-memoire', they give a detailed picture of some aspects of the operation, which have been fully researched.[4]

From these records it seems that Rashleigh was mainly concerned with two aspects of his business – the supply of timber and payment of wages. In the former he would plan several years ahead with one or more ships in mind. He bought a fifth part of a large stand of trees, mostly oak. Waiting until the winter before each was needed, he picked out specific trees for felling having in mind particular ribs or knees of the vessel under construction. These were then felled, trimmed and moved by cart or water to the assembly point.

Rashleigh kept weekly records of men employed, the hours they worked, and wages paid. In the example of the replacement *Success* the speed of construction and the economical use of labour were striking. Bearing in mind the highly skilled work involved and the still simple tools available – mostly adze and axe – to shape and assemble the many wooden members, sheathing, decking and fittings, it was a fine achievement for Rashleigh to set out on the maiden voyage on 11 October, 1606, having started work on 5 May.

For the first six weeks an average of ten men were employed on preliminary work, mainly setting out the site and shaping the various timber parts. Then Mr Bilton, the master-shipwright contracted to design and build the ship, and his men arrived. He was not local and appears to have been based somewhere along the north Cornish or Devon coast. Twelve weeks later the hull was complete and launched on or about 6 September.

Her superstructure was added over the next five weeks, the masts stepped and the rigging completed: the ship was painted, fitted out, ballasted and provisioned. She underwent and passed her sea trials. She was then loaded with a full cargo consisting of forty four tons of pilchards, more than two tons of white herrings, six firkins of butter, twelve slabs of tin weighing half a ton, and fifty three 'sows' of lead, weighing more than eight tons. *Success* set sail on her maiden voyage to Naples on 11 October, a remarkable achievement by any standard.

On the same day Mr Bilton was paid £10 for 'his charges in building my new ship' and was allotted a small consignment of the pilchards on board as part of the agreement. *Success* made three more trips to southern Europe before joining the Newfoundland fishing fleet. Her last recorded voyage was in April, 1621, when she returned from Naples. She certainly seems to have lived up to her name.

In the days of sail there were three routes which ships used to cross to North America. At first the northerly route was used – by the likes of the Irish monk Brendon and the Vikings. They 'island-hopped' by way of the Shetlands, Faeroes, Iceland, Greenland and the Labrador coast. The southern route was far longer following the trade wind, that great anti-clockwise circulation of wind and current which sweeps around the North Atlantic. Ships started down the coast of Europe and Africa to Madeira, the Canaries or Cape Verde, before heading west leaving the Doldrums to starboard. The route shifted during the year depending on the sun's position in its north-south motion. Ships would pick up the north-flowing Bahamas Current on nearing the West Indies, making sure to keep well west of Bermuda with its treacherous reefs. The homeward voyage in the Gulf Stream was direct and fast.

For the shortest distance by far from Devon to Newfoundland, fishing vessels had first to clear Start Point, then set a south-west or west-south-west course for about one hundred and twenty sea miles. After clearing Ireland close to the 49th parallel, it was then just 2,000 sea miles due west to Newfoundland, over the Grand Bank which gave due warning of land ahead. However, it was only in late spring that there was a reasonable chance of northerly or easterly winds to make this route practical. An average crossing would take three weeks, but exceptionally adverse winds could double this time.

The early established custom was that the first English shipmaster to arrive in any Newfoundland harbour would become Admiral for the year. It brought considerable advantages – the best anchorage and foreshore site for curing catches and a chance to 'acquire' the remains of structures abandoned the previous year. Over a period of time boats started to leave England increasingly early. But, as Richard points out in his book, it was to nobody's advantage. 'Ships hasting forward [about the end of February] greatly endanger themselves being many times beaten with rough and stormy windes. Oftentimes they are thereby forced to returne back with great losse both of mens' lives and goods, as it is well knowne. So that to get the superiority to arrive there first into an Harbour they will beare such an over-prest saile and in so desperate a manner, as there are no true understanding Sea-men that use the like to any other part of the world. Whereunto the Masters of divers ships have been often provoked, not only by their owne indiscretion, but also chiefly by the self-will ignorance of some careless Sailers of their Company. For albeit when the fogges are thicke and the nights darke that sometime they cannot discerne the length of three ships in the way before them. And the ice often threatening much perill to them. Yet on runnes the ship amaine so fast as possibly she may, when commonly most part of the company are fast asleep, even with extreme hazard of their lives. Thus many times both ships and men have been suddenly cast away, in divers places, to the utter undoing of many Adventurers and families. So had I myselve a ship lost, sailing to that Countrey, and divers others the like.'[5]

The state of ice on arrival off Newfoundland could vary greatly from one year to the next. Sometimes large icebergs sweeping down the coast in the Labrador Current would ground on the offshore banks and following bergs would pile up behind them. John Davis, an early explorer for the north-west passage, wrote in 1595 that Newfoundland Banks' fishermen met with such great quantities of ice that 'they are so noysomely pestered, as that in many weeks they have not been able to recover the shore, yea and many times recover it not until the season of fishing bee over'. In other years the coast would be relatively free of pack ice.

Richard recommended 'that they need not then goe forth in the said voyage until the twentieth day of March,[6] which is a time of the yeere to put to Sea from our Coast to that Countrey; the winter storms beginning then to cease.'

He goes on to say that an even later start – by about three weeks – would be in order if ships were to leave a fifth of their crew to over-winter. They could repair stages, rooms, boats and tackle. Fishing could start when the mother ship arrived the following year and no time would be wasted in repairs and preparations. Everyone would be forced to adopt it, or be out of business, were such a practice established.

The art and practice of ocean-navigation when Richard first sailed to Newfoundland was quite new to the English. Most mariners were used to trading along the west coast of Europe, rarely venturing into either the Baltic or Mediterranean waters. West Country fishermen would certainly go to the Irish coasts and as far as Iceland, a journey, nearly all within the bounds of the continental shelf. The art of navigation, or pilotage, was well established within the 100-fathom limit. There were calendars and almanacs in circulation giving a fund of information on sea- and landmarks, compass courses to follow, tide tables and currents. Particularly helpful was the 'line and lead' technique. Knowledge of the depth and sea-bed composition, obtained by using tallow held in the hollowed-ended lead plumb-bob, gave a good idea of the ship's position. Where necessary, there were many 'rutters' – from the French word 'routier' – printed or in private circulation that gave specific details of the sea-bed on the various shipping routes.

In this connection Richard wrote in 1623: '**I shall be better incouraged to set forth, what I have taken notice of, in my travels to that Countrey, concerning the severall depths of the water, and diversities of the ground in every severall depth that hath come in the Tallo, on the end of the Leade, when it has been cast into the Sea, which I conceive to bee necessary for those that shall henceforth trade thither because as yet no man, to my knowledge, hath undertaken: and whensoever it may please his Majesty, or the State shall seeme good to command me, I shall be ready with my life and meanes to make a perfect discovery and description of the several Head-lands, Bayes, Harbours, and Roads, for Ships to anchor; as also the Ilands, Rockes and Shelves round about the *New-found-land*; which as yet no man hath done:'**[7] His offer was not taken up.

It was on the high seas where experience was lacking. Usually hour and half-hour glasses where carried, not only to measure the time of each watch kept but also to plot the course taken by dead reckoning. The log could sometimes be used to measure the ship's progress. Alternatively, the sea captain would rely on experience to reckon his speed and drift. Results were unlikely to be accurate since the set of each current was unknown nor was the magnetic variation, which could change rapidly near the North American coast. Using a cross staff, or a quadrant, the altitude of sun, moon or stars was read, from which the latitude could be found, usually inaccurately. But there was no practical way of determining longitude.

After clearing Ireland ships sailed between west and northwest until North America was met. Sea birds and clouds would indicate land ahead as could soundings. By taking a slightly northerly course ships could, on entering the south flowing Cabot Current, drift down the coast along with the icebergs, until a familiar landmark was sited. Fog, particularly frequent in early summer, was a further problem.

Once a sea-captain or master became experienced, he would be able to sense where he was, like as not without knowing how he managed it. By then his chances of dying 'an old salt' in his bed back in Devonshire would have increased enormously.

7

The Bountiful Sea

'The seas, likewise all along that Coast, doe plentifully abounded in
other sorts of fish, such as Whales, Spanish Mackerel, Dorrelpoles,
Herring, Hogs, Porposes, Seales and such like royal fish, &c. But the
chiefe commodities of the New-found-land yet knowne, and which is
grown to be a settled trade . . . is the Cod fishing upon that Coast, by
which our Nation and many other Countries are enricht and greatly
comforted.'

Richard Whitbourne – 'Discourse and Discovery'

Nearly every existing report by early voyagers to Newfoundland and
her surrounds emphasised the abundance and variety of marine life.
John Mason, another sea captain and governor of Newfoundland's
first colony from 1615 to 1619, who published his own discourse on
Newfoundland in 1620 (the same year as Richard's book) wrote:
'Most admirable is the sea, so diversified with several sorts of fishes
abounding therein, the consideration whereof is ready to swallow up
and drown my senses, not being able to comprehend or express the
riches thereof.' He thought that an acre of sea during each of the
months of June, July and August would yield as much as a thousand
acres of the best English pasture. At that time of year 'Cods are so
thicken by the shore that we hardly have been able to row a Boat
through them.'[1]

Within a few years of Cabot's discovery, the Portuguese, Bretons
and Normans were fishing for cod there in considerable numbers. The
secretive Basques may have been hunting whales and seals in the
Straits of Belle Island, which divide Newfoundland from Labrador,
even before then. As long as Icelandic cod-fishing remained profitable

there was no need for West Country fishermen to look further afield and few English vessels were interested during the first half of the 16th century.

The Iberian nations had few readily accessible fishing grounds as the continental shelf lies close inshore and competition in the Mediterranean was fierce. England, surrounded by wide stretches of fish-filled seas, had little need for more. Her fleets fished the North Sea, in Irish and Scottish waters, around Shetland, Orkney and Iceland, besides her plentiful in-shore waters. Her problem was a lack of large markets to absorb the catches. Typical of the government's efforts to improve matters was Elizabeth's Act 5 of 1562. Under it, Wednesday and Saturday were declared meatless days to encourage the number of fishermen who would then be available to serve the navy in time of need. This law, being impossible to enforce, was ignored. After eighteen years it was repealed. Elizabeth imposed a duty on foreign-caught fish. Iceland, Shetland, Newfoundland and all parts of Scottish seas were exempt, as were fish taken and salted by her subjects.

Newfoundland was mentioned in a 1542 act of Henry VIII that regulated the sale of fish at sea, but excluded catches in 'Ireland, Shetlands, Orkneys and Newlands.' Clearly the English were fishing there by that time, but not in large numbers. With the Iclandic trade dwindling, through falling catches, competition from Hanseatic fishermen and objections from the King of Denmark, whose domains included Iceland, English participation in Newfoundland steadily increased, from mid-century onwards.

Anthony Parkhurst had made four visits to Newfoundland and reported in 1578 that there were generally 'more than one hundred sail of Spaniards taking cod, and from twenty to thirty killing whales; fifty sail of Portuguese; one hundred and fifty sail of French and Bretons, mostly very small; but of the English only fifty sail. Nevertheless the English are commonly lords of the harbours where they fish, and use all strangers' help in fishing, if need require, according to an old custom of the country.'[2]

The Spaniards who were involved in exploiting their West Indian, Central and South American colonies, sent few fishermen to North America. Only the Basque, then as now mostly coming under Spanish rule, went in large numbers. Known then as Biskaners, they were an ancient, proud but secretive people who kept to themselves. Within the Gulf of St Lawrence, they hunted whales and seals for 'train oil.' Used for lighting and in soap making, it was in ever increasing demand. There is little information as to where and how the Basque operated their cod fishing, and I can find no evidence that they frequented the southern shores of the island, later to be known as Avalon Peninsular.

Present day names of several Avalon features, and other evidence, indicates that the Portuguese, who had been cod fishing from as early as 1500, fished off this coast. It was from them that the English may have learnt how to cure the cod, using a minimum of salt. The result was known as 'Poor John' – an entirely different end-product from the air-dried stockfish of Iceland and Norway, cured without salt, only possible in low winter temperatures. It is curious that the most recent arrivals, the English, came to dominate the fishing stations of Avalon Peninsular, invariably becoming Admiral of each fishing site for a season at a time.

The Portuguese sailed in convoys. With each ship came a dog. Should fog come down, each dog would take up station in the bows and bark by turns, keeping all ships in touch so avoiding the risk of collisions. They shared the use of St John's with the English when selling their catch to sack ships, notably those that plied to Brazil where, according to Richard, there was a ready market. They also gathered at St Johns at the end of the season to make up home-bound convoys.

Richard tells us that the Grand Bank, lying due east of Newfoundland, started about 30 leagues off shore. A league, then, was commonly used at sea, equal to about three and a half miles. This sandy bank, mostly 12 leagues wide, stretched for 100 leagues. It is nowhere less than 20 fathoms deep. He reckoned that about a hundred French sails fished there yearly, winter and summer. Some ships made two trips a year, and still had plenty of time at home. Richard described how, as he sailed west at the beginning of April he would meet the homeward bound Frenchmen, deeply laden with fish caught in January, February and March: – 'which are the sharpest months of the year for storms and cruell weather.'

Pitie le miserable pecheur! He dangles in a wooden cage lashed to the ship's side, bucking up and down, now far above the sea, now nearly doused in waves; icy cold; soaked by rain and spray, wind whining through rigging; rattling clattering restless racket; bait the heavy hook with cod meat; pay out hook, line and sinker with raw numb hands, down through layer on layer of crowded codfish; soon a bite; haul up the line: wait the right moment when cage dips lowest, to hoist up aboard the struggling twenty pound giant of slithering, sliving fish; grab fast while your mate cuts out the hook; then together heave it onto deck above; re-bait the hook and repeat . . . repeat maybe twenty, thirty, forty times, each hour on weary hour, till the light fades. Then crash out below in dank, dark deck midst reek of dead fish and live, unwashed, shivering humanity; food, unvarying menu of salted pork – and cod – dull beans, weevily biscuits; wash down with sour Breton cider or the occasional sip of rough vin rouge; sleep comes swiftly, hard cold and restless, amid the creaking timbers; then tomorrow: – *demain est hier plus encore!* – *Pitie le pauvre pecheur!*

The French method was to gut the cod and stow the fish at once between liberal layers of salt, produced cheaply in saltpans along the coasts of Brittany, the only part of France exempted a crippling salt tax called 'la gabelle.' This so-called 'green' cod fetched a better price than Poor John and stockfish. The Bretons seldom had need to land on Newfoundland, except perhaps to replenish supplies for the homeward journey.[3] The French later became active along the south coast from whence, in the 17th century, they attacked English settlements.

In all, Richard reckoned that by 1620, there were more than 650 fishing boats upon the coast annually. By that time, something in the order of four thousand million cod would have been slaughtered. Yet if Cabot could have re-visited the waters around Newfoundland he would have found them still 'swarming with fish that they could be taken not only with a net but with a basket weighed down with a stone put in it, so that the basket may plunge to the bottom'.

Of the whole fleet, some 250 were English, mostly West Country ships. The numbers had increased steadily since Richard's first voyage in 1579 as had the size of the ships engaged. For historic and economic reasons the English used a technique different from the continental fishermen. Making salt by evaporating seawater in open saltpans and finally crystallising the concentrate by further boiling fell out of favour in England soon after the Norman Conquest. This was due to an ever-increasing dearth of firewood and a general lack of sunshine. In some places, like Cheshire where deposits of strong brine existed, salt continued to be made but in the West Country it was cheaper by far to import it from places in France such as Morlais and Rochelle. The English method of drying fish with a minimum of salt evolved from the Icelandic experience.

Cod swarmed onto the coast in early summer following bait-fish on which they fed when the latter migrated to the harbours, rivers and beaches to spawn. The West Country ships would arrive on the Avalon Peninsular in ones and twos during April and May. Between Trinity Harbour in the north and Trespassey Bay in the far south, lay scores of safe harbours and coves suitable as fishing camps. The first thing to be done was to secure a sure anchorage and sufficient working space. The long-established custom of the first comer becoming Admiral of the harbour for the year was touched on in the last chapter. The second arrival became the Vice Admiral and the third Rear Admiral. Latecomers could waste valuable days searching up and down the coast for a suitable unoccupied site.

It was a great advantage to be the 'Admiral' of a harbour for the year. He had the right to choose the best anchorage and shore-site. He would pick through the remains of staging and structures abandoned the previous autumn and 'acquire' anything else left lying around. With privileges came duties, chiefly to keep order and to arbitrate the inevitable squabbles that arose among those who arrived later. It was only with the creation by Royal Charter of the Newfoundland Company and the founding of the first colony in 1610 that an official attempt to establish law and order was attempted – without noticeable success.

Once at anchor the ship was unrigged and salt off-loaded while a large party went to fell timber for building, gather firewood, and skin birch trees of their 'rinds' as the strips of bark were called. A stage of strong posts and bracing with a deck of round timbers was built on the edge of the shore, extending out over the sea. Living quarters consisted of turf-covered roof and walls of brushwood sealed on the inside with 'rinds'. A cookhouse, flakes and a storeroom would complete a typical camp. While this was going on bait was gathered, workboats repaired or new ones built. All this preparation would take about three weeks.

James Yonge was the ship's doctor aboard *Reformation* when she went to Renouse, Newfoundland, to fish in 1663. The following edited account of the fishing operation is taken from his diary. Not much would have changed from the practices fifty years earlier.

'The three or four-ton fishing boats will carry over a thousand cod-fish yet three men will row these big boats a long way to and from the fishing ground. Two sit side by side while the boat's master in the stern uses his oar to steer. These three do the fishing with hooker and line while the other two – probably boys – 'save' the fish. When the boat is fully laden or the day spent, they row home and tie up under the stage. While the master is brewing up, two men are left to throw up the fish onto the stage-head using a pitchfork, known as a 'pear'. There, a boy gathers them up and lays them out on a table on the stage. On one side stands a 'header' who slits open the belly, takes out the liver and twines off the head and guts (which falls through the stage into the sea) with notable dexterity and speed. The liver slips through a hole in the table, into a 'cool 'or great tub. Later it is thrown in the train vat, which is a great square chest, where it is reduced to train oil that is drained off into casks.

Then the header thrusts the fish across the table, where sits a 'spilter' – or splitter – who splits it open with a strong knife and with a back-stroke cuts out the bones which fall through a hole into the sea. Some work with incredible speed, splitting more than 900 in the hour. Once split, the fish is dropped into 'drooge' barrows which, when full, are drawn to one side of the stage where boys stack them ready for the 'salter' who comes with salt on a wooden shovel. With a little brush he strews the salt on the fish that are then piled up in three-foot stacks. The salter is a skilful operator since too much salt burns the fish and makes it break and wet; too little makes it 'redshanks', that is it looks red when dried, and is not merchantable.

The fish lie for three or four days or (in bad weather) up to ten days. They are then washed by the boys in salt or fresh water and laid in a pile, skin upwards, on a platform of beach stones, which they call a 'horse'. After a day or two they are laid abroad on flakes which are boughs thinly laid upon frames, like a table, and here the fish dry. By night or in wet weather, they are made up into 'faggots', that is four or five fish with the skins upwards with a broader fish on top.

When well dried they are made into a 'prest' pile, where they sweat; that is, the salt sweats out, and 'corning,' makes the fish look white. After that, they dry one day on the ground and then are made into a so-called 'dry' pile, three times the size of the prest pile. There they stay until shipped out when they are dried for part of a day, then weighed, carried on board, and prest snug with great stones.'[4]

The hours of work were regulated by weather, what the fish did, and routine jobs. Only the Sabbath was kept as a day off. Bait was usually gathered every other day. Herrings, present nearly all the summer, were the standard bait, usually netted at night. Before their arrival, mussels could be used. The best bait were the 'small sweet capelin' that swarmed in astronomical numbers onto the beaches in June to spawn and die. Squid, 'a fish like soaked leather', was also used.

There was little enough time for recreation and no facilities. There were no permanent structures, no dwellings, no alehouses, except perhaps in St John's. The crews would, whenever possible, gather together and sing sea-shanties while the old salts told fishermen's yarns.

As normal practice was for the voyage to be based on profit-sharing nearly everyone worked with a will. A third of the proceeds each went to the owner, the victualler and the master and crew. It was the master who engaged the crew and agreed what portion each member got. The mate used to have two shares, while boat-masters, salters, headers and splitters received cash bonuses in descending amounts. One in six of the crews were 'lurgans' or boys who had to be content with twenty, thirty or forty pennies each.

Diet on the island was healthy but unbalanced. There was no bread or green vegetables, but fish aplenty. There were all sorts of birds' eggs early in the season and towards the end wild fruit such as small cherries and many sorts of berries such as strawberries, rasp-berries, blueberries, cranberries and partridgeberries. Deer, partridges, ducks and geese could be shot or trapped.

Sanitation does not seem to have been a problem. The tidal rise and fall was good so that cod offal would be carried away by the ebbing tide twice a day or eaten by scavengers, if it did not fall straight into the sea.

The crew would have stocked enough cured fish to fill the hold by about the end of July in an average year. Each ship could be loaded and sailed to St John's with a skeleton crew if there was no prior agreement to sell a fixed quantity of dried fish at a specified time and place.

Once there they would be unlucky not to find a sack ship waiting to buy up fish at eight or ten shillings a kentall. Sack ships would have arrived in ballast or with a load of salt for sale. After securing a worthwhile load they would sail for the Mediterranean where the fish could be sold in France or Italy – and in Spain after the conclusion of peace in 1604 – for twelve to sixteen shillings a quintal. The ships would load with high priced commodities such as wine, fruit, sugar and spices and head for home. This was an excellent arrangement for all parties, not least for England that gained rich imports for little outgoing currency.

Our typical fishing vessel, meanwhile, would have returned to her anchorage where the rest of the crew continued amassing dried fish. Once time started to run out in mid-August fish would be loaded 'green' into the hold, each layer being separated with a layer of salt. Casks of traine oil would go aboard from mid-September, together with dried fish pressed down with stones until the hold could take no more. Ships would gather together and return in convoy, a journey usually several days shorter than the outward leg. Some would head for home while others called in on the Atlantic seaboard of Spain, Portugal or France where a marginally better price for the fish would be expected. These vessels could load up with salt for the coming year or any other profitable-looking cargo on offer. They would be home in good time for Christmas.

8

The Years Between

'Omitting to speak of other Voyages I made thither during the late Queenes Raigne, I will descend to later times.'

Richard Whitbourne – Preface

It is quite common for the twenty or more years of a man's early working life to be scantily documented. He is no longer within the ambit of loving or doting parents and not sufficiently established to be of concern or interest to the world at large. He often needs to work hard to support a young family and climb the rungs of his chosen career. He has little time for recreation or reflection.

Perhaps the same held good four hundred years ago, for Richard seems to have fallen into this category. Richard tell us nothing, so this chapter aims to collect such scraps of information as there are about what happened to him after the defeat of the Armada in 1588 until the year 1612. We know that he went to live in the parish of Littleham, Exmouth, soon after completing his apprenticeship because the parish records show that, with Edmond Day, he was a churchwarden in 1589.

It is not known when he married as the register of baptisms, marriages and burials was not started until 1603 when Richard was in his forties. The most popular age for a man to wed was about twenty-seven. His wife Joane, who died in 1620, was buried in Littleham. Richard probably never remarried. Joanne was not mentioned in her father-in-law's will of 1597. Had they a son at that time he would have inherited at the least, one sheep. They certainly had one daughter, Katherine, who married the incumbent of Bishopsteignton, Mr William Hele, widower, on 23 May, 1612, in the parish church of St John the Baptist. Katherine was born not later than 1595, and may have been their only child.

The shipping records for that time are an obvious place to search. Exeter Customs Rolls, held in the Devon Records Office, are almost complete from 1579 to 1603 although often difficult to read. They cover all the ports in the Exe estuary, Dawlish and Teignmouth. The equivalent records for the reign of James I are held in the Public Records Office at Kew but there are few records for the first seven years of the reign. From entries found that include all variations of the name Whidborne I found John, father of Richard, William and John (2), entered as 'master' four times between 1591 and 1595. He died in 1597 aged about 60. It is just possible that the last of these entries refers to John (2) born about 1576, who had a son Gilbert in 1597. Richard was listed as ship's master three times and the importer of merchandise nine times and William was shown as a salt importer in 1587 and as master of *Endeavour* in 1602. When father John wrote his will in 1597, William was absent and his whereabouts unknown. For certain Richard either owned, wholly or in part, *Gift of God*, 40 tons, (1583–1597), *Mayflower*, 50 tons, (1593–1597), *Grace of God*, 30 tons, (1599, 1601), *Endeavour*, 120 tons, (1602), *Seraphine*, 70 tons, (1614–1617) and, perhaps *Truelabourer*, 30 tons, (1601, 1602).

The Exeter Customs Records do not, however, give anything like a complete record of all voyages. Only ships where duty was payable were included and fish was duty-free. While train oil was taxed at six shillings a tonne, fishermen would often sell their oil to a sack ship in Newfoundland. If the ship had first sailed to the continent and sold its catch there, it would not appear in the customs rolls. Occasionally, for some good reason, a ship would put in at a port not its own. Many fishing trips to Newfoundland were arranged through charters, which were a convenient way of spreading risks between the many merchants, engaged in the industry. Records of Exeter charters, however, do not appear to have survived. Richard was involved in many more ships and voyages whose records no longer exist.

Richard's father John died in 1597 and his will provides valuable information especially about relationships and property. (See page 2 for his immediate family tree). Richard, as elder son, was named as sole executor and inheritor of the residual estate. Joanne, the only other surviving child of his first marriage, and her husband Thomas

Cornelius were living at Kingsdowne and Haywardes Park, part of the old family farm at Radways in Bishopsteignton that John held on lease for an undisclosed term. The will allowed them to continue to live there until a year before the lease expired, when it would revert to Richard.

Thomas, John and Richarde's eldest son, was still a bachelor in 1597 having been set up on a farm in Ashcoombe. He married my nine-times great grandmother Francis Perriman in 1598. He eventually became the right heir of John, after Richard died leaving no legal heir. John's will granted Thomas possession of the properties known as Dawlishewater and Dawlishe Ford for life. These were extensive and it would seem that John had bought them, with others mentioned below, from the profits of many successful Newfoundland fishing trips during the 1590s. Since nothing in the will made mention of boats or fishing gear, it is probable that Richard had already taken over all John's shipping interests.

Richard inherited a house and half an acre of land at Exsone, 'being held by one deed of purchase with all the writings endorses and scripts belonging to the same.'[m9] During a weekend in October 2003, I found the cob-under-thatch Eastdon house still standing and little altered after four hundred years. The plot is shown on the large scale CX map as No.153 with a calculated area of 0.577 acres. It lies in a narrow strip ending to seaward in what would have been the high tide level in 1597. The Whitbourne ship at that time was *Mayflower* too large at 50 tons to operate safely from Teignmouth harbour. She could have had a safe anchorage in the main Exe channel two or three cables out from Eastdon. It is possible that *Mayflower* was built at the bottom of the half-acre plot. The cottage would certainly have been a useful base for servicing fishing vessels.

In his 'Synopsis Chorographical of Devonshire', Exeter's Chancellor John Hooker wrote in 1599 that the Devon yeomen were now 'also able and to daily furnish no small number of ships which from time to time do harbour themselves in the havens and creeks of that country, with beefs, barrows and porks but also with biscuits and beer and cider, beans and peasons' for outgoing voyages 'whether it be at the new found land for fishing or the lands and countries for merchandise'.

John also bequeathed to Richard 'all the house and lands which I have lying within the tithing of East Teignmouth'. There is but one

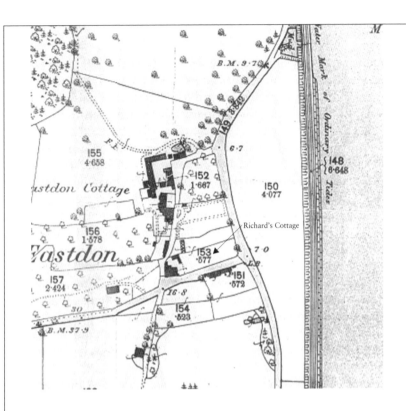

*The cottage at Eastdon, on the banks of the Exe estuary,
as it is today*

tenuous clue to this property. Many years later, in 1773, pioneering novelist and diarist Fanny Burney (1752–1840) wrote in her journal and letters, of her stay with a Mr and Mrs Rishton whom she said 'are turned absolute hermits for this summer. They have left Bath and are gone to Ting Mouth in Devonshire, where they have taken a cottage rather than a house.' 'But the country,' she writes, 'is beautiful.' She comments further that Mr Rishton's house is 'not in the town but on the Den which is the mall here: It is a small, neat, thatched and white washed cottage, neither more nor less. We are not a hundred yards from the sea in which Mr Rishton bathes every morning.' The cottage rented by the Rishtons was on Little Den and belonged to a Captaine Whitbourne.[1]

It happened that at that time there were Whitbournes still living in Teignmouth and trading with Newfoundland. Peter Whitborne was a powerful merchant trading out of Fermeuse while Thomas Whitborne, of Teignmouth, signed a petition of merchants dated 2 February, 1779, against the 1778 Act.[2] As young bridegrooms, both were described, as 'mariners' and either one of them could have become a captain.

Coombe Farm is not mentioned in John's will and one can only assume that Richard inherited it. It could have been farmed by either of John's daughters with their husbands. The only record is from a mortgage document dated 24 December 1675, when a James Smith (mariner) was in possession of Coombe on a lease for three lives from Richard Whitbourne of Bishopsteignton. It could be that John held Coombe on lease for his life only from Thomas of Ashill, perhaps John's elder brother.[3]

Former Devon archivist J.F. Chanter found, in 1924, among the Bishop of Exeter's Archives, a number of 'Testimoniales Litterae pro Navigantibus.' He quotes three, from the months of September and November, 1603, that are relevant to Richard's career:

'The ship called *Endeavour*, of Exmouth, 140 tons, Robert Perryman, master, Richard Whitbourn and George Troublefylde, merchants, crew 33 men or thereabouts.

The ship called *Mayflower*, of Exmouth, 60 tons, William Meare, master, John Borrough, merchant, crew 15 men and boys.'

On another date, not given, we have:- 'and *Endeavour*, of

Topsham, 140 tons, Richard Whitbourne, master, George Turberville, merchant, bound for various parts of Spain.'[4]

Regrettably the original documents, presumably letters of introduction to Spanish port officials, are missing. Whether Mr Chanter or Adolf Hitler, whose bombs caused havoc to the Cathedral records in 1942, was to blame it is hard to say. It is more certain that, following the peace with Spain of 1603, Richard made an exploratory voyage to Spain presumably to assess the commercial opportunities for resuming trade. In his book, he describes Spain's Mediterranean coast in considerable detail giving the impression that he had systematically explored it rather than just sailing to her ports.

'Likewise it is well knowne to all those that have travailed from thence [Portugal] all along its coast of *Spaine*, even to *Granada*, how barren and rockie those parts of *Spaine* are also in most places; and yet the people by their good industry, plant many of their Vines and other fruits, on the sides of some steepe Hils amongst the Rocks, where men are faine in divers place, even to creepe on their hands and knees to prune the said Vines, and gather the Grapes of them, to make their strong wines, and sweet Raysins withall, which we so much delight to taste. In those toothsome and delightfull Commodities, our Marchants bestow much money[5] . . .'

'Likewise from *Granada* to *Carthagena, Allegant, Denia,* and from thence even to the Citie of *Valencia*, which is a large circuit, the most part all along, as I have travelled, are very barren, rockie and mountainous; that very few Cattell, Sheepe, Goats, or any other beasts are able to live there;'

Here Richard is arguing that not only could Newfoundland be equally productive, given the will, but also that there was a huge market for fish in the Mediterranean countries, due to a general shortage of meat. While Richard was wide of the mark regarding the suitability of the Newfoundland climate for grapes, it is curious to note that the very place there named after him – Whitbourne Junction, now bereft of its railway and little more than a hamlet, has a flourishing winery. It is unusual, in that its wines are made from indigenous berries such as blueberry and cranberry rather than from grapes.

Grapes, coincidentally, are now being grown on the steep south facing hill that backs the Whitbourne ancestral homestead of Ashill

Farm, Bishopsteignton. Harvested by tractor, the rows of vines run up and down the slope. Years ago, people remember seeing faint horizontal furrows along the contours. Later fruit bushes were grown, and the lines disappeared. Roman coins have been found nearby so that it is possible that grapes were last grown on this site during the Roman occupation, when Exeter was a major port. The recent climate warming, from whatever cause, seems to give a promise of merry sunshine and some vintage years ahead.

It was not so warm at the beginning of the seventeenth century, when the Thames was prone to freezing over. There are few records of Newfoundland's winter weather, since people seldom stayed there, but clearly there were mild winters mixed with harsh ones, as is still the case. Generalising, it must be said that Richard was over-optimistic over the agricultural potential of the island and its climate. Even so, the crews managed to survive quite well through-out the summer months spent there, living on birds' eggs and wild fruits, game-meat and, of course, unlimited fish.

The plague, such a scourge in the English towns right up to the year 1666, although initially imported by ship-borne rats, was never a problem amongst the fishermen. This was probably due to the scattered nature of the fishing camps – and the colder summers. Deaths from the plague always peaked in the hotter weather from July to November, when the rats were most active and numerous. The West Country had major epidemics throughout Richard's lifetime, notably in 1564, 1570-71, 1589-91, 1625-28 and 1636. 1603 was a disaster year for London, when over 37 thousand burials were recorded that summer – at least 17% of the population. The infection spread slowly, and was dying out by the time it reached East Devon the following summer.[6] Richard's father, John, and stepmother almost certainly died of the plague and were buried together on 17 July 1597. Their grandson, Thomas of Mamhead and his wife Mablia were buried within ten days of each other in July 1629, also doubtless victims of the plague.

For his part, Richard counted one of his greatest 'comforts' the fact that he **'was never, as yet, in all my time beholding to any doctor's counsel or Apothecaries drugs for the preservation of my health.'**[7] A mere stripling of sixty summers when he wrote this, Richard lived for another fifteen years and even then may have died by mischance rather than from natural causes. He lived in an age when life itself was held in much less regard than today, when the newborn would, more likely than not, be dead within thirty years.

For those who made their living in ships on the high seas, there were extra dangers to be weathered, besides the hazards of storm and tempest. Starvation and disease were two. Once the Armada had fled in 1588, for example, the half starved and diseased remnants of England's victorious navy lay about the streets of some ports. From *Elizabeth Bonaventure* alone two hundred out of a compliment of five hundred, died.[8] This mortality was caused partly by the impossibility of provisioning ships on such a massive scale. But the practice of making up crew numbers by impounding inmates from prison led to the rapid spread of the deadly 'jail fever' typhus.

Scurvy was to remain an unresolved problem for many years. It was not, however, much of a worry for Newfoundland fishermen whose diet was largely one of fish. James Yonge, the ship's surgeon who spent the summers of 1663 and 1669 in Newfoundland, kept a fascinating diary describing his work in detail. He identifies two forms of scurvy: 'The one, soon caught, soon cured, the other a cachexy, or dry scurvy, which makes the patient look thin, yellow, squalled, with pain and paresis of the limbs, and is often mortal.' It was 'an acute scurvy, their gums rot, thick-breathed, swollen, black, indurated hams and thighs, tumours of the legs, yielding to the touch, exravasation of the blood; a disease not curable by all the medicines which can be carried there but easily by a few vegetables of the country.'

Yonge's prescription included the roots of stinking gladwin as a purgative 'which works violently both ways' and was followed by 'the tops of spruce, wild vetches, agrimony, a sort of wild succory (called here scurvy leaves) steept in beer, and bathing them in decoctions of the same'. While Yonge was spot on with the treatment he was somewhat adrift with the causes. These were, he thought 'partly from the great mutation of the weather, which when we first come is very cold, and in July shall be intolerably hot, partly from the aqueous and crude nourishment, fish, and from the sudden colds after fatigues of labour, but mostly from the air which is crude, foggy and scorbutick.' Then as now, the medical men liked to baffle the ordinary folk with obscure words.

Other maladies Yonge had to deal with included 'breaking out of the arm wrist', doubtless caused by processing so much fish; colds and coughs, 'vexatious haemorrhages of the nose' from 'eating much of the liver of the cods, which is here very delicious' and from a surfeit of herring that were 'the fairest, fattest, sweetest, and largest in the world'. He also had to deal with a little boy who had severely frost-bitten fingers, toes, both heels and the tip of his nose. All in all, Yonge was kept quite busy with largely minor ailments among his own and other crews, yet had leisure enough 'to study, to walk, to fish,' and to travel about the island. It is unlikely that conditions in Newfoundland were much different from when Richard was there half a century before.[9]

Richard never spent a winter on the island, where lack of good housing and the most simple amenities must have caused severe hardship. Richard maintained, mistakenly, that because it was some three degrees further south than England, Newfoundland's average winters would be milder. How he occupied himself in Exmouth we do not know. His ship was likely to visit France or Spain for the next year's salt, but there was no need for him to go in person and records suggest that he rarely acted as master of his own ship.

9

Peter Easton – Arch Pirate

'In the yere 1611, being in *New-found-land*, at which time that famous Arch-pirate, *Peter Easton*, came there, and had with him ten saile of good ships, well furnished and very rich.'

Richard Whitbourne – The Preface

Because of their occupation, pirates have always been a secretive breed not given to writing autobiographies. Indeed, many pirates would have been illiterate. The best written relic that one might hope to discover would be a much thumbed and rudimentary plan of an unidentifiable island with an 'X' marking the spot where great treasure was purported to be buried. In attempting to unravel the mysteries of their careers, researchers have to rely heavily on bureaucratic records that are often obscure and conflicting. Pirates tended to remain shadowy, legendary figures, bereft of human feelings and traits. To be successful in their career they needed to be a villainous bunch of unruly criminals. Peter Easton was not untypical.

Little is known of his early life. One source says that he was a 'man of low birth'. But the grant of a royal pardon by James I refers to him as 'late of London, gent'. It seems that he must have received some education as he wrote letters, which have not survived, to several Irish judges and officials. He was also expert in 'laying off guns' and, presumably, navigation.

He is first heard of somewhere off the coast of Ireland in 1608. It was a wild and sparsely peopled coast, a favourite haunt for pirates. A fellow pirate named Robinson limped into Cork harbour with his ship in very poor shape in June of that year. He complained that he had been 'treacherously overthrown by Easton,' among others, and offered to give himself up.

In another incident two years later, Easton killed Saukewell (or Salkeild) 'that petty rebel and pirate,' by throwing him overboard. Easton offered to give himself up to Lord Deputy of Ireland Sir Arthur Chichester. Uncertain of what policy the Privy Council would want him to follow, Chichester temporised, granting Easton and his fellow captains a protection order of forty days. Their ships were then lying off Munster port, probably Baltimore, and the order 'restrained them from coming ashore, other than two or three at a time, and then only for such as the vice-president [of Munster] shall allow of.' Easton, doubtless irked by these petty constraints, landed in numbers. The vice-president responded by sending a force to intercept the pirates but all, with the exception of a captain Gabriell, escaped.

The pirates promptly weighed anchor and sailed away. They probably spent the winter in or around Mamorra, a noted piratical bastion on the Barbary Coast of Africa. According to Easton, forty pirate ships manned by about 2,000 English men, regularly used the port of Mamorra as a rendezvous where they could safely dispose of their spoils to the local merchants. Easton may also have made a foray to Leghorn in the Mediterranean. There he talked to the Duke of Florence who appears to have extended a pardon and some degree of protection.

Easton and his followers are next heard of in the following February, 1611, near the Bristol Channel. A Captain Henry Mainwaring, who himself turned to piracy shortly afterwards, was commissioned to proceed to the area and confront Easton. Before any contact could be made, Easton quit the area, taking his fleet back to Limecon in Ireland. On 26 June, with a consort of at least six ships, he attacked and captured two large merchantmen sixty miles south of the Isles of Scilly. The prizes taken were the 240-ton *Concord*, of London, and *Phillip Bonaventure*, of the port of Dover. The latter was ransacked and released after about a week. Easton later claimed that it had been his intention to release *Concord* also.

But while Easton and a colleague, Hewes, slept in the main cabin of *Concord* they were set upon by some of the merchants remaining aboard her. The two pirates, despite being wounded, overcame their assailants, killing one while another three jumped overboard. Easton also relates that, at the same time: 'I lost my principal ship and all my wealth by the negligence of my own company'. It appears there was a mutiny while Easton was aboard *Concord*, with his crew making off with his flag ship. Extremely irate and set upon revenge, he decided to retain *Concord*.

He sent the remaining merchants and ships' crew to *Bonaventure* but promised to restore *Concord* and its cargo if the merchants could secure him the King's pardon, while at the same time threatening to land at Causton Bay [Cawsands] Plymouth, to take on supplies.

With a consort of nine warships and four prize ships, Easton set sail once more for Munster to renew negotiations for his pardon. He arrived at Limecon in mid-July and immediately started to refit his fleet, converting *Concord* into his new flagship. Port of Munster vice-admiral Captain Skipworth sent an ex-pirate named Bishop, also awaiting a pardon, to discuss terms with Easton. While the other captains in Easton's fleet begged for the King's mercy, Easton wanted to make for the Barbary coast, sell his assets and enter Duke of Florence's service. However, he agreed to surrender provided the pardon arrived by 'Friday seven nights'.

Throughout this time James 1 had been pondering the matter of a pardon with his Privy Council. The Venetian Ambassador in London wrote to the Doge reporting that the king was reluctant to compromise. But the great strength of the pirate fleet, compared with that of his navy, persuaded the king to send an envoy to negotiate with Easton. The envoy, Captain Roger Middleton, did not arrive in Ireland until 17 August only to find that Easton had left ten days earlier. According to Middleton, Easton had received intelligence that three ships, under the control of Dutch general Moy Lamber, were approaching Limecon.

While his ships were 'clean,' Easton made it clear he intended to spend time pirating off the north-west Cape of Spain before heading once more for Mamorra, trading any spoils, and retiring to Leghorn. Captain Skipworth's report was different. He maintained that Easton was afraid of being captured by the 'Hollanders' (as Bishop had been earlier) and had departed with a promise to return and give himself up.

Middleton promised to go after the pirates with the first favourable wind and it appears that he did. He did not return to Ireland until December and then left for London. However, it was not until the following February that the king, still much against his better judgement, granted a pardon on the conditions stipulated by Easton – who had changed his mind once more. He had probably found good pickings off the Spanish coast and North Africa and is known to have taken an English ship off the coast of Guinea.

Easton sailed from the Isle of May, in the Cape Verde Islands, captured a French fishing ship near the Banks on the way and arrived in Newfoundland with ten ships early in 1612. He proceeded to scour the coast from Renews in the south to Harbour Grace in the north, building a fort in the latter. His fleet captured nine ships and took two hundred pieces of ordnance and stores of all sorts, valued at about £10,400. Up to 500 English sailors were also taken 'although many are volunteers'. Easton's men attacked at least fifteen ships of the French fishing fleet to the value of £6,000, took a great Flemish ship worth about £1,000 and damaged twelve Portuguese ships to the value of £3,000.

Governor of the first Newfoundland settlement (established in 1610) John Guy gave a lively and interesting account of Easton's activities in a letter to John Slaney and other members of the council of the company of the Newfoundland plantation. His letter, dated 29 July, 1612, reads:

'Because the proceedings of one Captain Peter Easton, a Pirate, and his company, since are most fit to be known, before I touch our Plantation business, you shall understand what they have bin unto this time until the seventeenth of this present, the said Captain Easton remained in Harbour de Grace, there trimming, and repairing his Shipping, and commanding not only the Carpenters of each ship so do his business, but hath taken victuals, munitions, and necessaries from every ship, together with about one hundred men out of the Bay to man his ships, being now in number six. He purposed to have before he goes, as is said, out of the land 500 men; while he remained there, two several companies to the number of about 180 persons to each Company, being discontented, stole away from him in a Shallop, and took two ships that were fishing in Trinity Bay, one belonging to Barnstable and one other to Plymouth, and so intend to begin to be new heads of that damnable course of life.

As I sailed from hence towards Renews in a small Bark, I fell into one of their hands, and one of my company was hurt with a musket. There was one of their crew that wintered with me here the first year, by whose means, and because I was in the bark they made show, that they were sorry that they had meddled with us. And so they departed from us, without coming aboard. That which they sought after was men to increase their numbers.

Before the said Captain Easton's departure, he sent three ships into Trinity Bay, to store himself with victuals, munition, and men, who are said to be worse used then the Ships here. The said Easton was lately at Saint Jones, and is now, as far as I can learn, at Ferriland where he takes his pleasure, and thereabouts the rest are to meet him. It is given out, that he will send one Captain Harvey in a ship to Ireland, to understand news about his pardon, which if he can obtain in that large and ample manner as he expects, then he gives out, that he will come in. Otherwise, it is thought that he will get Protection of the Duke of Florence, and that in his course here hence he will hover about the Westwards of the Islands of the Azores to see whether he can light upon any of the Plate fleet, or any good rich booty, before his coming in.[1]'

Initially Easton made his headquarters at Ferriland where he detained about seven masters of English vessels. One fancies that by holding them captive but treating them well Easton was able to get all he desired from the English fleet. One of these masters was Richard, who in the preface to his Discourse recounts his time with Easton:

'I was kept eleven weekes under his command and had from him many golden promises and much wealth to be put into my hands, as it is well knowne: I did persuade him much to desist from his evill course; his intreaties then to me, being, that I would come for *England*, to some friends of his, and sollicite them to become humble petitioners to your Majesty for his pardon: but having no warrant to touch such goods, I gave him thankes for his offer; only I requested him to release a Ship that he had taken upon the Coast of *Guinnie*, belonging to one Captaine *Rashly* of *Foy* in *Cornewall*; a man whom I knew but onely by report: which he accordingly released.

Whereupon I provided men, victuals, and a fraught for the said Ship, and so sent her home to *Dartmouth* in *Devon*, though I never had so much as thankes for my kindnesse therein. And so leaving *Easton*, I came for *England* and gave notice of his intention, letting passe my Voyage that I intended for *Naples*, and lost both my labour and charges: for before my arrivall, there was a Pardon granted, and sent him from *Ireland*. But *Easton* hovering with those Ships and riches, upon the Coast of *Barbary*, as hee promised, with a longing desire, and full expectation to be called home, lost that hope by a too much delaying of time by him who carried the Pardon. Whereupon he sailed to the Straights of *Gibralta*r and was afterwards entertained by the Duke of *Savoy*, under whom he lived rich.²'

This account is of considerable interest, although Richard manages to cloud rather than clarify the course of events once Easton had left Newfoundland. Richard is careful to emphasise that he never profited from his contact with Easton. Nearly everyone who had dealings with pirates in those days was accused, sooner or later, of complicity. Captains Middleton and Skipworth were no exceptions but whether charges against these two officers were justified, the records do not reveal. Easton's move in releasing Rashley's ship was wise. Generally, he avoided taking English ships wherever possible. Rashley's may have been the only one taken since *Concord* and *Phillip Bonaventure*. The retention of Rashley's ship could have seriously delayed, or even prevented the granting of a pardon, while her release was a strong token of Easton's good intentions.

The pirate forces left Newfoundland towards the end of July. It appears that the majority of them made for the Azores in the hope of surprising the Spanish treasure fleets. At the end of September Easton was rumoured to be at Valentia Island, off the west coast of Ireland, and in considerable strength. He sent one of his lieutenants, Gilbert Roope, into Kinsale in the *Katherin of Oloone*, a ship taken the previous May and known as the *Isle d'Oleron*, his mission being to ascertain if anything had happened with respect to his pardon. However, Easton's control over his fleet was weakening. Two prize ships escaped and were brought into Irish ports. One was commanded by Latimer, who had been forcibly abducted by one Galton, and the other by Sneller, a consort of Peter Johnson.

Another pirate, Harris, came in and accused Easton and Roope of 'having spoken unworthily of the King and Queen in their cups': but when examined by Sir Arthur Chichester, Latimer declared: 'that the accusation is false and is invented out of malice against Easton by

Harris who has run away with one of his ships and pillaged a merchant ship of Wexford'. Another of Easton's captains, Baugh, and also a consort, surrendered, but there are no details available on this incident.

In a letter to the Doge dated 15th October 1612, the Venetian Ambassador to London wrote: 'A famous pirate who haughtily refused the pardon offered by his Majesty declaring that he would not bow to the orders of one King when he himself was, in a way, a King as well, has sailed with ten great warships to Newfoundland where there are usually to be found a large number of fishing craft. He has taken away every fifth man and also a fifth of the provisions, which were abundant and with these he has sailed towards the East Indies with the intent to lie in wait for the Spanish flotilla. This is reported by one of these ships on board of which were a large number of hands who wished to change their career, and so slew the remainder, and, aided by the wind, and parted by the storm, sought shelter here last week.'

Richard, whose London contact was probably the Lord High Admiral Howard, would have reached London about this time, only to discover that the first pardon had been granted as long ago as the previous February. On the 26th November, probably as a result of Richard's report to Easton's friends, the pardon was re-granted. There is a conflict of dates, since the Council had written to Chichester eight days earlier, on the 18th November, saying that they 'approve of his opinion that all who may now be admitted to the King's pardon repair to some port in England. They directed that Peter Easton, Coope [sic], and the others who have been pardoned, and whose pardons are sent to him by Captain Middleton, shall be required to bring their ships to Portsmouth, and for their countenance and assistance, Henry Skipworth, vice-Admiral of Munster, and Captain Middleton shall accompany them.'

Once again Easton seems to have a change of mind, and sailed for the Barbary Coast before Middleton could deliver his pardon. There is no corroborative evidence that Middleton was dilatory and his warrant may not have included another trip to the Barbary Coast. What is more likely is that Easton's 'longing desire' to be called home quickly fell away when he learned that the Duke of Savoy, Carlos Emmanual 1st, was making overtures to the Mamorra pirates. The Duke was short of finances, and thought that, by making his ports free, he might boost the trade through Nice and Villafranca to rival that of Leghorn. This he did by a proclamation in February 1613, which offered asylum and safe conduct to all, no matter what their crimes.

Before the end of March Easton sailed into Villafranca with four ships, 900 picked soldiers and over 40,000 crowns in coin. He made an agreement with the Duke whereby he, Easton, would pay a once and for all tithe on his wealth, provided he would be protected from molestation at the request of foreign princes. He stored his plunder safely, laid up his ships, including a further ten that arrived at a later date, and bought himself a palace and some fancy titles.

By August he was well on the road to enjoying his retirement when he was accidentally shot with a harquebus, from which he nearly died. Six months later he was again fit and went to Turin where he became a favourite of the Duke and the court. His life at court did not last long, for the Duke carried out a raid on a neighbour, the Duke of Mantua, in which he employed Easton in his siege train. Easton acquitted himself well, for it was said 'the Englishman has covered himself with glory, among his other achievements he is so skilful in laying guns that a few shots by him produce more effect than most gunners produce from many'.

When James 1 heard of Easton's new life style, he made representations through the Marchese Villa, the Savoyade ambassador, such that the Duke promised to do the King's bidding. Easton countered with an offer to re-commission his fleet under the aegis of the Savoy navy. This offer was accepted by the Duke as being a direct threat to Venice that had sided with the Duke of Mantua. Although Venice took the threat seriously, Easton's ships were reported to be 'no better than boxes, and valueless as ships of war.' They probably never sailed again, and when two were sunk and the rest badly damaged in a storm in November 1613, Easton finally retired from active service. He took the catholic faith, was ennobled by the Duke as a Marquis, and was also joined in matrimony to a very rich heiress.

So far as is known, Easton was never heard of again and possibly died about 1620. Richard's writings seem to support this theory since in his draft of the Preface written in 1619 he says Easton 'now liveth very rich,' but in the editions of 1620 and 1622 this became 'he lived rich'. It is omitted altogether from the 1623 edition.

Richard's involvement appears to have left him out of pocket, but perhaps by less than he tried to make out. In any event, by pressing Easton's case for a pardon to his friends and the Council, Richard may well have made contacts that stood him in good stead in later years.

As for the famous arch-pirate Peter Easton, he is scarcely remembered outside of Newfoundland. There he has acquired a rich aura of mystique and legend, while from the dusty pages of the Public Records Office he emerges as a volatile, charismatic character, intelligent yet vacillating, brave and boastful, who got far more from his life of crime than his just deserts: especially so, should his bride have turned out to have been comely and amenable – as well as exceeding rich.

10

First Court of Admiralty

'In the *yeare 1615* I returned againe to *New-found-land*, carrying with me a Commission out of the high Court of Admiralty, under the great Seale thereof, authorizing me to impannell Juries, and to make inquiry upon oath, of sundry abuses and disorders committed amongst Fishermen yeerly upon that Coast, and the fittest meanes to redress the same, with some other poynts, having a more particular relation to the Office of the Lord Admirall.'

Richard Whitbourne – Preface

It is not a little surprising that the first ever English Court of Law to be held in North America was not entrusted to a judge, lawyer or Justice of the Peace, but to a ship's captain with little or no formal education or experience of legal affairs.

To appreciate why this came about, some understanding is needed of the office and jurisdiction of the Lord High Admiral of England at the beginning of the 17th century. Even then the office was ancient, dating back four hundred years. Besides being one of great responsibility, it had become one with rich rewards to the holder from the 'privileges' that went with the job. So much so that the Sovereign, and later the government, spent the next two centuries clawing back as many of these perks as possible. The last Lord High Admiral was William Duke of Clarence, appointed in 1827; thereafter the office was merged with that of the First Lord of the Admiralty.

The High Court of Admiralty was to seafarers and to those whose business relied upon the seas, what common law courts were to landlubbers. The 'Sea Laws of Oleron', which applied in the courts of Admiralty, were a common law of the sea whose origins are lost in the mists of antiquity[1]. Matters maritime are frequently international in character so it is not entirely surprising that the laws of the sea of the various nations bordering the Mediterranean, Baltic and western seas had much in common. For want of a better – or less biased – alternative, the High Court of Admiralty played the role, notably in Tudor and Stuart times, of an international maritime court.

The story goes that Eleanor of Aquitaine, while consort to Louis VII of France, accompanied him to the Holy Land on a crusade. There she observed that the collection of customs of the sea contained in the 'Book of the Consulate' was held in high repute in the Levant. On her return she had a record made of the judgements of the maritime Court of the Island of Oleron, which related to the wine trade between Brittany, Normandy, England and Flanders, that it should serve as law among the mariners of the western seas. Richard I, Eleanor's son by her later marriage to Henry II of England, brought back a copy of these Judgements on his return from the Holy Land, which he then ordained to be observed in England as law. The High Court itself was established by either Edward I or Edward III.

The scope of the High Court of Admiralty was to try or settle:

1 criminal cases committed on the high seas, including piracy and high treason.
2 cases where the ownership of vessels was in dispute.
3 cases in respect of salvage.
4 wartime claims with regard to prizes.
5 wage-disputes and labour questions, such as desertion.
6 breaches of trading contracts.

Cases of smuggling and 'owling', the illicit export of wool or sheep, were considered as cases against the king's revenue and were usually tried by a baron (judge) of the Court of the Exchequer.

The need for an infrastructure to administer these laws arose in early Tudor times when the king's navy was being formed. It created a new class of officials known, from 1536 onwards, as Vice-admirals. Over the years a series of instructions on their duties – and perks – were issued, the final one during Queen Mary's reign. Every coastal county had its Vice-admiral. They had to appoint a deputy who was a trained lawyer, unless they were themselves. Among other matters they were required 'to proceed in matters of piracy and other offences according to the order of the laws'. Vice-admirals had no jurisdiction over pirates, however, being required simply 'to stay them'. They had to hold quarterly sessions of general inquiry and courts of judgement; also common courts to try suits between contending parties, as the need arose.

These courts had to be held at convenient times and places, in the presence of a registrar who kept the necessary records. Three record books were required, one of warrants and original actions, another of acts, constitutions, decrees and releases, and a third of processes, inquest verdicts and a record of casualties belonging to the admiral. They were also responsible for collecting all monies due to the king and admiral that accrued from flotsam, jetsam and lagon, from royal fish, deodands,[2] and other casualties, plus the fines and fees taken in their courts. For the honest performance of this work they had to give a bond to the admiral when he took office. Finally, each registrar was supposed to furnish the High Court of Admiralty with a 'fair and true copy' of the entire proceedings of his court during the previous year.

With the exception of Norfolk and Suffolk (1536), Lancashire and Cheshire (1635, 1636, 1639–42), and Essex (1636) no register has survived – indeed, most were probably never submitted. It is therefore little wonder that neither Richard's original commission nor his 'presentment' to the Lord Admiral on his return have come to light.[3]

West Country fishermen (and nearly all English fishermen from the 'out-ports') had harboured a grudge against rich City of London merchants for countless years. To them it appeared that the merchants had undue influence with government and repeatedly received monopolies and other favours from the Crown that whittled away fishermen's hard-won rights. By 1615, they were suspicious of what went on at court where, with Sir Walter Raleigh languishing in the Tower and the other West Country heroes Hawkins and Drake long dead, there was no one left to fight their corner.

Those in Whitehall were well aware of the English fishing industry's value as a source of mariners for the royal navy in times of war. Theirs was a careful balancing act between the need to preserve time-honoured traditions and the commercial opportunities presented by the expanding world of the early 17th century. This is well shown in the 1610 charter for the Newfoundland Company which was a joint venture between City merchants and those of Bristol for colonizing that country. While the colony's governor had the power to make laws for the maintenance of order, the ancient rights of the fishermen were to be strictly observed.

John Guy, a Bristol merchant and the first governor, was the mainspring of the Newfoundland Company. He was a strong believer in the advantages permanent settlements would bring to the fishing industry by the development of agriculture and the exploitation of the country's other natural resources. He wasted no time and his first settlement, well organised with about 60 chosen men, was established at Cupids in Conception Bay the next year.

This disturbing fait accompli was bad enough, but, a year later, Guy issued a set of laws, to be observed by all, on pain of penalty fines of £5 and £10. Cries of 'What did Oi tell 'ee?' and the virtual sound of cutlass sharpening, were heard in every fishing cove and harbour on the Avalon peninsular. The laws in themselves were sensible, curbing many abuses that had been going on for years – but as an exercise in tact and good neighbourliness they were a disaster.[4]

News of trouble brewing filtered back to the Admiralty. When Richard went to see the Lord Admiral seeking to help in gaining a pardon for another pirate, he was asked what all the trouble was about. Thomas Aylesbury had been secretary to the High Admiral for nine years. Conscientious and caring, he doubtless saw the wisdom of having a West Country fisherman investigating the disaffection of the industry and the abuses that were alleged. Thus the inquiry that followed lay strictly within the Admiralty's scope and stepped on the toes of neither the Privy Council nor the Secretaries of State. One suspects that Aylesbury's was the inspiration that led to Richard being offered the task. Given promises of proper recompense, he must have been well pleased and probably flattered to be entrusted with this Commission.

We have to rely largely on Richard's very full and 'grandoloquatious' description of proceedings. It is clear that his brief must have been to conduct an ordinary court of inquiry – an inquest or inquisition – something the High Court of Admiralty had not done previously. It enabled Richard to act on behalf of the Lord High Admiral, without having to be appointed a vice-admiral.

Richard first mentions the commission in the Preface and then in detail towards the end of the Discourse. It is also mentioned in a private letter to Lord Falkland dated 27 February 1625/6.[5] He set out from the Port of Exeter on 11 May 1615 in a bark, with a crew of 11 men and a boy, which he had hired at his own expense. He reached Trinity Bay on Trinity Sunday, being 4 June, and there anchored after a speedy voyage. He immediately issued a precept:- 'in the name of the holy and individual Trinity' summoning the masters of all English ships riding at anchor in the bay, and nearby, to attend the first Court of Admiralty ever to be held in North America, as was required by his commission. Many Trinity folk today think that the opening session was held on the foreshore close to the old Customs House.

For the next two months he sailed along the coast reaching Ferrilands, anchoring wherever English ships were fishing, and holding his court. Richard then retraced his course seeking out those ships which may have been missed on the outward circuit. He reckoned his voyage at 150 leagues – more than 500 sea miles. That was probably no exaggeration if all the creeks and inlets in Trinity and Conception bays were visited.

The Sabbath was strictly observed by Richard, while two days a week were needed to move from one harbour to the next. A further day was required to set up his court and give due notice of the court's next sitting. With thirty or forty locations to visit, nearly all sittings were completed in a day. There were few, if any, places with a permanent building suitable for a courtroom, except in St John's. Richard is likely to have brought a tent that would protect against sun, wind and rain but, with witnesses outside yarning while waiting to appear, camp dogs barking and gulls screaming as they fought over the offal from the gutted cod-fish, 'silence in court' was hard to maintain. A couple of the crew acted as court ushers, no doubt.

At first he may have attempted to empanel juries on pain of fine by those who defaulted. This was clearly a mistake that aggrieved the fishermen but produced no revenue. All he ever got – and that from two harbours which he had been particularly asked to visit by the masters – was a small contribution **'which was not able to defray half the losses and expenses which I had sustained'**. True, he took charge of **'two small boats, anchors and a small grapple that were found in the sea upon that coast,'** valued at two shillings and sixpence an item. However, these were 'droit' due to the Lord Admiral under the law and known as 'lagan'.

Inevitably, Richard could not please everybody and there were grumbles and groans when, on his arrival in some out-of-the-way creek, the masters and others were summoned to attend his hearings, thereby causing some disruption to the all important business of catching cod. In all, and '**according to course of law, as the tenor of my commission did warrant me therein**' he took evidence from 170 of the 250 ships' masters present that year, of the abuses and disorders that abounded among the fishing communities. He also 'settled such fit orders among them as they thought good under their hands and seals'.

On his return home in the autumn, he submitted his 'presentments' to the '**High Court of the Admiraltie, which was there by manie worthie men approved**'. He detailed the salient points of dispute and abuse in the Discourse, but no action was taken at that time and his report gathered dust. Ten years later, in his previously mentioned letter to Lord Falkland, he wrote '**although divers of them** (fishermen) **have yearlie since broken the orders, and spoyled the Harbours, burne the woodes, and done what they list there, it lyes not in me to remedie**'.

As the Whitehall government had no way of influencing affairs on the ground, it did what English governments have so often done with good effect – nothing. It just hoped that the difference between the two sides would go away and the fishing faction would realise that it was in their long-term interests to mend their ways. It is no surprise that the cash-strapped government did not compensate him for his troubles – other than by some words of thanks and praise. This oversight would not have worried him too much at the time when his career was full of comforts. Later, when crosses predominated and his fortune was all but gone, he certainly let everyone know how poorly he had been treated with a full and 'magniloquous' account in his '*Discourse and Discovery*'.[6]

It looked as if the government's do-nothing policy might work for a time. Yet the conflict between the western merchants and the settlers simmered on beneath the surface. A new Governor took over from William Colston (who had replaced Guy a year earlier) in 1615. He was John Mason, a sea captain of the no-nonsense school who had served King James well in the Royal Navy. The post of governor was his reward from a grateful, if impecunious, monarch. Mason had no more power to deal with unruliness than his predecessors. Perhaps his sharp tongue and determined attitude may have revived fears among West Country fishermen that the colony posed a real threat to them.

How a mere sixty settlers in a couple of out-of-the-way sites on the north side of Conception Bay could influence the 6,000 visiting fishermen, is not clear.

Fishermen from the western ports of Poole, Southampton, Plymouth, Bristol and Barnstaple petitioned the king in December 1618 against the settlers or 'planters' of the Newfoundland Company. They raised five issues to which the Company counter-petitioned on behalf of the planters. The fishermen complained that:

1 Before the arrival of the fishing fleets in the spring, certain planters had occupied the best sites on the shoreline for processing their catch. The company's response was that since there was no knowing if previous occupiers of any site would return, they had the right of first choice.

2 The planters had taken away great quantities of salt, casks, boats and stages left over winter by the fishing fleets. The company had no reports of any wrong done to fishermen and would never condone such actions. However, some localised pilfering, close to the two settlements, was to be expected.

3 Planters had prevented fishermen killing sea fowls in Baccalieu Island, needed as bait when no other is available at the start of the season. The company had heard of no such cases but would give orders that their planters must not interfere.

4 At the height of the season the company summoned a Court of Admiralty that exacted fees of fish and train oil from busy fishermen who had failed to attend. The Newfoundland Company replied that the fees had nothing to do with setting up the court.

5 Settlers harboured and had dealings with pirates thus encouraging their visits – to the great prejudice and hindrance of the fishermen. The Company replied that the plantation had suffered great damage from pirates through loss of provisions and men, and that the colony was on the point of being 'overthrown' because it was too weak to defend itself. It understood that the pirates had friends among the fishing fleet who encouraged them. The Company wanted to join the western ports' fishermen in resisting the pirates, as well to co-operating in the keeping of good order.[7]

In their reply to the Company, the ports' petitioners maintained that the charter to planters gave them no privileges for fishing before others and demanded that the liberties reserved for fishermen by charter be confirmed. Further, they knew how to manage their fishing better than the planters and would not be ordered about or co-operate with them.

The Privy Council, having heard all the arguments, issued an injunction on the Company dated 18 December 1618 to respect the fishermen's rights in future and restrain the planters.

This had no effect whatsoever and relations between planters and fishermen continued to deteriorate. The company treasurer wrote in 1621 about 'some few instances of certain misdemeanours and injuries committed by the fishers this last year', namely:

1 Certain English fishermen maliciously set fire to eight ships in several harbours, costing £180 to repair.
2 A man was killed while pulling up another's seine net.
3 A number of English fishermen boarded a Portuguese ship by night armed with swords and axes. They cut through ropes and stays before being restrained by a group of English masters.
4 An Englishman was dangerously hurt during a fight between English and Portuguese in Petty Harbour.
5 £40 worth of damage was done to a saw mill and a grist mill built by the planters.
6 Woods daily spoilt by fishermen taking rind and bark off trees. About 5,000 acres of woods were maliciously set on fire in 1619 by fishermen in Conception Bay, with thousands more acres burnt in the past 20 years.
7 There are yearly complaints of much salt, casks, train oil vats and boats stolen.
8 About forty harbours frequented by the English were in danger of being ruined by the casting overboard of ballast and fish-press stones.
9 Portuguese, French and other foreign fishing vessels were more law-abiding than the English.
10 The events listed were not a quarter of those that had been done. Letters from the Privy Council to the port towns' mayors had no effect.
11 Efforts made by the colony's governors have been ineffectual as they had no powers to punish miscreants.[8]

Whether these complaints had any connection with the debate in the House of Commons in 1621, there is no knowing but it seems likely. There was no Hansard and reliance has to be made on any notes that members made of what went on. Mr Neale, a merchant and member for Clifton, Dartmouth, spoke up strongly for the western ports. His speech was noted thus: 'Ed VI – free liberty for all subjects to go to the Newfoundland for fish: now make men compound for places: take away their salt: they cannot carry even portion but must leave or lack: *that the fishing there little above seven weeks: no leisure to attend an admiral court: pretence to reform abuses, but was to set fines: taxed an hogshead of train oil upon every master of ship that appeared not at his court*; that the Lords of the Council gave an order[9] against the planters have disobeyed: shot off ordnance against Kings subjects: that London merchants, by restraining trade and imposing upon trade, undo all trade.'[10]

Those parts of his speech that clearly refer to Richard's commission are in italics above. Richard's original 'precept' may have detailed the fines for non-attendance, in the way that such legal documents often do. With a crew of only eleven men, he was hardly likely to attempt the impossible. Yet from these few notes one can capture the flavour of the member for Dartmouth's oratory especially from his final well constructed parting shot, amid the desultory 'hear-hears' scattered thinly across the floor of the House as Mr Neal resumed his seat.

Twenty years of steady growth, following the peace with Spain in 1604, had seen the number and size of the English fleet more than double. The West Country prospered from this enterprise and the hard work of those involved. But the fortunes of the fisheries suffered several setbacks within a few years of the 1621 debate.

War was declared on Spain in 1624, following on the fiasco of the Spanish Marriage. Efforts were made by the government to 'stay' the western fishing fleet during the spring of 1625, so that there would be a source of sailors for the navy. But many slipped away before the ban could be enforced. Sailors were in demand in the autumn too when Buckingham headed an expedition to attack Cadiz. Ill-prepared, ill-disciplined and ill-lead, it was a dismal failure – in sharp contrast to Drake's earlier triumph in 1587. War against France followed in 1627, while losses from Turkish pirates increased sharply.

It was several years before the fisheries recovered from these setbacks but in 1632 Government and Parliament again focused on Newfoundland's problems. The several organised plantations that were set up had faded away by this time, leaving a scattering of small groups of independent settlers throughout Avalon. The need for law and order was apparent. The result was the Western Charter (issued by order of the Star Chamber on 24 January 1633). It re-affirmed the age-long tradition of authority through the 'fishing admirals' and included guidance for dealing with a list of abuses. This list differs little from that which both Guy and Richard had pin-pointed twenty years earlier and is thereby a justification of Richard's contribution.

11

Greatlie Wronged by Pirates

'For although I have by Pirates and other crosses received great loss, yet doe I acknowledge myself much bound to God my Creator, who has preserved me from many dangers in my time and always (praise be God) safely to return with my ship, goods and men, wherein I was:'

Richard Whitbourne – The Discourse

Pirates, like the poor, have been around since the dawn of history. They are still operating today – in the China Sea and elsewhere. They had become a real and increasing menace by the early part of the 17th century. Piracy had long been a problem around Britain's lengthy and mainly remote coastline. Local government in Cornwall, Wales and the west coast of Ireland in particular was weeks, sometimes months, away from Whitehall. Local officials were willing collaborators with visiting pirates, turning a Nelson-like eye on any business dealing even when not actively involved themselves. The law and structure for disposing of captured pirates was inherently weak and pirates were rarely punished, even when they were captured.

Piracy became a very rewarding business with the rapid increase in sea-borne trade that followed the surge of global exploration. The maritime powers of Spain, France, England, Holland and the Italian states, spent much time fighting among themselves during the 16th century. This exacerbated the piracy problem as the division between legitimacy and crime was parchment thin. A 'letter of marque' signed and sealed by the sovereign head of any principality – be it powerful or tin-pot – permitted the recipient to take reprisals against any enemy shipping. 'Enemy' was generally construed to mean 'foreign'.

Starting in 1585, and for the duration of the Spanish war, letters of marque were freely available to all English captains. James I made peace with Spain and cancelled these letters after ascending the throne in 1603. But neither captains nor crews knew a better way of making a living after so long a time and many of them turned from privateering to piracy without noticing the difference.

The coast of Barbary had become the unofficial capital of world piracy by then. It was named after the pirate king Khayr Ad-din, known as Barbarosa, who captured Algiers from the Spaniards in 1529 and Tunis in 1533. In time it came to include the whole coast of Africa from Tripoli to Agadir. Barbarosa handed over his realms for incorporation in the Turkish Empire in return for military support. The ruthless and cruel Turks would set out to wreak havoc on Christian countries across the Mediterranean from numerous bases along this coast, especially on Italy. Pirates took a greater interest in spoil to be had in the Atlantic, after Morocco was added to the Barbary Coast in 1609.

Legitimate trade to the Barbary Coast did not cease but ships needed to be well armed and to keep a weather eye open for sudden treacherous attacks, lest all the crew end up as slaves. Christian pirates, if they had booty to sell at discounted prices or stores to buy at a premium, were usually welcome and on good terms with their brothers-in-crime.

Richard became embroiled with pirates once more two years after his encounter with Easton, this time with Henry Mainwaring, one of the most successful of all the buccaneers of his time. He was born in 1587, the grandson of a vice-admiral and son of a Devonshire gentleman. He obtained his degree from Oxford when he was fifteen and was admitted to the Inner Temple two years later. Mainwaring spent most of the next six years on the continent, probably serving with the military. He was commissioned in 1611 to confront groups of pirates, including Peter Easton, who were 'hovering in the Bristol Channel'. Nothing came of this and a year later it was arranged that he escort the returning ambassador, Sir Robert Shirley, back to Persia.[1]

Mainwaring bought the 160-ton *Resistance* from naval architect Phinneas Pett yet he never made the voyage. He became 'by some mischance' instead, one of the most successful pirates of the time, setting out in August 1613, capturing his first prize soon after. Fiercely anti-Spanish, he got the better of fights with their navy on at least one occasion. He turned up in Newfoundland with a fleet of five, some say eight, ships the following June. It is possible that he got his intelligence from Easton, from whom he appears to have inherited the mantle of the 'Pirate King of the Atlantic'. He would have learnt that there were many good places for repairing and careening his ships without fear of assault from the fishermen.

Mainwaring's crews took from the Portuguese all the wine they could find as well as some 10,000 fish during their stay in Newfoundland. They captured one Flemish ship that was fishing at Carbonnier and left behind two hulks. They demanded of the English vessels a sixth of their crew (including carpenters), victuals, munitions and other necessaries. About eighty ships were involved but Mainwaring said it was easily done since the fishermen were disunited and put up no concerted opposition. Many of the pressed men went willingly. Many more who protested did so only as a blind to cover themselves in case they should ever be arrested, whereas they were quite willing to join the pirates for a share of any ill-gotten booty. Of more than 600 men pressed into his service, Mainwaring found only three 'perforce' men who genuinely objected to serving under him or his captains.[2] He sailed away on 14 September 1614.

While there he caused Richard '**to spend much time in his company and from him I returned into England although I was bound from thence to Marseilles . . .**'[3] Richard must have gone to London and seen the Lord Admiral Howard again, delivering Mainwaring's request, presumably for a pardon. At this time there was growing conflict between the West Country fishermen and Guy's colony. Howard may well have sought Richard's opinion and from this the idea of Richard carrying out an on-the-spot enquiry could have grown. How else would an untutored sea captain come to be entrusted with this task in preference to a qualified lawyer?

Mainwaring had to wait two more years for his pardon during which he wrote a treatise to 'My most Gracious Sovereign – Of the Beginnings, Practices and Suppression of Pirates – as some oblation for my offences', instancing occasions when he had protected English ships and freed English sailors from slavery. He gave a detailed account of some seventy haunts of pirates in twenty different countries; of their harbours and moorings, the friendliness or treachery of the locals, possibilities for selling loot, buying stores and watering. Mainwaring implied that he knew all the places detailed personally by listing Iceland and Friesland as haunts he did not know and thus could not say what went on there.

Mainwaring advised King James in his last chapter on how to handle the English and Irish pirates – and how he might combat the growing menace from the Turks. He had noticed in his travels that the best-governed countries are those where the laws were most severely executed, citing Tunisia: 'where no offence is ever remitted, but strictly punished according to their customs and Laws. In five months together when I was coming and going I never heard of murder, robbery, or private quarrel. Nay a Christian, which is more than he can warrant himself in any part of Christendom, may on my knowledge travel 150 miles into the country, though he carry good store of money, and himself alone, and none will molest him.'

Mainwaring maintained good civility and order in his fleet because he kept the most severe discipline among his own most uncivil and barbarous crews and never ever pardoned any notorious offence. 'It could not have been much better in a Civil state – for, as fear of punishment makes men doubtful to offend, so the hope of being pardoned makes them apter to err.'

At the same time he thinks the king should:

1 Make service in the royal ships more attractive for ordinary seamen than that of a pirate.
2 Grant no more pardons for pirates but put them to death instead.
3 station at least two ships off the west coast of Ireland to prevent pirates from landing anywhere there.
4 On no account allow any parleying or truck between pirates who might land in a port and locals or officials.
5 Combat the Turks, who usually go in fleets of eight or nine, with an adequate and well armed force which should lie in wait at places where they resort. When prisoners are taken they could be sold to Spain into slavery – worth about £30 a piece. Resourceful, experienced commanders were needed for this. Mainwaring reminds the king that 'He who would cheat the devil needs himself to be two devils in one.'

Having presented his 'Discourse' to the king, Mainwearing was soon back in royal favour. He was knighted in March 1618 and the same year became a Gentleman of the Bed Chamber to James. There followed, on and off, a distinguished career in the navy. Between 1620 and 1623 he wrote his 'Seaman's Dictionary' which he dedicated to the Duke of Buckingham, the newly appointed Lord Admiral. He sided with the Royalists during the Civil War and was with Prince Charles in Jersey and later in The Hague. He returned from exile in 1651 dying the following year.

Richard's next encounter with pirates was: '**In the yeere 1616. I had a Ship at New-found-land, of 100 Tun, which returning laden from thence, being bound for Lisbone, was met with by a French Pyrate of Rochell; one Daniel Tibolo, who rifled her, to the overthrow and losse of my Voyage, in more than the sum of 860 Pounds, and cruelly handled the Master, and the Company that were in her. And although I made good proofe thereof at Lisbone and represented the same also to this Kingdome, as appertained, after my returne from thence: yet for all this great losse, I could never have any recompence.**'[4]

The ship was a 'fly-boat', *Seraphine*. First recorded in the shipping records in 1609, she was in Newfoundland in 1609, 1611, 1615 and 1616. The records put her burden as, on average, 80 tons. When boarded on 9 October 1616, two of the company were dangerously wounded. The master and mate were '**bound about the head with boards very grievously, while the ship's boy had his hands bound together and powder put in them and then lit**'. Richard in his account lists many items taken and damage done which included £300 of dry fish either taken, spoilt or devalued in the forced sale later. They incarcerated the master and all the company in the cabin. Before abandoning their prize, the pirates loosened the one piece of ordnance, a 1,200 pound cannon. Before the crew could escape from the cabin, this gun, crashing to and fro as the ship rolled, made a great hole in the ship's side, allowing water to enter and wet much fish.[m1]

Richard, like many other people in a similar situation, seems to have been quite generous in his estimate of the total damage done. The *Seraphine* managed to make it to Lisbon where Richard went to straighten things out. With the ship's company he was able to see Lord Ross, the English ambassador extraordinary to Spain. All involved made statements on oath. The remains of the catch were sold and the *Seraphine* was repaired and returned to Exmouth under command of John Perry, where she arrived on 16 January 1617 with a load of eight tons of Spanish salt.

Richard, being in London, submitted his claim to the Council in March 1617, presumably with an accompanying petition that seems to be lost, asking that the question of compensation be taken up with the French authorities. Nothing appears to have been done and Richard submitted a further petition in July. As a result the Council sent a letter addressed to Sir Thomas Prideaux and six other Devonshire squires as follows:

'11 July 1617.
By this enclosed petition you shall understand the complaint made unto us by Richard Whidborne, of Exmouth, in the county of Devon, merchant, concerning the refusal of some adventurers with him in a ship of his to Newfoundland to undergo such fortune and adventure with him as befell unto him, but labour to shift themselves from the burthen thereof, and yet nevertheless doe require the performance of the conditions made on his behalf. Forasmuch that it appears that the petitioner hath heretofore been a good merchant and received great losses at sea, as well by French rovers as by Turks, and that we are informed that divers of the adventurers with him are willing to come to some reasonable agreement, we have been moved hereby to authorize you as the petitioner shall name unto you, and to mediate with them for some friendly and conscionable end as in equity shall be found, which if any of them shall refuse to agree unto you shall then certify their names unto us, that such further order may be taken as shall be expedient and with all to let them know that whatsoever shall be recovered of the French rover now lying in the town of Rochell by the instance of his Majesties Ambassador there shall be ratably divided amongst them towards the repair of their losses. And so etc,
                              Lord Archbishop of Canterbury & five others'[5]

It was all to no avail for Richard got not one penny in recompense. This is made clear in the following extract from Richard's draft preface, which differs from the printed book: '**And although I caused due proofed to be made thereof at Lisbon before the Lo: Rosse then His Majesty's extraordinaire Ambassador to the King of Spain, and represented the same in this Kingdome as appertained.**

Yet for this great losse I could never get any recompense from the French.

This year I myself went from England to Villa-nova in Portugal in a small Barke, and from thence by land unto Lisbon, to mete with my said ship. This barke also, being there laden with freight, was in her returne homewards taken by a Turkish man of ware, and carried away with all her goods in her, being of good value.'

Richard's final brush with pirates came in 1618 when he was in Newfoundland with two ships. Details of this and the consequences are told in Chapter 12. It marked the end of Richard's active life as a fisher-merchant. Pirates continued to be a menace to the industry but suddenly the Turks, who had learnt from their English counterparts to sail and fight in Atlantic waters, replaced the English 'errant captains'. At the same time, the number of English pirates lessened due to the liberal pardons granted by James.

Seven English ships in convoy for Italy were captured by Turks in the Mediterranean in 1617. Thereafter the Turks would lay in wait outside the Straits of Gibraltar and along the Atlantic coastlines. The Mayor of Weymouth reported that by 1622 so many ships had been lost that only eleven had sailed for the Banks that year.

A total of twenty seven English ships returning from the fisheries were captured by Barbary pirates in 1625[6] and Richard wrote in February 1626 that John Streate of Dartmouth, 'being long tyme a great adventurer to the Newfoundland, the last years he had seven or eight Shippes there for his owne accompt, and now afraide to sett any one Shipp there, and divers men are soe doubtfull to adventure there this years, and those that doe are likely to be in some danger.'[7]

Damage Done to Newfoundland Fisheries By Visiting Pirates 1612-1619.*

In 1612 *Peter Easton* came from the *Isle of May (Cape Verde Islands)* with 4 ships, later increased to 9. He seized 100 pieces of ordnance, all manner of victuals and munitions, all valued at £10,400, and carried away 500 English fishermen, of which many were volunteers, but most were taken by force .He robbed and spoilt 15 French ships fishing off the coast of Newfoundland, doing damage estimated at £6,000. He captured a great Flemish ship, valued at £1,000. He spoilt the voyages of 12 Portuguese fishing vessels doing £3000 of worth of damage.

In 1614 *Henry Mainwaring* with 8 men of war, seized from English ships, both on the Bank and from the harbours, one in six of all carpenters and mariners, and a sixth part of all victuals and munitions. From Portuguese ships they took 10,000 fish and all the wine they could lay hands on. They captured a Flemish ship and left behind the hulks of two other vessels. They arrived the 2nd of June and departed on 14 September, with about 400 mariners and fishermen in all, some going voluntarily.

In 1616 a Flemish pirate, Jacobs, with an English one, Ellis, captured a Portuguese ship from *Avero* in *Torbay*, and later a French vessel fishing off *Carboneir*: damage – £1500. They took all the ordinance from a ship of *Bristol* and a ship of Guernsey, fishing in *Witless Bay*, to the value of £200. Off other ships they collected £500 in beer, bread, candles, beef, pork, peas, powder and shot, and left with £2000 worth of fish and 50 men.

In 1618 two ships and a carvell, part of Sir Walter Rawleigh's fleet and under the command of errant Captain Wollaston, visited the island from the Orinoco, seized three French ships and the dried fish from four others, all of which they sold in *Lighorne,* Italy, for £5,400. They left one French ship in Newfoundland, which the Island's Governor sent home. It lost £500. Further, they 'taxed' the English ships in all the harbours of their powder, shot, and other necessaries to the value of £2,000 and left with 130 of the fishermen.

The same year a Flemish pirate from the West Indies, robbed ships in *Green Bay* and *Trinity Harbour*, of £1,300 worth of provisions and ordinance. This year, and last, two ships, one laden the other empty, from *Avero* in Portugal, together worth £1,500 along with three other ships, were rescued by the said Governor.

Assessing the damage by Mainwaring as at least £6,500, then the total loss over these 7 years was £40,800 with 180 pieces of ordnance taken away and 1080 fishermen, sailors, carpenters and gunners either taken by force or by absconding.

*Abstracted from a memorandum probably written by John Slany, Treasurer of the Newfoundland Company in 1621. Ref: CO 1/1.54. II.II.

12

Full Powers to Govern

'Shortlie after my returne from Lisbonne I was sent for by a Gentleman who about a year before had undertaken to settle people in Newfoundland. He acquainted me with his designes and after some conference touching the same we so concluded that he gave me a conveyance under his hand and seale for the term of my life with full power to govern within his circuit upon the coast.'

Richard Whitbourne – His Draft Preface

The gentleman was William Vaughan (1575–1641) a Welshman from Carmarthenshire. He had attended Jesus College, Oxford, receiving his MA in 1597 and went on to become a doctor of civil law. After spending three years travelling around Europe he returned to Wales in 1603, married, settled in Llangynddeyrn and was appointed a justice of the peace. His one son, Francis, died quite young and in 1608 he also lost his first wife.

Vaughan comes across as somewhat eccentric. He spent most of his time writing but much of his work is obtuse and peppered with classical allusions and conceits. He published his best-known book 'The Golden Grove' in 1600. In it, he considered the three phases of man's life according to the Aristotelian concept – the moral, economic and political. He expressed concern over the economic plight of Wales. Apathy, over-population and poverty abounded. He saw men starving while good land lay fallow and seafaring was ignored. Across the Bristol Channel he observed the West Country becoming ever more prosperous, largely on the back of the Newfoundland fisheries.

Like many of his contemporaries, Vaughan believed colonization to be the solution. In the ensuing years he considered several possible sites for a colony – Soldana Bay (a staging post north of Cape Town on the route to the East Indies), St Helena, Bermuda, and Virginia but finally lighted on Newfoundland. It was comparatively close to Wales and provided an inexhaustible store of saleable fish. He applied to the Newfoundland Company in 1616 to purchase a large block of their land, namely all that lay to the south of the latitude of Cape Boyle.[1]

This company, a partnership of merchants from Bristol and London, had received its royal charter in May 1610. Within two months it sent out forty colonists under Governor John Guy, an established Bristol merchant. A settlement was started on the west side of Conception Bay at Cupids. Two years later a further party of settlers arrived and it was intended to start a second colony at Renews, fifty miles south of St John's. This plan was never executed due to the presence of Peter Easton and his large pirate band. The colony was still struggling five years later – the fibre of the settlers was probably not up to the formidable conditions they found there. By 1616, funds were running low and the Newfoundland Company must have been happy to replenish its coffers by selling off part of its massive land grant.

Vaughan sent out his first batch of settlers to Aquafort, a small harbour on the east coast close to Cape Broyle, the following year. There is no record of how many went but at least thirty seems likely since Richard talks of a 'great number', sent in this and the following year. It is not known how they were selected nor who was in charge. No instructions appear to have been given as to what they were to do.

We do not know who advised Vaughan to contact Richard, but it turned out to be a sound choice. From Lisbon, Richard would have gone to London to make a claim for his losses suffered when *Seraphine* was rifled. He was there in March 1617 and again about June. Vaughan and Richard were men poles apart in every way. Vaughan was well born and an intellectual but with no practical experience in organising men or events. Richard, with his yeoman background and thirty years of seafaring and merchandising, had no formal education. He was essentially a practical man used to managing men and getting things done. Despite these differences, they would appear to have come rapidly to an understanding and a common objective.

Richard did not meet the party of emigrants before they left in 1617 and was prevented by other events from going himself that year.

It was agreed that the following year he would take over the colony as governor. He would take two ships to Newfoundland with further colonists and supplies. The ships would engage in fishing while he was organising the settlement. In this way they expected to pay, at the least, for the expedition. It was a joint venture, victualled and financed by Vaughan, Richard and some others.

Ill chance crossed Richard's path once more. It came about because King James agreed that Sir Walter Raleigh, who had been charged with treason and unjustly imprisoned in the Tower for thirteen years, should lead a last desperate expedition to find the elusive gold of Elderado. Raleigh believed it to lie up Guiana's Orinoco River that nominally belonged to Spain. The Spaniards, forewarned of his arrival, lay in readiness. Everything went horribly wrong. Sir Walter's son was killed in battle while Raleigh's devoted lieutenant Keymis, feeling that he was responsible, took his own life. Two captains, Whitney and Woolaston, whose vessels were temporarily disabled, deserted with their ships. Raleigh returned home, badly beaten, without the gold for James that would have saved him from the reluctant headsman. The king sacrificed him to appease Spain. Sir Walter took his 'sharp medicine that is a physician for all diseases,' with courage and dignity.

On his arrival at Newfoundland in the spring of 1618, Richard learnt that his second ship had been intercepted **'by an English erring Captaine that went forth with Sir Walter Rawleigh'** The Captain was Whitney **'who tooke the Master of her, the Boatswaine, and two other of the best men, with much of her victuals (the rest of the ship's company running into the woods in fear) and so left the ship as a prize, whereby our intended fishing-voyages of both our ships were overthrowne, and the Plantation hindered'.**[2]

Richard's priority was to set up camp and start fishing as soon as possible. He almost certainly chose to do this at Renews (now spelt Renouse) with its harbour normally used by about twenty ships, many of which were from Teignmouth and Exmouth. Here lay an island just off-shore that commanded views of the harbour entrance as well as the land-approaches. He believed that, if Woolaston and Whitney were still around, this island could be quickly fortified and the fishing fleet defended.

Once the stages and other structures had been built and fishing started, Richard had time to go over to Aquaforte and find out how

Vaughan's colony, of which he was now governor, was faring. By land, Aquaforte was less than ten miles from Renews, rather longer by sea. The situation of the Welsh settlers filled him with despondency. He had met none of them before and it was a shock when he found that after a whole year they 'had not applied themselves to any commendable thing; not so much as to make themselves an house to lodge in, but lay most shamefully in such cold and simple roomes all winter, as the fishermen had formerly built there for their necessary occasions, the year before those men arrived there. Such persons are not fit to advance your Majesty's most worthy intended worke there, but rather much disgrace and hinder the same.'

'Yet entering into consideration, how injurious I should be to God, and (as I did conceive my conscience) treacherous to your Majesty, and my country, having once as it were laid hold of the plough, I should take it off and look back: I did then encourage my retiring spirits, notwithstanding all my former wrongs then sustained by pirates.'[3]

He interviewed these men, most of whom were disgruntled and quite useless. The only thing to do was to ship these 'Welsh fools' back to England – together with many of the new recruits who were reluctant to stay. Some time in the summer they went in the second ship, under command of the master from his own ship.

Only six suitable settlers remained. Although a good base for fishing, Aquafort was not a good site for a settlement. It had very little flat ground for cultivation and no natural defences against attack by pirates. Richard decided that the colony needed a fresh start at a new site. He chose nearby Renouse.

Whether he gave consideration to Fermeuse, lying half way between Aquafort and Renouse, he does not say. He is fulsome with his praise for Renouse as a site for settlement. It had one of the best fishing harbours in all Avalon, and attracted visits from sack ships that visited yearly to buy cod and train oil. These could be useful in future years for transporting people and stores to the budding colony.

There were several open valleys at Renouse with more than three hundred acres of open land with good deep soil and without trees and rocks. He believed these would be suitable to grow corn or for use as pasture. They were well supplied with fresh water with several brooks that fed into the harbour. The brooks were plentifully stocked in the spawning season with salmon, salmon-peale, trout and other species.

Deer roaming the woods and open land close to Renouse, were fit for 'profit and delight'.

There were also infinite numbers of land- and sea-fowl and in summer an abundance of fruits, herbs and wild flowers. Earlier settlers and fishermen had brought seeds of cabbage, lettuce, beets, and carrots which they had grown 'very fair' while 'for turnips, I never saw better than there, both for greatnesse, relish, and goodnesse; I esteeme them to be the equal with any potato roots which are growing elsewhere.'⁴ There were fine stands of spruce, fir, pine, birch, and many long rushes for thatching houses. Richard also believed he had found limestone, an invaluable resource when starting a plantation.

The six planters moved to Renouse were given careful directions for building a house and how to employ themselves gainfully 'until they heard from the gentlemen that sent them thither'. They lived there pleasantly all the next winter. Nothing further was heard of them and the colonists probably dispersed the following summer.

Vaughan, by then 'finding the burthen too heavy for my weak shoulders', assigned parts of his grants to Henry Cary, later Lord Falkland, and to Sir George Calvert, later Lord Baltimore. He may have tried again, in 1621 or 1622, with a colony at Trepassey Bay, but hardly anything is known about it and did not last long. It is unlikely that Vaughan ever visited Newfoundland but he continued his writings encouraging others. *The Golden Fleece* (1622) was written under a pseudonym 'Orpheus Junior', while the *The Newlanders Cure* (1630) was a medical work containing remedies for maladies such as scurvy and seasickness.

Having lost many of his best crew, Richard's fishing operations had been seriously disrupted, but he was doubtless exaggerating somewhat when he wrote later that 'the voyages of both his ships had been overthrown.'

The fishing had been reasonable, for he took command of his own ship, probably the repaired *Seraphine*, and sailed for Lisbon where he had made contacts the year before. Richard knew there would be a market for his catch, such as it was.

So ended, before it had really begun, his mandate as life-long colonial governor. He spent much time that summer thinking about the question of plantations and 'the fittest course whereby to advance that work which was formerly so worthily intended.'⁵ He was the one person who could see all three sides of the fierce conflict that divided London merchants and the would-be colonists from the West Country fishing community, with a reluctant Government watching indifferently from the sidelines.

He could see well enough what had gone wrong and thought he knew how matters might be managed in the future to the advantage of all. He was clear about what he should do. He would write a book: 'A Discourse and Discovery of the New-Found-Land' setting out how matters could be put right. Now facing financial difficulties, lacking the sort of education that would embellish his simple style, and with no idea of how to go about getting a book published, Richard could only trust that God would show him the way forward.

An Exceeding Brief History of Syon Abbey

In:-

1378. The Pope affirmed the new closed "Bridgettine" Order, founded by saintly and high-born Birgitta of Sweden.

1399. Henry Bolingbroke rebels against Richard II, who abdicates. Richard is imprisoned where he dies from starvation. Five years later, Archbishop Scroope is 'judicially' murdered by Henry IV. Pope excommunicates him.

1481. Henry IV craves pardon and is exonerated, but as penance he must found three strict religious Houses. One will be the Bridgettine Syon Abbey.

1413. Henry V succeeds and decides to site these near Shene Palace, Richmond.

1420. Foundation Day sees 27 nuns and five brothers profess their vows.

1423. Site is too small and marshy. It is moved a mile downstream to Isleworth.

1431. Full complement of 60 nuns and 13 brothers go to new site, where building works continue for many more years.

For the next hundred years, Syon Abbey flourishes, & becomes richly endowed with many estates in Devon and elsewhere. It soon gains reputation for virtue, devotion and a mixture of erudite learning and plain-spoken, popular preaching on Sundays, to all-comers. It has a famed library.

1534. Five years after the Bill dissolving the Monasteries, Cromwell ousts the nuns. The Abbess and nine nuns go to Flanders, the rest disperse.

1557. With Mary on the throne and Syon restored, the nuns enjoy a brief year there before being exiled by Elizabeth I. Hoping to find safety in the Low Countries, they are forced to move – usually by incessant fighting – five times in 23 years. In 1580 they move to Rouen in France until in

1594. Rouen is captured by Henry of Navarre. The nuns flee to Lisbon by boat.

1599. With protection from the kings of Spain and Portugal, and through local generosity, they acquire a new permanent Abbey – 'Sitie de Mocambe.' Only one monk remains, Father Seth, alias Forster, who is the Father Confessor.

1661. Most of Lisbon is consumed by a huge conflagration, including the Abbey. All the nuns escape and a new Abbey is built.

1775. World's biggest-ever recorded earthquake devastates Lisbon, leaving the Abbey in ruins, yet all the nuns escape. The Convent is rebuilt.

1791. English Parliament passes Catholic Relief Act, restoring freedom of worship.

1809. Abbess & 11 nuns return to England, but fail to get financial support. They sell all the Abbey's treasures, but to no avail. Without funds, they disperse.

1816. Convent reduces to three ailing sisters; then ten postulates arrive due to efforts of a Lancastrian priest, Dr. Gadwell.

1861. Popular anti-clerical feelings in Portugal increases. The Abbey returns to England, settling firt at Spottisbury in Dorset.

1887. Move again, this time to 'Filleigh' – a house in Chudleigh, Devon.

1925. A further move to Marley House, South Brent, Devon.

1992. Marley House gets too large; is sold & sisters move to smaller building nearby.

13

The English Nunnery at Lisbon

'And thereupon by order of his late Majestie, your Grace's Suppliant brought the said Robinson to his great charge before the right Honourable Sir Robert Naunton, then Secretairie to his Majestie to whom the said Robinson related so much as he formerly had to your Suppliant.'

Richard Whitbourne – in a letter to the
Duke of Buckingham, 10 November 1626

In his long and obsequious petition for employment, Richard tells how he met Thomas Robinson. He was walking the streets of Lisbon in the company of fellow merchants one day during the winter of 1619, when they came across a young man and a priest, both obviously English, who were close to blows. Robinson turned to the merchants beseeching them for help as he feared for his life. The priest, he said, one Joseph Foster who was father confessor to the nuns of the exiled Syon Abbey, had threatened to have his throat cut if he did not leave Lisbon immediately.[m7]

After being rescued by the merchants, Robinson told Richard his story which in today's world seems, at the least, biased and exaggerated. But in the early 17th century, with its disparate and strongly held religious view-points, there were many who believed his assertions to be 'God's truth', and some who were utterly outraged by them.

At its core, his story related to Syon Abbey, the Bridgettine order of nuns whose origins were in Sweden and Rome but had long since become essentially English, as it so remains. King Henry V created the Abbey as part of the penitential imperatives imposed on his father,

Henry IV by the Pope, following the murder of Richard II and Archbishop Abbott. It is a tale of the power of the Spirit, as exemplified by the nuns who for six hundred years have endured and surmounted wars, tyrannies, fire, earthquake and pestilence. Guided by the virtues of poverty, humility and chastity, the Abbey remains today a centre for prayer and contemplation par excellence. It is the only English pre-Reformation Roman Catholic order with an un-broken record[1].

Thomas Robinson, Richard learnt, was born in King's Lynn in about 1595. Evidently a bright boy, he acquired a patron, Thomas Gurley, who was later to be Mayor of Kings Lynn. Gurley paid for Robinson to attend Cambridge University, a quite common arrangement in those days. Robinson squandered his time there and failed to gain his bachelor degree. Leaving Cambridge, he became a seafarer and probably spent two or three years in travel.

He met 'by divers accidents' while in Lisbon father confessor of the Syon Abbey Joseph Foster, also known as Father Seth. He was befriended by this priest who persuaded him, 'by his subtle and wily fetches', to join him living at the abbey where his clothes were taken and he was required to wear a 'foolish habit'. Robinson was put to work copying out 'treaties of obedience', composed for the nuns' benefit. Seth, the abbess and some of the sisters worked on him 'by deep dissembled entreaties and persuasions', to take Holy Orders. Eventually he agreed to become a 'holy brother and mass priest' and was soon 'adept in the rubric and knew each mass from its initial letter'. He could 'sing *Ave Regina* and *Salva Sancta parens* which is learning enough for any abbey-lubber'. Only his age prevented him taking vows since the order's rules required men to be at least twenty-five years old before admission.

As time passed Robinson grew uneasy about the way the convent was run. He felt imprisoned by its walls and after two and a half years he decided to escape from Father Seth – yet feared that, his life would be endangered if he were caught. He drew up a list of six 'articles' that he would present to the Chief Inquisitor of Lisbon in the hope that the authorities would act against Seth, although fearing that they might not.

His list of 'articles' was, briefly that:

1 Father Seth compelled youths like him to stay in the nunnery against their will.
2 Seth frequented the nuns' cloisters, which was against the rules.
3 The confessional grating could be taken down 'with a sleight', allowing nuns to pass through to his bed at night.
4 No official visitor had come to hear grievances for many years.
5 The election of the Abbess was conducted improperly.
6 Working in the nuns' garden Robinson had chanced upon a newly 'daubed up' hollow in a wall which contained 'sundry bones of some dead children'.

One morning, while making a copy of these articles, Father Seth caught him unawares and snatched up a blotted first draft from his table. In panic, Robinson fled down the stairs and out of the convent but Seth soon overtook him, hauled him back inside and demanded what he intended doing with the articles. When told, Seth turned as pale as ashes and begged Robinson not to proceed with his intent. Seth agreed to let him go so long as Robinson promised not to breath a word to anyone. Robinson left the convent but a few months later he was back in Lisbon and met Seth in the street. Seth accused him of telling tales about the goings-on at the convent and threatened to have him killed. A row ensued just as Richard and his companions arrived on the scene.

Robinson also told Richard about a plot of the Jesuits of Lisbon to land some 'treacherous people' from Spain and Portugal in England to do some 'mischief' there[2]. Richard, ever steadfast in his loyalty to country, king and the Church of England, decided to take Robinson back with him to Exmouth and hand him over to the authorities. On returning home, Richard wrote to the Lord Admiral's secretary Thomas Aylesbury, his contact in the administration. Richard was instructed to bring Robinson before Sir Robert Naunton, one of the two secretaries of state who was close to the king. One of Naunton's duties was to see that the legal restrictions on Catholics were enforced according to the dictates of the king.

'Sir Robert Naughton did much commend your Suppliant thereon, and did forthwith imploye the said Robinson to seeke where hee could finde out anie of such treacherous people as hee had said were come from Spaine and Portugall to do some mischief unto the state of this

Kingdom, but what the said Robinson did therein after – your suppliant heard no more of it.[m7]'

Nothing else seems to have been recorded until 1622 when Robinson published, by Authority: 'The Anatomy' of the English Nunnery at Lisbon'. In the book he details his experiences and the immoral carryings-on of Father Seth and some of the nuns. He further names many English Jesuit priests working on the continent and what they were up to, all of which would be lapped up and blindly believed by the large following of anti-Catholics who were strongly against the 'Spanish match' between Charles, Prince of Wales and the Infanta Maria, sister to King Philip III of Spain.

The evolving ideologies and forces resulting from the Reformation and the subsequent Counter-Reformation, combined with the enigmatic nature of King James, makes it difficult to understand all the ramifications of this 'Spanish match' affair.

With the popular marriage of James' only daughter Elizabeth to Frederick V, Elector of the Palatinate of the Rhine, in 1614, James aligned England with the Protestant states of central Europe. For a brief time a fragile peace was kept with the Catholic Alliance, the remnants of the Holy Roman Empire. The pluralist Bohemians, who had first opted for the Catholic side, became dissatisfied and literally threw their rulers out of the window. In 1618. They asked Frederick, the titular head of the Protestant faction, to become their king. In August 1619, without waiting for his father-in-law's advice, Frederick accepted and moved to Prague. By the following spring Frederick and Elizabeth were refugees, defeated by Catholic Emperor Ferdinand. Austrian and Spanish forces occupied Bohemia and the Palatinate. Thus started the Thirty Years War, that was to tear the heart out of central Europe, leave a third of its population dead, ruin Spain and put paid to the Holy Roman Empire. James, who felt slighted by Frederick, was unwilling to give the Protestants more than moral support while Parliament, although all for war, would not vote the subsidies that would have made it possible.

Meanwhile, in 1615, Spain had appointed a new Ambassador to England. Count Gondomar had instructions to woo James and, through him, the fifteen year-old heir to the throne, Charles, into marrying the Infanta Princess Maria. Spain's long term hope was that, in due course, the future king Charles would turn to Rome and bring England back to the 'true faith'. To James this was unthinkable, but he was attracted to the plan if Spain could be persuaded to restore the status quo in the Palatine. The promise of a £60,000 dowry was an added spur. For five long years, plot, intrigue, pretence and counter-plot ensued, while the young Charles, by slow expectation, was caught spellbound by calf love for the young princess.

When the machinating and unpopular Gondomar was recalled in 1622, he invited Charles to visit Spain, there to finalise the arrange-ments. Charles, with his friend and his father's latest favourite, the Duke of Buckingham, travelled overland to Madrid, supposedly in disguise. A frosty reception by the Spanish Court greeted their arrival. Having caught their fish, the Spaniards intended to dangle him as long as necessary. Charles was not allowed to meet his 'match', who, just eighteen, ran screaming away when Charles finally caught her un-awares.

After three months of negotiations, a treaty was agreed in which all Spain's demands were accepted, but left the question of returning the Palatine to Frederick unresolved. When Charles broached the matter he was told that Philip would never take arms against the Catholic Emperor Ferdinand, however obdurate he might be. Charles retorted that: 'there is an end of all; for without this you may not rely upon either marriage or friendship.' Bride-less, Charles left Madrid in August. Various delays meant that he did not reach England until October 1623. The populace then went wild, rejoicing in their usual boisterous fashion over Charles' escape from the popish trap. James was relieved and delighted by the return of the 'dear boys.' King and parliament abrogated the treaty and, some time later, a marriage was arranged between Charles and the French king's sister, Henrietta Maria, also a Roman Catholic. Buckingham, not surprisingly, came out strongly against Spain, advocating war.

Among those who would have been bitterly disappointed with the breakdown, were the sisters of the nunnery at Lisbon. When they learnt of Charles' presence and purpose in Madrid, they saw an opportunity opening for their return to England. They set about composing a petition 'To The Most High Lady the Princess of Wales whose God preserve' begging her help in persuading her brother, Philip III, to act on their behalf. They painted nine exquisite miniatures depicting incidents in the history of Syon Abbey. Of course, these could never be presented and they ended up in Arundel Castle, home of the Earls of Northumberland.[3]

The opening gambit to the following slice of dramatic history happened on Wednesday, 5 August 1624. Enter the King's players to stage centre. For nine days continuously (Sunday excepted) they packed the Globe theatre, on London's South Bank, with a new political drama by Thomas Middleton, a popular, talented and prolific poet and playwright, nowadays largely forgotten. The play – 'A Game at Chess' – was the talk of the Town, although only one eyewitness account survives[4]. John Hollis wrote on 11 August to the Earl of Somerset, with whom he had just stayed, that on returning to London: 'I was saluted with a report of a facetious comedy, already thrice acted with extraordinary applause: a representation of all our Spanish traffic, and accordingly yesterday to the Globe I rowed, which house I found so thronged, that by scores they came away for want of place, though as yet little past one; nevertheless loath to check the appetite, which came so seldom to me (not having been to a playhouse these ten years) & such a dainty not every day to be found, I marched on, & heard the pasquin,'[5] Daily audiences topped 3,000 and total takings amounted to over £1,500 – a lot of money considering the entrance to the pit cost but a penny.

In the play, Middleton cleverly deals with the burning political question of the time by disguising the leading politicians of England and Spain as chess pieces. He highlights the king's reluctance to make war on Spain in accordance with Parliament's demands following the ignominious failure of the 'Spanish Match.' Much of the abundant detail – and some of the wit – is drawn from several contemporary tracts, including Robinson's 'Anatomy.' Using the game of chess as a play within a play, Middleton hoped that the real characters involved would be able to ignore the true nature of his plot. It is no surprise that Spain drew the Black pieces.

A dramatic allegory spiced with topical satire, Gondomar, the Black knight, replete with sedan chair, is lampooned without mercy, to the delight of the audience who knew all about him. De Dominis, Archbishop Spatola, is readily identifiable as the Fat Black Bishop, but was a late addition to the script and not essential to the plot. He was possibly added to make a part for one of the leading players, the amply girthed William Rowley, who was noted for his clownish acting. The other pieces, both black and white, are not so easily identified and are not treated harshly. The plot itself has as many sub-plots, twists and turns, as in any real game of chess. The game –

and play – ends with the black pieces being put back in the 'bag' – by way of the trap door, centre stage.

Given the anti-Spanish sentiment at that time, Middleton might have got away with this daring play – and garnered a few guineas at the same time – had not the new Spanish ambassador taken exception. On 7 August he wrote to king James about the presentation of 'a comedy so scandalous, impious, barbarous, and so offensive to my royal master . . . that this comedy has forced me to put my pen to paper . . .' He complained that his predecessor, Gondomar, amongst others, was portrayed 'in a rude and dishonourable fashion' in this 'very scandalous comedy acted publicly by the king's players.' James was conveniently absent, in Leicestershire, at the time, but etiquette is well as prudence required him to take action as soon as he heard. On 12 August, he brought down the fire curtain on a very embarrassing and potentially inflammatory scene. Through Secretary Conway, he wrote an indignant letter to the Privy Council requiring it to summon forthwith and punish the poet and actors.

One can imagine the next scene, the following Wednesday, being full of impact, with the Council Chamber crowded with a motley bunch of players arraigned before the most august body of men in the land. Awaiting their fate, the players would be in fretting rather than strutting mode. Middleton himself was nowhere to be found. Confronted by their Lordships, the King's Players produced an 'original and perfect copy' of the play duly seen and allowed by the Master of the Revels, Sir Henry Herbert. Playing Innocence herself, they vowed not to have 'ad libbed' the script by so much as one line. In the face of this evidently convincing performance, the Council could do no more than dismiss the company with a 'round and sharp reproof,' forbidding any performances whatsoever until the king's pleasure be known and binding them over for three hundred pounds to appear again before the Council, whenever required. A warrant was issued for the apprehension of the missing poet and a report sent to James on 21 August.

So far as the players were concerned, the king was soon mollified, for, six days later, the Lord Chamberlain could write to the President of the Council that 'in consideration of these his poor servants, his Majesty would have their Lordships connive at any common play licensed by authority, that they shall act as before.'

As for Middleton, history is divided on his fate. When he could not be found, his son Edward was arrested in his stead – 'and his indemnity formally recognised.' Nothing further is recorded, so perhaps Middleton suffered but trivial punishment, if any at all. There was one dubious source that reported him as committed to the Fleet prison, where he lay some time and at last got out upon sending 'a petition to the king in six verses.' that read:

'A harmless game, coined only for delight
was played betwixt the black house and the white
the white house wan: yet still the black doth brag
they had the power to put me in the bag
use but your royal hand. 'twill set me free
'Tis but removing of a man that's me '6

A novel type of 'Get out of Jail Free' card!

14

Discourse and Discovery

'Although I well know, that it is a hard matter to persuade people to
adventure into strange Countries, specially to remaine there, though
the conditions thereof be never soe benefitiall and advantagious for
them:'

Richard Whitbourne – Draft Preface

Richard started a draft manuscript of his book, which is preserved in
the British Library[m2], with the above words some time in the late
spring of 1619. It was not the first draft, since the back of remnant of
an earlier one is used here. Nor was it the final draft that was
addressed to 'Your Majesty', and for here he writes about 'His
Majesty' and 'the Royal Progeny'. Most likely, there were several
other drafts and copies written out by Richard in his neat and legible
hand that have not survived.

Richard took Thomas Robinson 'at my great charge' to London at
the behest of the government in March 1619. At the time he was still
pondering the reasons why both Vaughan's and Guy's Newfoundland
colonies were on the point of failure. If English plantations could be
established there prosperity for her fishermen must surely follow.
How could this best be done? Richard's long-time contact with
officialdom, the Lord Admiral Charles Howard, had just retired. He
had been replaced by the king's current favourite, George Villiers, Earl
– later Duke – of Buckingham. The Admiral's secretary, Sir Thomas
Aylesbury, stayed on until Buckingham was assassinated in 1628.
Aylesbury comes across as a loyal and sympathetic man who might
easily have befriended and encouraged Richard in his endeavours.
Equally, Sir Robert Naunton, who was appointed secretary of state in

January 1618 on Buckingham's recommendation, may have become Richard's chief mentor, encouraging him to write down his ideas in an address to the king.

It was Naunton who would have arranged Richard's audition with King James six months later, on 17 October 1619[1]. James, who liked to hawk and hunt, was then a guest of Sir Oliver Cromwell, uncle of the future 'Lord Protector' at his country mansion, Hinchingbrooke, near Huntingdon. James had stayed there often since his first visit in October 1603. On that occasion he was on his way to London to assume the throne, and was right royally entertained for one extravagant night[2].

Naunton would have coached Richard in the appropriate protocol and warned him of the king's often ill and graceless manners. He would have hoped that Richard would get at least a sympathetic hearing, perhaps recalling the occasion when a delegation of English religious dissidents from Dresden had petitioned James. They sought a licence to emigrate to the new American colony. According to Winston Churchill: 'James was sceptical. He asked how the little band proposed to support itself in the company's territory in America. 'By fishing,' they replied. This appealed to James. 'So God have my soul' he exclaimed in one of his more agreeable remarks, 'It is an honest trade! It was the Apostles' own calling.'[3]

The King granted a licence and in due course the *Mayflower* sailed for America with these and other emigrants, got lost and ended up in Cape Cod Bay where the Plymouth colony was founded. Eventually it flourished. Thus do the whims and moods of princes influence the tide of history.

At Richard's audition, Naunton recommended that the king should consider recompensing Richard for his expenses in carrying out the 1615 Court of Enquiry in Newfoundland and for bringing Thomas Robinson back from Lisbon. Apparently the king also promised to look at the book that Richard presented to him before deciding on a course of action.

About ten weeks went by and Richard heard nothing. In January, he wrote again to the king with an abstract '**of some material points in my book, humbly beseeching your Majesty to peruse it**'[m3]. This letter, or a copy of it, is now housed in the unlikely archives of Harrow School. He wrote a similar abstract to the then Governor of Guernsey, Sir George Carew, who may have been known personally to

Richard.[m4] Carew (1555-1629) – later Baron Clopton and Earl of Totnes – was a man of many parts but it was as a member of the Privy Council that Richard asked him to make a presentation of the book to the Council. This letter is printed here in full to the point where the texts diverge. It gives a fair summary of the book's contents and is less deferential than that to the king.

'Right honourable,

1 First the discovery tends to the glory of God for reducing the Pagans in that Island to behold the Comfortable beams of their salvation &c and for a perpetual honour and benefit to the Kings Majesty and the state to unite such a spacious and beneficial Island to the royal Crown without charge or bloodshed by settling of an orderly plantation there and it will be also a general benefit for all his Majesties' subjects and not hurtful to any.

2 Secondly, it tends that there may yearly be sent some of the superfluous branches of all his Majesties' subjects from all his highness kingdoms which now live idly to do his Majesties service and themselves good and to be very beneficial for those that shall send them thither.

3 Thirdly it shows that the trading now to the New Land with 250 sail of his Majesties' subjects ships with 5,000 persons in them is worth to his Majesty and subjects above one hundred and thirty thousand pounds yearly besides many families thereby set to work and maintained.

4 It shows that if an orderly plantation were there settled the trade to that Land only in fishing may in little time be worth to his Majesty and subjects double the value what now it is. Besides the great riches in that Country which is supposed to lie hidden because not sought for and may with gods assistance appear to be of great value to his Majesty and subjects.

5 It shows that it will be a great means to increase the numbers of Shipping and multitudes of mariners in all his Majesties kingdoms in short time if the said Book be printed and dispersed abroad in all his Majesties Kingdoms to every parish and which ships and mariners will be ready on all occasions to be called home from thence, lusty and strong to do his Majesty and their Country service in less than 15 days warning if the wind serve when such Ships and Mariners are abroad in the voyages to the East and

West Indies and other places will not be so quickly called home, neither so lusty and strong if there be never so great cause to defend their King and Country.

6 It shows that whenever Spain or France should break league with his Majesty or royal progeny how there may be a great advantage against either of them by having an orderly plantation.

7 It shows how commodious it will be to those that trade to and from Virginia and the Isle of Bermuda and from the bay of Mexico and other parts of the west Indies because it lies near half the way between Ireland and Virginia which ships do often in their return from those parts come near the said Island.

8 It shows that how near the Islands of Azores and Flores lie to the said Newlands and what Commodities may chiefly be had from there to further the desired plantation.

9 It shows a part of such fruit as the earth there naturally yields and what abundance of deer and other beasts are there and what variety of land fowl and sea fowl and what multitudes of several kinds of fish that coast yields whereby his Majesties subjects may be willing to adventure there either in person or with their purses and how from thence to seek out the supposed north west passage towards China and the northern parts of the world.

10 It shows that the climate there is health full and habitable and the waters exceeding good. Fuel for fire such great abundance that there is never like to be any want and if Iron mills may be there set to work it may yield infinite wealth to his Majesty and subjects in that kind. Furs Spruce Birch and Pine trees fit for masts boards and timber for building to be transported from thence into Spain Portugal and other places with other commodities and be of great benefit to his Majesty and subjects in that trade only.

11 It shows a part of what great and insufferable abuses are yearly there practised by our nation who trade thither and most of them approved by presentiments of 170 masters of English ships there sworn for that purpose and order set down by them under their hands and seals for reformation which orders are not looked into, although the presentiments are delivered into his Majesties high Court of the Admiralty under their hands and sealed by the Author hereof at whose great charge and travail the same was performed.

12 It shows that if his Majesty should not hold an orderly plantation

there it is to be feared that some other Prince may undertake the same and so not only reap the harvest of his Majesties subjects labours which trade thither but also have some great advantage against his Majesty and kingdoms.

13 And if his highness be pleased to give order that 2 good ships and 2 Pinnaces should be yearly kept on that coast to guard the fishermen and Plantation from Pirates and that such which adventure thither be willing to contribute thereunto which will tend greatly for the benefit and safety of the subjects whereby that no Pirate should henceforth molest them there or hinder the desired plantation as formerly they have done for the Pirates have to my knowledge carried from thence perforce many a sea faring man Into Barbary and the other parts beyond the Sea to the great hurt of his Majesty and the loss and undoing of many a good subject and thereby made many a poor widow and fatherless child most miserable.

14 To defray the charge of 2 good ships and pinnaces for that purpose half the value of a good days fishing from every of his Majesties subjects ship that yearly trades thither will aquit the said charge which is a very small matter for their safety henceforth in that trade and be very beneficial to his Majesty and subject and a most worthy business to be under-taken.'m4

In his letter to the king, Richard goes on to relate how he brought Thomas Robinson before Sir Robert Naunton: **'For which service and great charge it pleased the right honourable Mr Secretary to commend me well for the same, etc. leaving the consideration thereof and other my good endeavours to your Majesty's most gracious favour and reward etc.'**

There were a further four paragraphs in Richard's letter to Sir George Carew, expanding on some of his ideas for planting Newfoundland, that are considered in chapter 20. The abstracts must have been effective for, on the 14 February 1620, the Star Chamber of the Privy Council met and:

'Upon a Proposition made, and a book this day delivered to the Board by Captain Whitbourne for a plantation in Newfoundland, to the benefit of the fishing there and the good of his Majesties Subjects otherwise. It is ordered that [seven named councillors⁴] or any four of them shall take as well that Proposition and Book as what is likewise offered by Mr Guy of Bristol and others in that behalf into their serious consideration, and upon Conference with such persons as they shall think fit to call before them, and due Information of the Condition of that Country and the benefit of a Plantation there to make report to the Board of their opinions and what course shall be most requisite for establishing that Plantation in case the same be found fit to be entertained and proceeded in.'[5]

There is no record of those interviewed by the sub-committee, other than Guy and Richard, nor how often it met. At some time Richard may have brought up for discussion his list of 'crosses' and expenses and his expectation of recompense, namely:

1 His help in getting pardons granted to the pirates Peter Easton and Henry Mainwaring.
2 His costs in time and money for carrying out the 1615 Admiralty Commission into abuses by fishermen in Newfoundland.
3 Losses from the attack on his ship *Seraphine* by French pirates. The Government had not taken the matter up with the French authorities while the Privy Council's attempt to have the loss shared with Richard's charter partners had come to nought.
4 Losses at the hand of the errant sea-captain Woolaston .
5 The cost of bringing Thomas Robinson from Lisbon to London.

The sub-committee reported at a meeting in Whitehall on 23 July 1620, The report started: 'Whereas Capt. Wytborne haveing spent much time in Newfoundland has set down in writing divers observations and notes, touching the state and Condition of that Plantation; which he desires may bee published, for the furtherance and advancement of the said plantation, and to give encouragement to such as shall adventure.' Then it gives 'good approbations' of all of Richard's efforts, designs and desires, agrees he should have the printing of his book and recommends the Archbishops to act[6], as related in Chapter 16.

There appears to have been no immediate financial support for Richard. None-the-less, he went ahead and prepared his manuscript ready for printing. However, within six weeks his wife Joane died and was buried on 4 September in Littleham churchyard. Soon afterwards, Richard moved to live in London during the production of his book.

A
DISCOVRSE
AND DISCOVERY

OF Nevv-Fovnd-land, WITH
many reasons to prooue how worthy and bene-
ficiall a Plantation may there be made, after a far
better manner than now it is.

TOGETHER WITH THE LAYING
OPEN OF CERTAINE ENORMITIES
and abuses committed by some that trade to that
Countrey, and the meanes laid downe for
reformation thereof.

Written by Captaine *Richard Whitbourne* of
Exmouth, *in the* County *of* Deuon, *and pub-*
lished by Authority.

As also, an Inuitation: and likewise certaine Letters sent
from that Countrey; which are printed in the
latter part of this Booke.

Imprinted at London by *Felix Kingston.* 1622.

Title page of 'Discourse and Discovery'
(actual size)

15

At the signe of the gilded Cocke

'It hath always beene my chiefest studie and practice, to serve your Maiestie and my Countrey: The intent of my best labours that way, I have put into the following Discovery, and, upon good approbation thereof by divers of your Maiesties most Honourable Privie Councel, have beene incouraged to offer up the same worke unto your Maiestie. I confesse my weaknesse such, that I cannot put so fit a Garment upon it, either of stile or method, as I conceive the matter it selfe deserveth. The substance of the worke, I submit to your Maiesties wisedom and iudgement; the errors and things needlesse, to your Highnesse pardon.'

Richard Whitbourne – Dedication to his 'Most Dread Soveraigne'

Some say that the wheel, others the printing press, was the single invention that most changed the world. The wheel developed through the input of a great many people but we don't know who, where or when. The first successful printing press is usually attributed to goldsmith Johannes Gutenburg, of Maintz, in the middle of the 15th century. It was only made possible by the Chinese inventions many centuries earlier of both paper and ink. They would certainly have invented the printing press at an early date, had it not been that their language is represented by 80,000 characters.

Printing caught on rapidly in Germany and continental Europe, so that by year 1500 more than nine million books had been produced. England was slow to get going. It was not until 1476 that William Caxton brought his printing press from Bruges and started to print books in England. He printed about ninety titles, all but sixteen in English. He personally translated twenty-two of these books into

English. It is for bringing a large measure of cohesion and uniformity to the English language and its spelling that he should be remembered, rather than for introducing the printing press.

In London, only members of any one of the ancient craft guilds were allowed to practice. Caxton was a mercer (textile merchant) although there had been a small Guild of Stationers since 1403. Membership included scribes who copied out existing books onto parchment, limners who did the illustrations, bookbinders, and stationers who attended to the business side. More so than now, books were comparatively heavy, bulky and easily ruined by rain and damp. They were not a commodity to be trundled around the countryside in a tinker's cart. This created a need for a shop or stall – a 'station'. The stationery trade was limited to London and the universities of Oxford and Cambridge.

By the time Richard came to write his book, the printing and publishing industry had grown into a powerful, rich and exclusive monopoly. Once a sufficient number of native craftsmen had been trained, foreign labour was excluded by an act of 1523. With the Reformation came the need to clamp down on the production of 'heretical' books and tracts, as well as 'naughty printed books'. Outsiders were soon pirating books to the detriment of the first printer or publisher. A form of copyright was introduced to protect both the Crown and the emerging guild in 1534, followed four years later by a law requiring new books to be licensed by the Privy Council.

The Stationers' Company received its charter from Queen Mary in 1557. Under it, only company members and those with special privileges or patents from the Crown had the right to print matter for sale within the kingdom. Privileges included the exclusive right, 'copy right', to publish classes of material, such as grammars and primers, almanacs, church literature, dictionaries and legal matters. All books had to be entered in the company register on payment of a small fee after licensing by the authorities. The first stationer to enter a book acquired the 'right' to the title or 'copy'. This right was negotiable. The Charter was confirmed and strengthened by Queen Elizabeth by injunction in 1559 that also allowed certain church signatories the right to grant licences.[1]

A decree by the Star Chamber in 1586, confined printing to London, except the two universities which were allowed one press each. The company gained the power to inspect printing premises and destroy any offending material, a right it exercised zealously in defence of its monopoly[2]. Nevertheless, secret presses abounded largely expounding the complaints of both puritans and papists.

A member of the Stationers' Company was initially both a publisher and printer. The system of privileges and copies meant, in practice, that a few merchants dominated the company to their own advantage. They found it most advantageous to contract out the printing, concentrating on the more lucrative commerce of publishing and selling. Soon, ordinary members of the company had little say in how it was run. This led eventually to a lowering of standards, although this was not obvious when Richard wrote his book.

Initially, most books produced fell within a class of privilege, or were by foreign or classical authors. English authors had to find a 'copy-holder'. This was a member of the company who, on payment of a sixpenny 'fine', registered the title before a licence was granted on behalf of the Privy Council for it's publication. Copyright being negotiable, it could be acquired by the author at a price.

When Richard heard that the Privy Council had given 'good approbation' for the printing of his Discourse on 23 July 1620, he arranged for the registration of the title with the Stationers' Company. For this he had to engage a publisher and printer who together drafted out a title page for his book. Accordingly, this entry was made on 26 August 1620 in the Company's register:

'Master Barratt Entered for his copy under the hand of Master Doctor Goade and Master Lowdes Warden, a book called 'A Discourse and Discovery of New-found-land' with many reasons to prove how worthy and beneficial a plantation there may be made after farre better manner then now: it is written by Captain Richard Whitmore of Exmouth in Devon.'[3]

Not much has come to light concerning William Barratt, other than he was a book-seller from about 1608 until his death in 1624. He left a widow called Hannah. He had a shop at the *Green Dragon* in 1608 and another at the *Three Pigeons* between 1614 and 1618, often publishing jointly with others. A notable partner was Edward Bloute of the *Black Bear*. However, as will become clear, few copies of the book would have been sold in the market place.

Richard moved to London while the Discourse was being

published shortly after burying his wife in Littleham churchyard at Exmouth. He had chambers 'at the sign of the Gilded Cocke', in Paternoster Row near St Paul's yard.

This address was that of his printer – Felix Kingston – later to become Master of the Company of Stationers for two years (1635 to 1637). Antony Kingston, possibly Felix's grandfather, traded as a London bookseller from 1548 to 1551 at the west door of St Paul's. John Kynston was almost certainly Antony's son. He had been apprenticed to a grocer, Richard Grafter, but was freed from that Worshipful Company in 1542. He may have worked for his father and was first mentioned as a printer in 1553. John continued in practice until his death in 1584 when his business passed to his widow Joan. She married Thomas Orwin in 1590 and the business continued under his name until 1593, when he died. Joan carried on for another four years when her son Felix succeeded her after being freed from the Grocers' Company. He operated from Paternoster Row, at first at the sign of the *Checker*, later at the *Gilded Cock*. For a short time, he operated in Dublin where he was appointed one of the king's printers.[4]

Richard's first task was to make any revisions to the Preface and Discourse, including any suggestions that may come from the reviewing committee of the Privy Council. They were both extensively revised and the Discourse much enlarged from the draft that has come down to us. As the book was being authorised through the King's instructions to the Privy Council, the use of the Royal Coat of Arms and a 'Dedicatory Epistle' addressed to the 'High and Mightie Prince, by the grace of God, King of Great Britain, France and Ireland, Defender of the Faith,' were incorporated.

As the preface consisted almost entirely of a 'curriculum vitae' of the author, some form of introduction was needed. This was addressed 'To his Majesties good Subjects' and explained Richard's motives and objectives in writing the Discourse and his reasons, in brief, for advocating a renewed effort to 'plant' Newfoundland. The type was set and proofs were run off and corrected where necessary.

The first (1620) edition of the Discourse consisted of:

1 Title Page and the Royal Coat of Arms
2 Dedicatory Epistle to the King
3 Introduction, addressed to H.M. Subjects

4 The Preface
5 A Relation of the Newfoundland. (The Discourse)
6 A Conclusion to the Former Discourse.

How many copies were made and bound of this edition was not recorded – probably only a few hundred. While its appeal was limited to the high and mighty already interested in England's territorial expansion, it was published at a time when the North American settlements of Virginia, Plymouth and Bermuda were beginning to become established and many of the initial problems overcome. At least two leading figures in government, Sir George Calvert and Sir Henry Cary, decided to plant settlements in Newfoundland as a result of what they read.

The next edition of the Discourse was published in 1622. The following was added to the Title Page: 'As also, an invitation; and likewise certain letters sent from that country; which are printed in the latter part of this Book.' The words 'for William Barratt' were omitted. There is much more matter in this second edition, including a fair amount of repetition by Richard. Three items were added following after the Coat of Arms (1):

7 A reference from the king.
8 A letter from the Privy Council to the archbishops dated 30 June 1621
9 Names involved in Newfoundland plantations. (By RW)

Then, following 5, the Discourse:

10 The second motive and inducement. (By RW)
11 A loving invitation to His Majesty's subjects. (By RW)
12 A letter from Governor Edward Wynne dated 28 July 1622.
13 A letter from Capt. Daniel Powell dated 18 August 1622.
14 Another from Wynne, dated 17 August 1622, with a list of settlers.
15 A copy of a letter from NH to WP dated 18 August.[5]

Both the Preface (4) and the Discourse (5) are considerably altered and the Discourse much enlarged, as is the Conclusion (6). The letter from the Privy Council of 30 June 1621 has twelve signatories.

Interestingly, Captain Richard Whitbourne is now described as a 'gentleman'. In some copies there is a letter from the archbishop or diocesan bishop (16) setting forth the details for a 'brief', namely a collection in church for Richard to off-set his costs of publishing the Discourse. It appears to be a standard letter with just the name of the bishop, his diocese, and the signature and date varying. That from the Bishop of Norwich is dated 2 December 1622. My copy of the 1622 edition does not have a bishop's letter. This suggests that it was printed and sold before the bishop's letter was received by the printer.

The intention was for a copy of the book to be sent to every parish in the country – in all about 9,000. It may be that the stock of books was used up and a further edition was needed. In this new (1623) edition, numerous small alterations and corrections were made. It brought up to date what was happening regarding realisation of Richard's proposals for settlements.

The story of the 'Brief' is told in the next chapter and I shall conclude this one by recounting the subsequent history of the 'Discourse'.

While it was most unlikely that it would ever be a popular 'read' it did attract the interest of geographers and historians. In particular, it was reprinted by Samuel Purchas in his classical work: 'Haklutus Postumus or Purchase his Pilgrims'. This was printed by William Stansby for Henrie Fetherstone in 1625. In the fourth of five parts, all of the preface and the first fifth of the Discourse, 1620 edition, are included in full. Then follows: 'After this the author useth reasons to persuade to a Plantation there, which I have omitted, as busied in history. The book is common to such as desire to read it. I have also omitted the Admiralty commission and proceeding.' Purchas then adds a section of the 'Conclusion', including the description of the 'natives of those parts' and the encounter with a 'mermaid'.

The Discourse, abridged and translated into German, appeared in 'Grand Voyages,' (1628) a collection by Theodor de Bry, of international explorers' writings. It is here that his imaginative picture of Richard's encounter with the mermaid is to be found. When de Brys work was produced in Latin in 1634, a small section based on Richard's book was included under the heading 'De Terraes reperta situ.'

John Smith, governor of Virginia and Richard's contemporary, included excerpts of the 'Discourse' on the needs of colonies and how to conduct the fishing trade, in his 'Generall Historie of Virginia, New England and the Sunmmer Isles' published in 1624.

'Westward Hoe for Avalon' was published in 1870. Edited and illustrated by Thomas Whitburn, this 47 page book is culled exclusively from Richard's Preface and Discourse. Whitburn (1802 to 1889) lived for many years in Guildford but had also worked in Paris and Italy. He was interested in antiquaries, natural history and anatomy. He was responsible for a house, The Hermitage, being decorated by a process known as xylography, evidently a form of wood engraving or possibly a technique which embellished walls and doors with wood-block prints.

The Haklyut Society published 'Newfoundland Discovered – English Attempts at Colonisation 1610 – 1630', edited by Gillian T. Cell in 1982. In this scholarly work she is much more than just an editor. She sets the scene in a detailed fifty-nine page introduction, followed by fifty carefully edited pages of letters, books and other documents that include the entire text of Richard' book, 1622 edition, with foot-notes detailing the differences in the text in the other two editions.

Finally, within the last few years, a transcribed, unabridged 1620 version of the Preface and Discourse has been placed on the Internet by Dr Hans Hollmann on behalf of the Centre for Newfoundland Studies of the Memorial University of Newfoundland.[5]

16

A Brief for Richard

'Then the Curate shall declare unto the people what Holy-Days, or
Fasting-Days, are in the week following to be observed, and then also
(if occasion be) shall notice be given of the Communion: and Briefs,
Citations and Excommunications read.'

The Book of Common Prayer

The Anglican Church has been experimenting for many years with a
variety of alternative forms of worship. The Book of Common Prayer,
for so long second only to the Holy Bible in popularity, is today
seldom used. First drawn up by Archbishop Cramner in 1549, revised
in 1552, it was withdrawn a year later when Mary came to the throne.
With Elizabeth came the third Book of Common Prayer in 1559.
Thereafter it was revised but once, in 1662, and remains an Official
Order of Services to this day. The directions quoted above will
be found under the Communion Service, just after the Creed,
traditionally printed in red ink – hence the name 'Rubric' for such
instructions.

It is hardly surprising that few people today know what a church
Brief is, or was, since an Act of Parliament in 1828 abolished this
venerable system for gathering alms at the sovereign's command. The
system started centuries before the Reformation when the pope used
to issue Bulls and Briefs. Both were pontifical letters of Authorisation,
Bulls being by far the more important. The ritual attendant on their
issue was different, including the paper used and script. The date was
abbreviated for Briefs, which could be the origin of the name *brevis*,
from the Latin. Following the English Reformation, the prerogative
for issuing Briefs passed to the Sovereign and from this time onwards

they seem to have been entirely charitable in nature. By the time Charles 1 came to the throne the scope and procedures had been fairly well standardised as is illustrated by a Royal Warrant issued in 1625:

'Whereas we have been, and are likely to be much troubled with the pitiful Suits and Petitions as well of divers of our loving subjects that have sustained great Losses and Damages, either by Casualties of Fire, Shipwreck, Losses by Sea, or by being taken by Pirates or Enemies, or for other occasions, as also by Strangers, Christians of other Nations, who have been, or shall be for their Religious Sake, enforced to fly hither for Succour and Relief, some Extremities offered unto them in foreign Parts; That We would be graciously pleased to grant them Letters Patents to make collections.' The warrant goes on to entrust the Lord Keeper with full discretion in considering petitions for charitable collections and issuing the necessary Letters Patent under the Great Seal.

Later on, once the insurance underwriting business had become well established, the emphasis was almost entirely on the repair of churches and other religious buildings, and the building of new churches to serve a greatly increased population.

Only five 'foreign' Briefs are on record between 1581 and 1651. A Brief was issued in 1603 for the defence of Geneva, at that time the stronghold city of the Reformation, when it came under threat from Charles Emanuel, Duke of Savoy. In 1618, one was issued for the relief of Wesel, Germany, which had been spoiled by war.

One was issued in 1621 for the Huguenots, French Protestants, many of whom 'came by Rochelle, some to Jersey, Guernsey, and many fled out of France for fear of persecution unto England.' Their flight followed the civil war that broke out in the spring of that year, having been disarmed by the French king. Another was issued in January 1627 to relieve the (Protestant) inhabitants of the Isle of Rhé where Buckingham was fighting his unsuccessful campaign on their behalf.

A Brief was issued in 1627 in aid of the 'poor exiled Ministers of the Palatine.' As this Brief is quite typical, it is worthwhile looking at it in more detail. Brief was the one thing it was not. Some thousand words long, it started: 'Charles, by the grace of God, King of England [etc, etc.] . . . Greetings [etc] . . . WHEREAS WE . . .'. There follows a discourse on the parlous state of the Ministers, their wives and children 'who falling into the power of their cruel enemies [in this case the Spaniards] have been spoiled of all their Temporal estates, and exposed to inexpressible miseries' . . . and much more in like vein.

'We taking these things into our Princely consideration, and being moved with the bowels of compassion towards them' etc, etc. Having been assured that his subjects' bowels will be moved in a like manner to the king, it continues: 'KNOW ye therefore that WE of our princely grace, doe order and grant, that a general collection be made of the charitable devotions . . . of all our loving Subjects' throughout England and Wales, . . . which Collections we will and command be made and ordered in manner and form following. That is to say, Wee first will and grant, that by the discretion of the Lord Bishop of London, Our own Printer at Our own charge, shall forthwith print so many Briefs of these Our Letters Patent, as shall bee sufficient to disperse them unto every Church and Chappel where public and Divine Service is usually celebrated, in, and throughout this Our whole Kingdome and Dominion, And that the Letters Patent themselves under our great Seal, be left with the said Bishop of London.' He was to distribute them through every Parish Church and Chapel: 'and in the time of Divine Service on some Sunday publish them, with an exhortation to the people for the stirring up of their Christian devotion to a work so full of charity, that the Churchwardens and Overseers of the poor make diligent collection of all the Parishioners, and persons present, that after the money shall have be collected, the sum collected be indorsed on the back of the Brief, and that it be publicly declared unto the Congregation what the Sum doth amount unto.'

Detailed instructions followed as to how and when the collections were to be sent, first to the local dean, then to the bishops and thence to the Bishop of London. He was to hand over the total to the elders of the Dutch Congregation in London who were to arrange for the supervision of the distribution 'among these poor distressed souls' for their relief and sustenance. Careful accounts were to be kept at every stage and receipts given so that finally a 'perfect account' might be shown to the king.

It was the Keeper of the Great Seal who dealt with the Briefs on the king's behalf, and he had a 'clerk' or 'secretary of the Briefs' under him, a post which was a sinecure for the most part. 'Our own Printer', forerunner of HM Stationery Office, had to work hard, no doubt, to print all His Majesty's requirements. It was a most lucrative monopoly. Briefs were printed on one side of the paper only so that they could be endorsed on the reverse side with the certified amount collected in every church and chapel.

A register of the Stationers' Company records, on 29 January 1587: 'Allowed unto Thomas Purfoote the imprinting of all letters Patents to be granted under the Great Seale of England for gathering by reason of Casualties and losses happening as well by sea as by Land. The printing of which Briefs is authorised to the said Thomas under the Archbishop of Canterbury his hand and both ye wardens viz: master Bishop and Mr Denham.'

Thomas Purfoote kept his monopoly for well over thirty years. The same register records that, in the year ending July 1618, Purfoote printed Briefs at the rate of nearly one a week. Records of only a small number of these have survived, of which the following are the more interesting:

1611 Fire at Cullumpton in Devon.

1611 A great fire in Tiverton (They had had a devastating fire there in 1598). Losses were estimated at £200,000.

1616 Stratford-on-Avon. 54 dwelling houses consumed by a fire.

1617 Two for church repairs, at East Greenhithe, Kent and East Greenwich.

1618 For repairing the haven at Dunwich, Southwold and Walsberwick (including a house collection by the church wardens – an alternative to collecting in church sometimes used.)

1619 Repair of ancient water-course, the Foss-Dyke, at Lincoln.

1620 Repair Hastings' pier.

1623 Repair church at Rochester.

1624 Redemption of captives (of the Turks)

1625 Six for repairing churches at Chiddingston (Kent), Folke (Kent), Lemmington, Woolpitt (Suffolk), Guildford and Clarkenwell.

1625 Repair of wharf & sea breach in Polperrous in Cornwall. August: Plague in London and surrounds.

1628 Repair of steeple in Maldon (Essex) – used as a beacon.

1630 Plague in Cambridge.

1631 Repair of St Paul's. Another for Doddington church.

1633　　Marlborough (Fire)
1634　　For a new church at Kirk Andrews (Cambs)

Richard died in 1635 and with the start of the civil war five years later charities went by the board, with few Briefs issued under the Commonwealth. The numbers rose sharply with the Restoration, Briefs being issued for repairing the ravages caused by the Civil War as well as rewards for 'services rendered' in the royal cause. So great was the number that Samuel Pepys recorded: '30 June 1661 (Lord's Day). To church where we observe the trade in Briefs is come now up to so constant a course every Sunday, that we resolve to give no more to them.'

It might be thought that surviving churchwardens' accounts would contain many instances of monies collected on Briefs. However, since these collections were specific to one cause and the money was sent away soon afterwards, there was no need to include them in the general accounts. There are many instances of money given to shipwrecked mariners and maimed or wounded soldiers. These were not Briefs but 'protections', issued as individual licences by Justices of the Peace. Without a licence those found begging were likely to be hounded out of the parish as vagabonds or suffer a session in the stocks. Also issued were 'protections' under the Privy Seal of the Sovereign, but in these cases the Church was not involved.

The extremely unusual Brief granted to Richard was initiated by the committee of the Privy Council in their report of 23 July 1620 dealing with his draft Discourse. The report ended: 'Their Lordships did give good approbation of his good endeavour and purpose. And ordered that according to his desire he should have the printing of that Book, with the further addition of favour that the Book so printed bee recommended to the Archbishop of Canterbury and the rest of the Lord Bishops, to bee distributed to the several parishes of the Kingdom for the encouragement of such as shall be willing to assist that Plantation ether in their persons or otherwise.'[1]

The Privy Council's letter to the archbishops, dated the last day of June 1621, sets out Richard's background, his losses through pirates and others, the costs in carrying out 'commissions', and his diligence in writing about Newfoundland which the Council duly approved, and gave permission for his book to be published. The Council thought that once the book was published it should be distributed to every parish in the land. A collection was to be taken in each church to defray the cost of printing and as compensation for his losses and expenses. The Council asked the archbishops to arrange for this collection.[2]

One can only assume that the archbishops said something to the effect of 'Hang on a day or two. We are happy to do as requested but we need the king's permission in writing first, because he is the only person in these circumstances who can authorise a Brief.' Master Secretary Calvert had signed both Privy Council documents and knew that the king had agreed this course of action but it was not in writing. Soon the days became weeks and then months. This is surprising, for it would not have taken Calvert long to draft a suitable document or for the wily cash-strapped James I to see clearly that here was a way to get the debt settled by his loyal subjects without having to dip into regal coffers.

Eventually, the Council received a 'Copy of a Reference from the Kings most Excellent Majesty, dated at Theobalds, 12 April 1622: 'His Majesty is graciously pleased, that the Lords Archbishops of Canterbury and York, doe in their several Provinces proceed according to the Letters of the Lords of the Council, bearing date the last of June 1621 as well in recommending *Captain Whitbournes* discourse concerning *New-found-land*, so as the same may be distributed to the several Parishes of this Kingdome, for the encouragement of Adventurers unto the Plantation there; As also by furthering (in the most favourable and effectual manner they can) the collection to be thereupon made in all the said Parishes, towards the charge of printing and distributing those Books, and the said *Captain Whitbourne's* good endeavours, and service, with expense of his time and means in the advancing of the said Plantation: and his several great losses received at Sea by Pirates and otherwise, of which his Majesty has been credibly certified; And further his Majesties pleasure is, that the said *Captain Whitbourne* shall have the sole printing of his book for one and twenty years.'[3]

Some cleric on the archbishop's staff produced a standard letter for all the bishops to sign, in duplicate, one copy being bound with Richard's book and the other to be returned in accordance with the 'Brief'. Here is a typical example:

'Samuel, by Gods providence, Bishop of *Norwich*.

To all and singular Archdeacons, Deans, and other Officials, Parsons, Vicars, Curates, Church-wardens, and all other Ecclesiastical Officers and Ministers within my Diocese of *Norwich*, and the several Parishes thereof, Greetings.

Whereas letters have been addressed unto me from the most Reverend Father in God, the Lord Archbishop of *Canterbury*, his Grace, recommending, according unto special directions, by him received from his Majesty and the Lords of the Most Honourable Privy Council, the publication of a Discourse written by *Captain Richard Whitbourne*, concerning *New-found-land*, and a collection to be there-upon made in all the several Parishes within this Kingdome of England; And that by myself and my Officers I would give my best furtherance thereunto. Now, for as much as the publication of the said Discourse tends principally to the advancement of his Majesties' Plantation already there begun, by inciting Adventurers thereunto, as well for the propagation of the Gospel in that Country, as also for many great benefits that may be there gotten to all such as will be Adventurers therein; and likewise for the general good and enriching of the whole Kingdome, and not by any way burdensome, or hurtful to any of his Majesties' subjects, as by the Discourse itself, herewith sent unto you, does more at large appear. And for that his Majesty and the Lords of the Council.

I have so well approved the said Captains good endeavours herein, as to recommend him in an extraordinary manner; That towards his great travails, charge, and expense of time, with several Commissions, and otherwise in this business; and towards the Printing and free distributing of his Books, and his several great losses received at Sea by Pirates and otherwise, in adventuring to further the said Plantation, and partly discovering the good which may come thereby unto all his Majesties subjects; The voluntary bounties of all his Majesties subjects should be collected by his use and behoof, as by their Lordships Letters, and His Majesties pleasure thereupon signified, which is printed in the forepart of the Book, doth appear.

These are therefore to pray & require you my Brethren of the Ministry, in your several parish Churches and Chapels, throughout my Diocese of *Norwich*; That within one month next after the said Captain *Whitbournes* Book, with this my Letter, which I do allow to be Printed, shall be by him, his Assignee or Assignees brought unto any of you, you signify unto your Parishioners in so friendly and effectual manner as possibly you can, upon some Sabbath day, in the time of Divine Service, and when no other Collection is to be made, this my letter, and the scope and intent of his Discourse, and seriously stir up and exhort them to extend their bountiful liberality herein; which you the Churchwardens are to collect, after the due and usual manner from seat to seat; and such of the Parishioners as shall be then absent, to collect their gratuities thereunto at their houses, and then jointly with the Minister endorse the sum and place where it is collected, in letters, and not in figures upon these Letters. So as his good endeavours, several great losses and expense of his time and means therein, may be friendly considered, and speedily return all such money and Letters unto your Archdeacons Registers, by a trusty friend, who may speedily return all such Letters and monies so paid over unto either of them, unto my Chancellor in *Norwich*, or his lawful Assignee or Assignees by whom all such Letters and money so Collected may bee repaid to Mr *Robert Christian* Gentleman, or his Assignees in Knight-rider Street, near unto the Cathedral Church of Saint Paul's in London. So as both money and Letters may be repaid unto the foresaid Captain *Whitbourne* or his lawful Assignee or Assignees. *Given at my Lodging in the* Doctors Commons at London, *the 2. day of December* 1622.'[4]

This Brief is unusual in several ways:

1 It appears to have been instigated by the Privy Council and endorsed by the King, rather than the other way round.
2 It was unusual to have three distinct purposes, namely to defray printing costs, compensate Richard for his great losses at sea by pirates and otherwise, and to reimburse his costs in undertaking several commissions.
3 It has unusual instructions for collection in that it was to be made only when no other collection was made. Additionally, the church-wardens were 'to collect their gratuities at the houses of those parishioners as shall be absent when the collection in Church is made.'

Why this method was used rather than the more normal way of collecting on a number of Sundays is uncertain. Perhaps it was a precaution against the Cuffes of this world, for:

Cuffe comes to church much; but he keeps his bed
Those Sundays only when Briefs are read.
This makes Cuffe dull: and troubles him the most
Because he cannot sleep i th' church free cost.
  ['Upon Cuffe' – Roberk Herrick (1591–1674)]

No doubt, Richard had hoped to recoup a large part of his losses but he appears to have been disappointed. In a letter to Lord Falkland in 1626, he wrote: **'besides that I am out about my bookes, that are printed & dispensed the summe of 90 pounds to the printer & 150 pounds of my charge in 5 yeares attendaunce thereon & know not how to recover it again;'**

Only a few parochial records are known, as follows:

> *Prestbury , Cheshire*; '1623. For Captain Whitburnes booke
> . . . xij^d [One shilling] Towards his collection . . . . . viij^d' [Eight old pennies]
> *Morton, Derby.* '1624. 2 May – pd this day to Mr Brandreth the collection for New found land. (no amount stated)
> *Youlegreave, Derby.* The Church Wardens' Account Book between 1604 and 1745, contains (undated) 'A Memorial of all ye Books belonging to ye Parish Church', and in the list is included 'A discovery of ye new-founde land, written by Captain Richard Whitbourne.'

With more than 9,000 parishes in England and Wales, there was undoubtedly much more collected than shown above. This is borne out by the later history of a Brief for the poor sufferers of Teingmouth in 1690, as in the following account: 'Brief Encounter for Teing-mouth.[5]

Brief Encounter For Teingmouth

The year was 1690 and, not unusually, England and France were at war. Known as the War of the Grand Alliance, it had broken out when the 'Ancient Enemy' under Louis XIV had given refuge and support to James II, ousted as king a year earlier by William of Orange and Mary.

About 4 o'clock in the morning of 26th July, the defenceless inhabitants of East and West Teingmouth were rudely awakened when several French Galleys, having drawn off from their fleet riding in Torbay, took up station close by the shore and played their cannon upon the town, firing near to two hundred shot thereinto. In panic, the townsfolk hurriedly dressed, gathered up their most precious and portable treasures and fled onto the surrounding hills and fields as far and as fast as their legs would carry them.

From there, they watched an estimated seventeen hundred French land and, for three hours, ransack and plunder the town. Out of a total of some three hundred houses they destroyed by fire 116. With their traditional thatched roofs, it would have been an awesome as well as heart-sickening sight. Adding sacrilege to barbarity, the French defiled the two churches, broke down the pulpits and overturned the altar tables. They tore in pieces the bibles and prayer-books, scattering their leaves about the streets. Finding no folk to rape or murder, they set about the cattle and hogs, leaving very many dead. They destroyed eleven ships and barks that were in the harbour, as well as boats, nets and fishing-craft, consumed in the common flames. As the English relieving force drew near, they gathered up as much loot as they could carry and fled back to their ships.

The stunned inhabitants crept back to the ruins of their houses to contemplate a bleak future with their principal means for earning their living by fishing, destroyed. This was the second time that their town had been sacked by the French – exactly 350 years earlier pyrates had "set fire to the Towne and brent it up."

Then the poor suffering townsfolk petitioned the Lord Lieutenant and Justices of the Peace for speedy "relief by your honours' charitable assistance" in this their great extremity. The Justices examined witnesses and made an inventory of the damage, which they estimated at £11,000. Their Majesties, William and Mary, issued an impressive Brief – in 1,600 well chosen words and dated 13th November 1690 – urging the Kingdom's clergy and church-wardens to stir up the charitable hearts of their congregations upon next Lords Day and during the following week make house-to-house collections for the great losses suffered by the citizens of Teingmouth.

According to the meagre surviving records only five parishes donated a total of £6.19s.2d. or an average of £1. 8s. each. It may be noted that had eight thousand parishes each donated a like amount, it would have totalled £11,200.

According to a Mr Lake,5.Ch:16 the exact amount collected was £11,030 6s 10d.

17

Of Wolves, Water-Dogs, Flies & Flightless

'In the yeare 1615 it was well knowne to 48 persons of my company
and divers other men, that three severall times, Wolves and beasts of
the Countrey came downe neere them to the Sea-side, where they
were labouring about their Fish, howling and making a noise: so that
at each time my Mastiffe-dogge went unto them (as the like in
that Countrey hath not been seene:) the one began to fawne and play
with the other, and so went together into the Woods, and continued
with them every of these times, nine or ten dayes, and did returne
unto us without any hurt. Hereof I am no way superstitious, yet it is
something strange to me, that the wilde beasts, being followed by a
sterne Mastiffe-dogge, should grow familiaritie with him, seeing their
natures are repugnant:'

Richard Whitbourne – The Discourse

Firstly, consider the wolf: to the European, at least, he has never been
the friendliest of beasts. He hangs about in the forest and has a
propensity for grandmothers and little girls in red riding hoods – to
such an extent that the latter are believed to be extinct. He has a huge
lung capacity and has been known to do as much damage as a tornado
with his huffings and puffings. He is either a solitary animal – the
Lone Wolf – who steals up in the still of the night and swipes your
lambs, or he goes around in packs scaring the day-lights out of poor
souls trying to go to sleep. In either case, he is like the Hosts of
Midian who prowl and howl around.

Four hundred years ago there had been no wolves in England for a long time and nobody could remember any of his good qualities. Of all the mammals, he is socially the most organised, the pack coming before the individual. The pack is a highly efficient hunting unit able to take on prey many times the weight of a single wolf. The Rudyard Kipling tale of Mowgli, a small child in India reared by a wolf pack, was based on more than one real life incident. After the primates he, with other species of the family of *Canidae*, is the closest to that of man. Other members of this family include the jackal and fox and coyote.

The dog, as everyone knows, is man's best friend. How this friendship arose is still argued. The popular wisdom is that the dog, *Canus lupus domesticus*, is a sub-species of the Euro-asian grey wolf, *Canus lupus.*. It is unrelated to the endangered African wild dog, *Lycoan pictus,* or the extinct Dire dog, *Canus dirus*. The Dingo appears to be a 'feral' animal – a domestic dog gone wild, probably brought by man to Australia long ago from Borneo.

Bones of a small dog or wolf have been found at a site of early humans, dated at around 100,000 years ago. It is thought that orphaned wolf cubs became domesticated ten to twenty thousand years ago, probably at several different sites across Eurasia. Recent DNA evidence suggests that both man and dog only narrowly survived extinction following one of the cataclysms that shook the world at the end of the last ice age, roughly twelve thousand years ago. Thereafter, man and dog re-colonised the world together, the dog developing different attributes to suit the life style of his master.

Today there are many more than four hundred distinct breeds. Of these one hundred and fifty are pure bred and are strictly defined and regulated by national bodies such as the American Kennel Club. Every thoroughbred dog has to be registered along with a pedigree going back many generations. The range of physical differences, abilities and character between all these breeds is staggering. Who would think that a St Bernard weighing 200lb is the same species as a Chihuahua weighing less than five? The proof is that any dog will have his day with any other of the opposite sex. That is why the world is so full of half-breeds, crossbreeds and Heinz-dogs. And that is why the law in more enlightened countries has dealt severely with owners who fail to keep their dogs under strict control.

Richard owned the 75-ton flyboat *Seraphine* in 1615. She returned from Bordeaux on 15 January with a load of salt and John Hilley as her master and he sailed again, probably early April, for Trinity Bay in Newfoundland with a compliment of forty eight men, more than usual for a ship of this size, and more than Richard recommended in his book for a fishing voyage. At the same time Richard sailed in a specially hired barque, arriving at Trinity Harbour on 4 June, Trinity Sunday. He immediately opened his Admiralty Court of Inquiry. His plan seems to have been for *Seraphine* to employ a larger than usual crew for fishing and towards the end of the season to use the barque to ship home the extra catch. The *Seraphine* returned to Exmouth on 24 October – unduly late for a ship coming straight home from Terra Nova. Richard Whitburne paid six shillings duty an estimated two tons of train oil.

Richard had taken his 'stern mastiff-dogge' with him. It is reasonable to assume that its presence while he was trying to hold his Court on the beaches of Trinity Bay was highly disruptive to the proceedings. So when Richard caught up with *Seraphine*, at or near Heart's Ease Bay[1], he left the dog in the care of one of the apprentice boys. Relieved of his other duties, the lad spent the ensuing days exploring the shoreline on either side of the anchorage. One day, while he was some distance from the *Seraphine,* a pack of wolves (or so it was thought) descended upon him, and he was, naturally enough, terrified. When the dog began to 'gavort' with the wild animals and finally went off into the forest with them, the boy slunk back to the camp in fear and trepidation. Admonished and much chastened, he returned to his former chores.

About ten days later, the dog reappeared, seemingly unharmed. Everyone was greatly relieved. The lad was again put in charge with strict instructions to keep within sight and earshot of the men working on the stages or in the boats. When the wolf pack returned many saw what happened but were too afraid to intervene. Once again the stern mastiff absconded. This time there was an expectation that he would come to no harm and no fuss was made when the dog returned after a further ten days. After the third time, any apprehension about Richard's reaction on being told what had happened, would have melted away. Indeed, Richard found the behaviour strange almost beyond his belief. So unnatural did it appear that many of the men must have felt that some dark and ominous power had been at work. Richard could offer no other explanation for the fraternisation of such disparate and mutually repugnant animals.

The pack could have been of wolves but this seems improbable. The Newfoundland wolf is, or rather was, since it is no longer, a defined sub-species. It had been around for a long time, possibly from before the last Ice Age. Most of the early writers mention its presence, including Anthony Parkhurst (1578), Edward Hayes (1583), William Colton and John Guy (1612). Wolves may not have been common but they certainly made their presence known. There is no known instance of a wolf attack on a human but they were often blamed for live-stock killings. They were constantly hunted as a consequence. The Newfoundland Government passed 'an Act to encourage the killing of wolves in this colony', in 1839. A bounty of £5 per animal was on offer but in the next fifty-five years, it was claimed less than two hundred times. By then wolves were getting quite rare. Their main diet was caribou (reindeer) and the wolf population was closely linked to that of its prey. When the caribou herds started to dwindle during the first decades of the twentieth century, for reasons not yet fully understood, so did the wolf packs. There were very few sightings after 1930 yet the 'Killing of Wolves Act' remained on the statute book until 1963.[2]

The Encyclopaedia Britannica states that: 'Wolves and dogs will mate willingly'. True, a lot of dogs are like that but, as Richard remarked, it is strange that a 'stern-mastiffe-dogge' should grow familiar with them. Today's mastiff is believed to be much like the original guard dog of the steppes – very big with fighter instincts. The breed was known in Egypt and the Romans introduced them into England where the locals used them to hunt wolves. In Rome they were Coliseum star-turns in combats, particularly against lions. In England in the Middle Ages they were bred especially for bear fighting.

Dr John Maunder, of the Newfoundland Museum, says in a personal communicaton that there were a few recorded cases of male wolves and bitches mating, but he had never heard of a dog and a she-wolf doing so. If the pack was not wolves what else could it have been? The natives who inhabited Newfoundland in Richard's day were *Beotucks*, the original 'Red Indians' who covered their bodies and, wherever possible, their possessions with red ochre. Never in large numbers, and faced with yearly invasions by hundreds of cod-fishers, they had more or less retreated from the Avalon Peninsular where most of the fishing took place. There is no firm evidence that the *Beothuks* ever kept dogs and none of wild dogs roaming the island.

The only other possibility is that it was a pack of feral dogs. Dr Maunder says that there were such packs about at the time but he does not think they could survive the severe winters which were, and still are, quite frequent. Of the nations fishing Newfoundland waters in the 16th and early 17th centuries, the Portuguese, who used to sail in convoy, would regularly take at least one dog per ship with them. In foggy weather the dogs would sit in the bows and bark at regular intervals so that the helmsmen would know when they strayed off their station.

These dogs were called Portuguese Water Dogs.[3] It is believed that they were introduced to Portugal when the Moors invaded Iberia in the eighth century. They had centuries of practice being the 'fishermen's friend'. Web-footed and strong swimmers but not over large, they could herd fish into nets, catch those that escaped, take lines ashore and generally make themselves useful around the fishing grounds. Other nations might also have taken dogs along. There is little evidence one way or the other. If they did, it is quite likely that now and again the odd animal would be accidentally left behind in the autumn, although one lone animal would not have a dog's chance of surviving the winter.

When Bernard Drake was sent to Newfoundland in 1585 to warn English settlers and fishermen of the Spanish embargo he was to round up all the Spanish fishing boats. However, he failed to find any Spaniards (who were usually only Basques fishing in St Lawrence Bay far from the Avalon Peninsular.) Portugal was occupied by Spain at that time. Drake therefore took over about sixteen Portuguese ships, imprisoning their crews. The captives, who held their water dogs in high regard, would have turned them loose on the island to fend for themselves. These dogs, reverting to their instincts of long ago, would have formed one or more packs. A pack leader would have been chosen and, thereafter, the survival imperative dominated their every action.

Maybe the pack survived for thirty years, roamed the island and, on coming across Richard's stern mastiff, welcomed him into the pack, where he served his purpose, and that of the pack. Thus it may be that the present day breeds of Newfoundland dogs have some of Richard's mastiff's genes in their make-up.

A Very Nimble Fly

Richard takes the writing of his book and the view he hopes will influence those in high places very seriously. So it comes as a bit of a surprise that, while describing all the beasts, birds, fish and other fauna and flora, he includes the following gem:

'For no man that I ever heard of, could say, that any Woolfe, Leopard, Beare, or other beasts did ever set upon any man or boy in the *New-found-land*, although divers times some men have been by themselves in the Woods when they have suddenly come neere unto them, and those Beasts have presently upon sight of any Christian, speedily runne from them. Neither are there any Snakes, Toads, Serpents, or any other venemous Wormes, that ever were knowne to hurt any man in that Countrey, but onely a very little nimble Fly, (the least of all other Flies) which is called a Muskeito; those Flies seeme to have a great power and authority upon all loytering and idle people that come to the *New-found-land*: for they have this property, that when they finde any such lying lazily, or sleeping in the Woods, they will presently bee more nimble to seize on them, then any Sargeant will bee to arrest a man for debt: neither will they leave stinging or sucking out the blood of such sluggards, until, like a Beadle, they bring him to his Master, where he should labour: in which time of loytering, those Flies will so brand such idle persons in their faces that they may be knowne from others, as the Turkes do their slaves.'[4]

Forty years after Richard wrote this, James Yonge, ship's doctor on the *Reformatione* of Plymouth, came to Newfoundland during the fishing season. As we saw in an earlier chapter, he was a keen and critical observer who kept an interesting journal for most of his adult life. Discussing health on the island, he wrote: 'In July, the muscetos (a little biting fly) and garnippers (a larger one) will much vex us. Sometimes the boys are so tired with labour they will steal off and hide under the flakes, or get into the woods and sleep three or four hours, so hearty that they feel not the muscetoes, who by the time he wakes shall have swoln him blind, and then he knows not to get out. I have seem them prodigiously swollen by them; their cure usually is by *populem*' (an ointment made from buds of the black poplar).

'When the fishermen lade, or sometimes moor in the day, it's hard work for the shore men, so as they rest not above two hours in a night. Nor are the fishermen better to pass, who row hard and fish all day, and every second night take nets and drive to catch herrings for bait.'[5]

From this, it is clear that all those engaged in fishing were expected to work long and hard. Ships' company would usually include up to three 'boys' who needed to be exceptionally tough to stand the pace and it is understandable, if not excusable, for the weaker ones to sneak off for a rest once in a while. As the sale of fish was divided among all concerned in the trip, everyone would be expected to pull their weight. But the boys and those called by Yonge 'lurgens' (possibly lurdan – a sluggard, vagabond or loafer) would get the smallest portions. Possibly no further punishment was meted out other than that inflicted by the nimble mosquitoes.

These Penguins

There are no penguins in the northern hemisphere nor have there been. When Richard wrote of penguins he was referring to the Great Auk, (Pinguinus impennis) a bird that, in his time, seemed plentiful in Newfoundland. Haklyut reported a very early visit to the island, in 1536, by Master Hore:

'Shaping their course north-eastwards' (from Cape Breton) 'until they came to the Island of the Penguins which is very full of rocks and stones, whereon they went and found it full of great fowls, white and grey, as big as geese, and they saw infinite numbers of their eggs. They drove a great number of the fowls into their boats upon their sails, and took up many more of their eggs: the fowles they flayed and their skins were very like honeycombes full of holes being flayed off. They dressed and ate them and found them to be very good and nourishing meat[6]...'

By the sixteenth century there were only about six Great Auk breeding sites world-wide with, it is thought, one in Newfoundland – Funk Island. This lies off the east coast well north of the parts frequented by the early fishermen. A tiny flat island of about fifty acres, it is estimated that 100,000 pairs once bred there. The indigenous Beothuks had harvested their eggs for centuries. Before the 18th century visits by fishing vessels were infrequent although killings probably far exceeded the needs of the crews. Thereafter, the rate of slaughter rapidly increased particularly when it was found that auk feathers were ideal for stuffing mattresses. Gangs started to stay on the island throughout the breeding season just to pluck feathers. In 1785 there still seemed to be plenty of birds, but fifteen years later they were no more. By 1845, the Great Auk was 'as dead as the Dodo'.

In retrospect, what Richard wrote, no doubt typical of the attitude of his day, has for us a chilling poignancy: 'These **Penguins are as big as Geese, and flye not, for they have but a little short wing, and they multiplie so infinitely, upon a certaine flat Iland, that men drive them from thence upon a board; into their boats by hundreds at a time; as if God had made the innocency of soe poor a creature, to become such an admirable instrument for the sustentation of man.**'[7]

Richard Whitbourne and The Mermaid(s) – Theodor De Bry. 1628

Theodor de Bry died in 1598, aged about seventy. Born in Liege near Brussels, he followed his father's calling and was apprenticed as a goldsmith. His Calvinist family suffered persecuting under the occupying Spaniards and fled to Strasburg when he was about thirty, later moving to Frankfurt. In 1586 he went to England on commission to produce copperplates for its first ever sea atlas. Through Sir Philip Sidney's family he became friendly with Jacque le Moyne, who had been with the French Huguenots who started their first ever American colony in Florida twenty years earlier. He was the official artist and was lucky to be among the few to escape when the Spanish overwhelmed the colony after fifteen months. His paintings were lost but de Bry agreed to make copper plates from new drawings from Le Moynes memories. He died the following year but de Bry was then set on a huge project to publish the writings and pictures relevant to all voyages and explorations to the New World. After consulting with Haklyut, he started with the drawings of John White and the writings of Thomas Harriot on Raleigh's Roanoke enterprise. Published in 1588, it was an immediate success, initiating a massive series of illustrated volumes spread over more than forty years. After de Bry's death his sons took over. While the illustrations were works of typographic brilliance they bore little resemblance to reality, to which the above mermaid picture bears witness. Only one mermaid was seen; Hawridge, (on left) and Richard would never have dressed in such finery; nude sailors would never be taking baths and no natives canoe would be anywhere near St John's harbour

18

Something of a Strange Creature

'This (I suppose) was a Maremaid. Now because divers have writ much of Maremaids, I have presumed to relate what is most certaine, of such a strange Creature that was thus seene at *New-found-land*, whether it were Maremaid or no, I know not; I leave it for others to judge, &c.'

Richard Whitbourne – The Discourse [1620 Edition]

When Richard is quoted, which is not very often, it is usually his account of 'a strange Creature, which I first saw there in the yeere 1610. In a morning early, as I was standing by the River side, in the Harbour of Saint *Johns* . . .'

His memory after ten years is not likely to have been much impaired and one suspects that in the intervening years he would have told the tale on many occasions. Mermaids were in their heyday at the time; the Mermaid theatre and Mermaid taverns well known. With voyages of exploration commonplace, many a good yarn would be told of encounters with various fabulous creatures. Here is Richard's description in full so that readers may judge for themselves:

'It very swiftly came swimming towards me, looking cheerfully on my face, as it had been a woman: by the face, eyes, nose, mouth, chin, eares, necke, and forehead, it seemed to bee so beautifull, and in those parts so well proportioned, having round about the head many blue streakes, resembling haire, but certainly it was no haire, yet I beheld it long, and another of my company also yet living, that was not then farre from mee, saw the same comming so swiftly towards me: at which I stepped backe; for it was come within the length of a long Pike, supposing it would have sprung aland to mee, because I had

often sene huge Whales to spring a great height above the water, as
divers other great Fishes doe; and so might this strange Creature doe
to mee if I had stood still where I was, as I verily beleeve it had such a
purpose. But when it saw I went from it, it did thereupon dive a little
under the water and swam towards the place where a little before I
landed, and it did often looke backe towards mee; wherby I beheld the
shoulders & back down to the middle, to be so square, white and
smooth as the backe of a man; and from the middle to the hinder part,
it was poynting in proportion something like a broad hooked Arrow:
how it was in the forepart from the necke and shoulder, I could not
well decerne; but it came shortly after, to a Boat in the same Harbour
(wherein one *William Hawkridge* then my servant was[1]) that hath
been since a Captaine in a Ship to the *East Indies,* and is lately there
so imployed againe; and the same Creature did put both his hands
upon the side of the Boat, and did strive much to come in to him, and
divers then in the same Boat; whereat they were afraid, and one of
them strucke it a full blow on the head, whereby it fell off from them:
and afterwards it came to two other Boates in the said Harbour,
where they lay by the shore: the men in them, for fear fled to land and
beheld it. This (I suppose) was a Marmaid, or Mareman. Now
because divers have writ much of Maremaids, I have presumed to
relate what is most certaine, of such a strange Creature that was thus
then seene at *New-found-land,* whether it were a Maremaid or no, I
leave it for others to judge:'[2]

Before making our judgement as to what sort of creature Richard
saw, we need to look at the wider picture. Of all the strange creatures
to emerge from the ark of antiquity, mermaids (or, more correctly,
mer-folk) are the most familiar and credible. Sightings of centaurs,
sphinxes or salamanders have been so rare as to be virtually unknown
but there are scores of encounters with mermaids on record. They
began over five thousand years ago when pen was first put to paper –
or rather stylus to clay tablet – in what is now the Persian Gulf.
Oannes was an amphibian, part man part fish, that lived on land by
day instructing the Sumerians in letters, science and art. At night he
returned to the sea. In due course he was revered as a god, adapted by
the Babylonians and later by the Phoenicians, who first dwelt on the
Palestinian coast. Three thousand years ago they called him *Dagon*
and he had acquired a wife, known as *Atergatis* or *Derceto.* As the
Phoenicians were seafarers par excellence, sailing to all parts of the

known world, mer-folk would have spread their territorial limits at the same time. The Phoenicians became Carthaginians and were liquidated by the Romans, winners of the Punic Wars in 202 BC. By then, mermaids would have become established in many folks' lore.

The Romans were an unromantic lot. This may sound a contradiction in terms but 'romance' was created long after the Romans had passed away following the collapse of their empire in the 5th century AD. They appear to have left no reports of mermaid sightings.

Christianity gradually brought enlightenment to the subsequent 'Dark Ages'. With its spread and the building of churches, the natural artistic appreciation of the human feminine form found expression in many examples of mermaids carved in stone and wood. Hundreds have survived throughout Europe, not only along the coasts but also far inland. It may be that woodcarvers and stonemasons were able to avoid censure by the holy Christian hierarchy by hiding the sexual explicitness of these creatures beneath scales of propriety. Nevertheless, reported encounters with reputed mermaids continued although the records are sporadic and poorly documented.

The known world was expanding as never before by the 16th century. Hundreds of thousands of new species of animals and plants were being recorded with indigestible speed. Thanks to travellers like John Mandeville and Baron Munchausen with publishers such as the Hakluyts, Andre Thevet and Theodor de Brys, some pretty unlikely mythical beasts were being recorded. There was a marked increase in the number of sightings of mermaids and they became quite commonplace creatures. A measure of this lies in the number of London Mermaid Taverns and Inns. Only one was listed officially in 1553 but by the Great Fire of 1666, a further eleven had been founded. Most famous was the one in Bread Street where Sir Walter Raleigh reputedly started the 'Friday Street Club' in 1602, a forum for writers and poets who included Ben Johnson, Francis Beaumont, John Fletcher and, maybe the Bard himself.[3]

It was not long before the tricksters and con-men got in on the act and several 'genuine' examples of mummified mermaids went on exhibition around the world during the next three hundred years, some at such well known establishments as the British Museum and the 'American' Museum of showman P. T. Barnum.

The most eminent man of letters and science to study the subject seriously was Sir Joseph Banks. (1743–1820) As a young man he spent three years circumnavigating the world with James Cook, captain of the *Endeavour*, collecting and later classifying many scores of new plant species. For forty years he was the formidable President of the Royal Society. At one stage he believed that mermaids might exist and studied many sightings then being reported off the coasts of Scotland. But he never encountered a specimen, alive or dead, from which he could classify the species.

Gradually, as the populace at large became better educated and worldly-wise, the belief in mermaids waned, so that, by the end of the Second World War, mermaids were on the verge of extinction – excepting for the ever popular artists' models.

Regarding Richard's 'Maiden of the Deep', a search for other sightings of mer-folk in the area at that time reveals only one other credible record. This is from the log of explorer Henry Hudson during his second voyage in search of a North-West Passage. On 15 June 1608, when Hudson was well into Baffin Bay and 1,800 sea-miles north of St John's, the log read: 'This morning one of our company looking over board saw a Mermaid, and calling up some of the company to see her, one more came up, and by that time she was close to the ship's side, looking earnestly on them: a little after a Sea came up and overturned her; From the navel upwards, her back and breasts were like a woman's (as they say that saw her) her body as big as one of us, her skin very white, and long hair hanging down behind of colour of black: in her going down they saw her tail which was like the tail of a Porpoise, and speckled like a Mackerel. The names that saw her were Thomas Hilles and Robert Ragnar.'[4]

No one else has spent more time studying Richard and his writings than Professor Gillian Cell. Her praise is generous, as when she says: 'What particularly singles Whitbourne out from other writers on Newfoundland, indeed from most writers on other parts of the New World, is the authority which informs every page. This is no armchair propagandist making extravagant and improbable promises. Notice the absence of reference to mineral wealth and the scathing comments about those who had believed that gold lay in chunks on the beaches of Guiana or could be found by the barrowful in the West Indies. Only rarely is he credulous, as in his story about mermaids. No propagandist, of course, can be entirely free of exaggeration and inflation. Whitbourne is less culpable than most.'[5]

Jonathon Raban, in reviewing 'The Faber Book of Reportage' in the Observer of 1 November 1987 is less generous. Under the headline: 'Mermaids And Slippery Truths' he comments: 'Many of the stories in this book are unwitting fictions. William of Newburgh, writing in the twelfth century, reports on green extra-terrestrials sighted in a field near Bury St Edmunds: Benvenuto Cellini sees a salamander in the heart of a log fire; Richard Whitbourne is visited by a mermaid in the harbour of St John's, Newfoundland, in 1610. The truth of each of these accounts is established by the web of contingent details with which they're surrounded, for readers, unlike magistrates, are happy to accept purely circumstantial evidence.' Surely, on the recorded evidence, the magisterial coroner would be bound to return an open verdict?

Others, like the Rev. M. Harvey, writing in 1874, took a more light-hearted view. 'Our dear old captain was not afraid of the devil or of Spaniards but he had a sailor's dread of mermaids, especially after a narrow escape he had from being carried off by one in the harbour of St John's. He has left for posterity in his book a full and faithful account of his interview with one of these bold unscrupulous sea-nymphs who, in the exercise of 'women's rights', evidently designed to hurry him off to her sea cave, there to make a merman of our stout Devonshire captain leaving Mrs Whitbourne a disconsolate widow. The event he tells us took place at River Head.'6

Several others I have spoken to, considered him gullible. In 1959, Richard Carrington quoting Richard's story, was nearer the mark: 'It would be impossible to accuse such a sober and straightforward witness as Whitbourne of fraud or sensationalism. The episode obviously occurred as it was described and it was the identity, not the existence, of the 'strange Creature' that a later and more sophisticated generation was to question.'7

One thing is sure, the four mariner witnesses would have been familiar with all the sea mammals common in those western waters – such as whales, seals, sea lions, and walruses (then called sea horses). The wise men of science have suggested that the sea-mammal family called *sirenids* – manatees and dugongs – were impersonators of the mirror-holding, hair-combing charmers of so many seas. Today, these sea mammals are to be found only in tropical waters. I have seen manatees close-up in Florida and it is inconceivable that anyone, whatever the state of mind, would willingly consort with such an incredibly ugly beast. The same would apply to dugongs. The only species of sirenids known to have existed in temperate or Arctic waters was Steller's Sea Cow, first discovered in the Bering Sea in 1741. Never in large numbers nor found alive anywhere else, it was extinct by 1770, killed for its meat and train oil. Since a fully grown the sea cow was over eight metres in length and weighed more than three tons, even a calf would have been a trifle outsized as a mermaid look-alike.

As we discover more and more about this incredible world in which we have been born, the intellectual arrogance of our Victorian forebears is giving way to a more humble attitude. The more we know, the more we realise how little we know. Someone has estimated that there are in the order of two million species of fungi; a mere seventy thousand have been identified so far. The Okapi, a large and not all that rare mammal, was not discovered until 1900. 'Old Four-legs' – the 50 million year-old Coelacanth – waited until 1938 before proving that he wasn't just an extinct fossil of a fish. Ten years later, a large flightless bird, the Takahe, came back to life in New Zealand; only ten years ago, 1995, a breed of horse, previously known only through cave drawings, turned up in Tibet, alive and kicking. While we think that there is little more to discover on land, we are just beginning to realise that we have not begun to explore what lies in the depth of the sea beyond the continental shelf, that covers more than half the planet's area. Bill Bryson puts it well: 'We are astonishingly, sumptuously, radiantly ignorant of life beneath the sea.'[8] Only a handful of humans have been to any depth to see for themselves and, as yet, only a minute fraction of the seabed has been explored by remotely controlled submersibles.

There will have been more genuine sightings of mermaid-like creatures by humans, than of humans by all the denizens of the Deep, of which it is thought that there may be up to fifteen million species still undiscovered, any one of which could turn out to have been the strange creature that Richard saw and described in detail. Whether or not it was a mermaid, he knew not, leaving it to his readers to make up their own minds.

How dare anyone call Richard naive, gullible or credulous!

19

An Ingenious and Tractable People

'The naturall Inhabitants of the Countrey, as they are but few in number, so are they something rude and sauvage peoples: having neither knowledge of God, nor living under any kinde of civill government.'

Richard Whitbourne – The Discourse

Newfoundland lay deep beneath the ice during the most recent ice age. The soft fertile topping was slowly ground away by the weight of ice and ended up in the surrounding sea. When the ice melted about eleven thousand years ago, what remained was a bare island 112,000 square kilometres in extent (only slightly smaller than England) and now colloquially known as 'The Rock.' With its jagged jigsaw of a coastline and many thousands of 'ponds' in all shapes and sizes it was inhospitality itself. The surrounding sea, enriched by so much goodness, soon spawned an abundance of aquatic life scarcely equalled anywhere else in the world. It took far longer for trees, plants and land species to become re-established.

Man began to live there in small, scattered groups about five thousand years ago. Firstly, across the frozen sea came people descended from the earliest settlers of America. Archaeologists now call them *'Palaeo-Indian' (Southern branch)*. They became hunter-gatherers as the harsh climate and poor acidic soil made tilling the land a forlorn task. In due course, they occupied coastal sites around nearly all the island and developed a sophisticated sea-oriented technology. Many artefacts of stone, bone and antler were recovered from a site at Port au Choix. These included arrowheads, harpoons, bird darts, spears and lance points. Caribou bone was used for scrapers and split bird bones as needles for sewing hides while beaver incisors were made into chisels and knives. Many examples of ornaments and animals carved from various materials were found, some appearing to have a religious significance. These people disappeared after about seventeen hundred years for reasons yet unknown.

The next major occupation was by people of *Palaeo-Eskimo* origin, often referred to as Pre-Dorset. They came from the high Arctic or Greenland. Important sites on both east and west coasts have been excavated. They lived, like their predecessors, as hunter-gatherers greatly dependent on the sea. They used small tools, often serrated, carefully fashioned and extremely sharp. These people arrived about 500 BC and stayed for about three hundred years. They were the precursors of Recent-Eskimo Dorset people who occupied the island in considerable numbers for the first eight hundred years AD. Adept and skilled in hunting harp seals, the Dorsets made man-pulled sleds and kayak-like boats. They probably lived in igloos for part of the year, made vessels out of soapstone and used seal-oil for lighting. They too disappeared for no known reason.

There appears to be a gap of two hundred years before the arrival of the *Vikings* just a thousand years ago. They established a settlement known as 'Vinland' on the northern tip of the island, at L'Anse aux Meadows. The substantial remains mark the furthest known point Vikings reached in their explorations. But they were gone after a few years, perhaps returning to Greenland or maybe moving on further south.

Recent Indians of the Beaches Complex appeared at about the same time. followed by those of the *Little Passage Complex*. Both groups were ancestors of a third tribe, the *Beothuks* who were living there when the 'new found land' was discovered by John Cabot in 1497. The three complexes differed mainly in the way they made tools and the materials used. The Basques were well-established within a few years of Cabot's landing, catching whales in the Strait of Belle Island at the northern end of the Gulf of St Lawrence. French and Portuguese started to fish each summer off the Avalon Peninsular at the southern end of the island a few years later.[1]

Richard wrote extensively about the Beothuks who smeared their bodies and clothes with red ochre and were known as 'Red Indians'. His introduction to this chapter continued with **'in their habits,** customes and manners, they resemble the Indians of the Continent, from whence (I suppose) they come; They live altogether in the North and West part of the Countrey, which is seldom frequented by the English: But the French and Biscaines (who resort thither yeerely for the Whale-fishing, and also for the Cod-fish) report them to be an ingenious and tractable people (being well used:) they are reedy to assist them with great labour and patience, in the killing, cutting. And boyling of Whales: and making the Trainoyle, without expectation of other reward, then a little bread, or some such small hire.'[2]

It is now thought that they were indeed few in numbers, possibly totalling less than a thousand. As Richard wrote, there was 'not the least signe or apperance'[3] that they ever adventured to or lived permanently on Avalon Peninsular, except at Ferrilands where a Beothuk cook site was found recently thanks to a systematic archaeological exploration lasting many years. It proved to have been contemporaneous with summer campsites of early 16th century French fishermen. The natives seem to have come in the winter to pick over the sites, particularly for any ironware left by fishermen. They quickly learnt to re-work iron into fishhooks, spearheads and such-like. Richard also wrote that many of them 'secretly come into Trinity Bay and Harbour (from the Bay of Flowers, not three miles overland,) in the night time, purposely to steale Sailes, Lines, Hatchets, Knives and such like.'[4]

Richard referred to the widespread, wilful and wanton destruction of many good trees bordering the sea by English crews, such as 'no nation else doth the like'. He added 'neither do the savage people, after such time as our Countrey-men come from thence, either hurt or burne any thing of theirs, that they do leave behinde them.'[5]

The Beothuks were hunter-gatherers who followed their food sources. They would camp by the coast in the spring and summer, when seals, fish and birds' eggs were abundant. They returned to the interior in the autumn, primarily to hunt caribou as they migrated south. In this they demonstrated the ingenuity which Richard attributes to them in several passages. By the skilful, if laborious, felling of trees using only stone axes, they would create lengthy barriers that guided the migrating herds into chosen river crossings where the huntsmen's arrows were most effective. They lived in small groups of about fifty and the yearly maintenance of these fence lines must have required good organisation and considerable labour.

Adaptable and dexterous, the Beothuks lived close to and in harmony with nature, not having yet 'eaten of the tree of knowledge', as one might say. As the island became more and more settled during the next two centuries, they suffered persecution, notably from fur-trappers who accused them of stealing their traps. Little attempt was made by the authorities to befriend or protect them with the result that when, at last, an effort was made to find out more about the native people and their way of life, it was too late. Their numbers, small by any standards before Europeans arrived, had fallen below the level of self-sustainability. The last of the tribe, a woman called Shanawdithit, died in 1829, after giving the only comprehensive description ever of her tribe and its ways.

Before then, Richard had written: 'Now it may be well understood, there is great hope that those parts of the world will yeeld severall commodities of exceeding worth, whereon divers good imployments may bee made for great numbers of his Maiesties Subiects. For it is well knowne, that the Natives of those parts have great store of red Okar, wherewith they use to colour their bodies, Bowes, Arrowes, and Cannowes, in a painting manner; which Cannowes are their Boats, that they use to goe to Sea in, which are built in the shape like the Wherries on the River of Thames, (but they are much longer) with small timbers, no thicker nor broader than hoopes; and in stead of boards, they use the barkes of Birch trees, which they sew very artificially and close together, and then overlay the seames with Turpentime, as Pitch is used on the seames of Ships, and Boates: And in like manner they use to sew the barkes of Spruise and Firre trees, round and deepe in proportion, like a Brass Kettle, to boile their meat in, as-it-hath been well approoved by divers men; but most especially to my certaine knowledge, by three mariners of a ship of Tapson, in the Country of Devon; which Ship, riding there at Anchor neere by mee, at the Harbour called Hearts-ease, on the North side of Trinity Bay, and being robbed in the night, by the Savages, of their apparell, and divers other provisions, did the next day seeke after them, and happened to come suddenly where they had set up three Tents, and were feasting, having three such Cannowes by them, and three pots made of such rinds of trees, standing each of them on three stones, boyling, with twelve Fowles in each of them, each Fowle as big as a Widgeon, and some so big as a Ducke: they had also many such Pots so sewed, and fashioned like leather Buckets, that are used for quenching of fire, and those were full of the yolkes of Egges, that they had taken and boyled hard, and so dryed small as it had been powder-Sugar, which the Savages used in their Broth, as Sugar is often used in some meates. They had great store of the skins of Deere, Beavers, Beares, Seales, Otters, and divers other fine skins, which were excellent well dressed; as also great store of severall sorts of flesh dryed, and by shooting off a Musket towards them, they all ran away naked, without any apparell, but onely some of them had their hats on their heads, which were made of Seale skinnes, in fashions like our hats, sewed handsomely, with narrow bands about them, set round with fine white shels. All their three Cannowes, their flesh, skins, yolkes of Egges, Targets, Bowes and Arrows, and much fine Okar, and divers other things they tooke and brought away, and shared it among those that tooke it; and they brought to mee the best Cannow, Bowes and Arrowes, and divers of their skins, and many other artificiall things worth of noting, which may seeme much to invite us to indeavour to finde out some other good trades with them.'[7]

It is easy to visualise these natives, scared by the sudden firing of the muskets, running away clad only in their hats. Richard is less credible when he alleges that 'the Savage people of the countrey that live in the North parts, endure it so well, that they live there naked Winter and Summer.'[8] Here, as in other places, he is trying hard to persuade his readers that the Newfoundland's climate is at least as good as England's. He continues: 'And also myselfe, that have been there often, and divers others of our Nation, that have traded there, endure the greateste colde we have met withall there at any time, in our faces, neckes, and eares, as well as any Gentlewomen in England doe the colde in their naked bosomes, neckes and faces in the Winter time, when they go so uncovered; and therefore I doe conceive, it is but a little needlesse charie nicenesse used by some that trade there, that complaine any thing of the cold in that Countrey, by keeping themselves too warme: which cold (I suppose) some that have bin there, may feel the more, if they have beene much accustomed to drinke Tobacco[sic], stronge Ale, double Beere, or have beene accustomed to sit by the Taverne fire, or touched with the French disease, such peradventure may, when they come to a little cold, wheresoeuer they bee, feele it the more extremely then otherwise they would.'[9]

He argues that: 'it has been in some Winters so hard frozen in the

River of Thames, above London-bridge neere the Court, that the tenderest faire Ladies and Gentlewomen that are in any part of the world, who have beheld it, and great numbers of people, have there sported on the Ice many dayes together, and have felt it much colder there, then men doe that live in New-found-land.'[10]

England was having some exceptionally severe winters at the time. The Thames froze over in 1620 while Richard was living in London. Even so, with the hindsight of four hundred years of recorded weather, we can say with certainty that, miserably cold as an English winter often is, Newfoundland's is far colder on average. Yet it is true that in many years one can live there as pleasantly and healthily as in England – provided one is suitably clothed: as the Eskimos say, there is no such thing as bad weather... only bad clothing.[11]

Richard thought that 'some other good discoveries of trade may be made in some other parts of that Countrey, and also with the natives there: not only with those which live in the North and Westmost parts of the land, but also with those which border in the maine Continent of America, neere thereunto. For it is well knowne, that they are very ingenious and subtill kinde of people (as hath often appeared in divers things) so likewise they are very tractable, as has been well appooved, when they have been gently and politickly dealt withall: also they are a people that will seeke to revenge any wrongs done unto them, or their Woolves, as hath often appeared. For they mark their Woolves in the Eares with severall markes, as is used in England on Sheepes, and other beastes, which has been likewise well approved: for the woolves in those parts are not so violent and devouring as Woolves are in other Countries. For no man that I ever heard of, could say, that any Woofe, Leopard, Beare, or any other beasts did ever set upon any man or boy in the New-found-land.'[12]

When Richard talks of 'wolves' he must mean 'wolf-dogs' kept by the native tribes. All modern authorities agree that the Beothuks in Newfoundland did not possess dogs. Richard must be referring to the natives employed by French and Basques in the Straits of Belle Isle who were of a different tribe. He remarks that the ear-tagging to mark their dogs was just like that used on the sheep at Coombe Farm where he grew up – and much the same as used now-a-days to mark cattle. Although he never says so, I feel certain that he came into close contact with these natives on the one and only occasions that he was there – in 1579 – aboard the *Edward Cotton*, as quoted in Chapter 2.

It is a hundred pities that no account of this unusual voyage, other than Richard's, has survived. Certainly, the ship was large enough for whaling but what was the captain's indiscretion that seems to have 'blown' it so far as the Basques or French were concerned? Without their co-operation there was little hope of a successful enterprise. It seems that *Edward Cotton* arrived in the gulf in late spring when the right whales migrate through the Strait of Belle Isle. It was an unusually cold year, not at all to the liking of the faint-hearted gentlemen who had come for the sport. Was Trinity Bay a planned second option or was it by chance that they landed there? They would not have expected to meet any Englishmen there in 1579. How did they managed to kill 'a great store of Fish, Deere, Beares, Beavers, Seales, Otters and such-like'?

Among the crew would be many experienced fishermen and it was necessary only to drop a line and hook into the sea to get a bite in double quick time. So the company would not starve, although without plenty of salt it was impossible to keep the fish edible throughout the long homeward passage. But who aboard had the experience, knowledge and skill needed to kill 'great numbers of deer, bears, beavers, seals, otters and such like' and to skin and cure the pelts?

Is there a curious similarity here between the: **Deere, Beavers, Beares, Seales, Otters, and divers other fine skins'**,[13] that Richard says were found in the Indian camp thirty seven years later?

The Beothuks almost certainly still occupied summer camps along the northern shore of Trinity Bay and close-by to the north, at Bonavista Bay. Surely, Richard's ship would try to trade seeing that they had on board **'sundry commodities'** intended for this very purpose? Why then did Richard not say openly that they had traded with the natives for the furs and skins that appear to have turned the voyage from disaster to profit? Was it just a slip of the pen, when he wrote, 'killed' instead of, say, 'acquired'?

There is one other another aspect concerning Richard's writings about the Beothuks. Many times he mentions **'their savage and unbeleeving'** state. He seems sincere in the hope that **'the propagation of the Christian Faith, which has ever been your Majesties principall care,'** may **'bring the poore unbeleeving Inhabitants of that Countrey to the Knowedge of God, and a civill gouernment; and it is not a thing impossible, that from those slender beginnings which may bee made in**

New-found-land, all the Regions adjoyning (which between this place,
and the Countries actually possessed by the King of *Spaine*, and to the
north of *New-found-land*, are so spacious as all Europe) may be
converted to the true worship of God.'[14]

'I need not inforce this any further, or labour to stirre up the
charity of Christians therein, to give their furtherance towards a work
so pious, every man knowing, that even we our selves were once as
blinde as they in the knowledge and worship of our Creator, and as
rude and savage in our lives and manners.'[15]

However, 'if they might be reduced to the knowledge of the true
Trinity indeed, no doubt it would be a most sweete and acceptable
sacrifice in God, an everlasting honour to your Majesty, and the
heavenliest blessing to those pore Creatures, who are buried in their
owne superstistious ignorance. The task thereof would prove easie, if
it were well begun and constantly secounded by industrous spirits:
and no doubt but God himselfe would set his hand to rear up and
advance so noble, so pious and so Christian a building.'[16]

Whether conviction or cant, this zealous attitude has prevailed in
the relevant parts of the British Empire right from its inception, until
quite recently.

20

Planting and Withering

'In many respects Whitbourne's books are just what one might expect: straightforward and highly practical, in the tradition of the seamen's narratives preserved by Richard Hakluyt. His style, totally free of conceits and learned allusions . . . is infused with the vigour which is characteristic of so much prose written in the sixteenth and seventeenth centuries by men with no great amount of education.'

Gillian Cell in 'Newfoundland Discovered'

Gillian Cell reviewed Richard's book with clarity and learning in her introduction to a book she edited for the Hakluyt Society, sub-titled 'English Attempts at Colonisation[1]'. It would be pointless for me to try and emulate her scholarship. All of Richard's printed book is reprinted. Foot-notes detail the differences between the three editions. Instead, I have made a modern transcript of Richard's draft manuscript (Appendix), hitherto unpublished. This, or a very similar draft, would have been that which Richard presented to King James in 1619. It has a flavour and taste of the printed work.

It was no small achievement for Richard to have his book available to be read in every parish in England and Wales. In this respect it must stand alongside the Bible, the Book of Common Prayer and possibly Fox's Book of Martyrs, which headed the 'top ten' books for many years. However, few of the populace were literate and of those who were, fewer still would have read his 'Discourse'.

Had the West Country fishing captains and merchants studied it they would have felt that Richard was a turncoat, not prepared to fight the fishermen's corner. Richard demonstrated that the establishment of stable and thriving settlements would bring about a rapidly expanding fishing fleet, more efficient working practices, and greater prosperity all round. What he put in his draft, though slight in words and vague in detail, showed that he knew that success was entirely dependant on the Crown taking control.

All colonising enterprises up to that time had been by way of royal charters which empowered private enterprise to act 'in loco regis'. Governors of settlements had the power to grant title of land without which no settler could feel secure. The same happened to hold good for Newfoundland, except that the fishing community, by prior occupancy, had established foreshore rights they were prepared to defend by all possible means. But the tradition whereby the first ship arriving in a harbour in the spring became 'admiral' for the year, caused trouble. It often led to petty tyranny, waste of resources, abuse and disorder.

Richard, in the draft, wrote that these practices: **'necessarily require a reformation: some other things there are which tending to the advancement of the trade, order and quietness amongst the fishermen, which must be settled by government there: but neither of them can be done but by means of a plantation. So that there is after a sort necessity, as well as honour, or profit inviting us into this plantation.**

Much more might be said to this purpose: but it is above my reach to invent or enlarge matters beyond my observations. Yet this much I may truly say, that the fishing on the coast of Newfoundland is the best and most surest trade that Great Britain has.'[2]

In another context he says: **'This plantation as it has divers considerations of a higher nature than some others which we hold abroad, so to make it effectual, it would be managed by the special direction of his Majesty & his Council & not left to the care of private men.'**[3]

Richard saw that the participation of the West Country fishing merchants in such settlements was essential for a successful colony, adding substantially to their profits at the same time. By leaving a fifth of a ship's crew to over-winter in Newfoundland annually, there would be a 20% saving in victuals on all voyages and increased cargo capacity for the return journey. Those that stayed behind would remain members of the crew ensuring that the stages, rooms, boats and other facilities were kept safe and ready for the return of their ship the following spring. Thus they could start fishing within a day or two, saving up to three weeks that they might otherwise have spent in repairing storm-damage and cannibalisation by earlier arrivals. With better housing for both crew and storage of cured fish, Richard reckoned a ship's yearly takings would increase by as much as 50%. When rival ships came to see how successful this policy was, they would soon follow suit and: '**by this means will the burthen and numbers of your Majesties subjects shipping bee greatly increased, and strengthened, and great numbers of Mariners yearly augmented; and then our shipping may trade thither two voyages in every yeere, and more, whereas now they goe but once.**'[4]

There would inevitably be problems and arguments over rights but with 250 miles of coastline and many good harbours and anchorages, there was more than enough room for all fishermen and other settlers. Unfortunately, in those troubled times neither King nor Council was willing to be involved in an entirely new way of administrating budding colonies. Certainly, the Lord High Admiral could have been the agent for implementing control. Many times advocated by those with experience, the idea of a naval squadron being stationed at the island to guard the fishing fleet was sound. A Vice-admiral could be appointed to settle disputes and empowered to grant leases for limited periods to established settlers. Alas, the king's navy had been allowed to run-down and providing such a squadron would have seriously depleted the home fleet.

The aged Lord Admiral Howard had retired in 1615 and was replaced by the young Duke of Buckingham, George Villiers. Good looking, intelligent and the king's latest favourite, he believed that there were far more urgent matters deserving his attention. The king, aging rapidly, was more concerned with problems on the continent and those involving his children, Charles and Elizabeth.

Richard, in editing and enlarging the Discourse for publication, would have been swayed by the opinions of influential members of the Privy Council. Several of these, persuaded by his arguments and those of other Newfoundland propagandists, were considering adventuring their energies and capital in settlements of their own. The opportunity was on hand to purchase large tracts of land from the ailing Newfoundland Company. Richard felt obliged to devote his pen to expounding the best ways for private adventurers to go about their tasks. These were practical and commonsense but meant that the key problem of the conflict between settlers and fishermen was neglected.

Sir George Calvert bought a strip of land from William Vaughan known as South Ferryland in 1619. An Oxford graduate, Calvert started his career as secretary to Sir Robert Cecil in 1606 and was then 'esteemed to be a forward and knowing person in matters relating to the state'. He worked his way up the civil service of his day becoming, on Buckingham's recommendation, a secretary of state in 1619. Two years later, the French ambassador described him as 'an honourable, sensible, well-intentioned man, courteous to strangers, full of respect towards ambassadors, zealously intent for the welfare of England, but by reason of these good qualities entirely without consideration or influence.'[5]

Although Calvert had taken a fairly active interest in new world plantations, his motives in becoming fully committed are not obvious. At the age of 20 he married a Roman Catholic, Anne Mynne, and was gradually persuaded towards Catholicism. But so long as he held high office, he was prepared to wait. He had taken a small part in earlier New World plantations and now he pressed ahead with his Newfoundland plans with determination. Army captain Edward Wynne was in charge of an advance party that left Plymouth on 26 June 1621. He immediately set about building and establishing a base upon his arrival in Ferryland on 4 August.

Wynne was a no-nonsense, energetic and efficient leader. Unexpectedly, he was welcomed and helped in various ways by the masters of at least six ships. By the end of October the first building, measuring 44ft X 18ft, was habitable and much other work was underway. Many trees were felled and, after Christmas, enough timber amassed to enclose four acres of the homestead with a palisade seven feet high. Two more buildings and a forge were ready by mid-June. A salt works was completed by the end of July and about two acres of land sown with trial crops of wheat, barley, oats, peas and beans. A vegetable garden was established with lettuces, radishes, carrots and many other crops.

The settlers were lucky in having a winter even milder than the average back home. This enabled Wynne, in a postscript of the letter to Calvert dated 28 July 1622, to write 'all things succeed beyond my expectations.'[6] Encouraged by the progress, Calvert obtained a royal charter in 1623. It confirmed title to his now enlarged Newfoundland possessions. The charter gave Calvert, as governor, extensive powers to act as he pleased. But the rights of fishermen were explicitly reserved: 'saving always and ever unto all our subjects, free liberty of fishing, as well in the sea, as in the Portes and Creekes and... of salting and drying their fish unto the shoares . . . as heretofore'. This rider ensured that the conflict between settlers and annual fishermen would smoulder on into the distant future.[7]

Records thereafter are meagre but it seems that the settlement grew steadily so that by the winter of 1624/5 a hundred men and women were established. It was reported by Sir William Alexander that 'the industry of the people, both for buildings and making trial of the ground, have done more than was ever performed of any in so short a time, having on hand a brood of horses, cows, and other bestials'.

Early in 1625, Calvert retired as secretary of state, James 1 died, Charles 1 succeeded him and married Henrietta, a French princess. With Charles' 'princely approbation' and in his 'good grace', Calvert retired to his Irish estates. He was created Baron Baltimore and turned Catholic. Financially he had done very well. He now had the time and means to attend more closely to his settlement.

Then things started to go wrong both with Ferryland and the fishing industry generally. The Barbary pirates, now roaming the western approaches outside of the Straits of Gibraltar, were making serious inroads into the fishing fleet. In 1625 twenty seven English ships were captured by them while returning from Newfoundland. Earlier in the year, when war against Spain was being actively considered, the Council attempted to 'stay' the fishing fleet, intending to press some of the crews into naval service. However, anticipating the problem, many ships had set out unusually early. Two London ships, which Calvert had hired to carry 80 settlers and supplies to Ferryland, were stayed although later released along with others. Calvert had hoped to go there himself that year with the new governor to replace Wynne – Sir Arthur Aston, a Catholic gentleman. They were delayed for two years.

Thereafter, shipping restrictions were imposed in most years. Merchants found it very hard to sell their catches within the Mediterranean and prices dropped. In February 1626, Richard wrote to Lord Falkland that **'divers men are soe doubtful to adventure there that it is not like there will be anie English Shipps there this yeare and those that doe are like to be in some danger.'**[m6]

When Calvert reached Newfoundland in 1627 he remained only a few months, although returning in 1628 with many members of his family to take up residence. With him went two Catholic priests, thereby effectively making his colony the first in the New World to allow freedom of worship. England was at war with France by then and Calvert found himself and his ships heavily engaged in staving off French marauders. The following winter was exceptionally severe and Ferryland fulfilled its reputation of being the coldest harbour in Newfoundland.

Calvert had had enough. He told the king that from mid-October to mid-May 'there is a sadd face upon all the land, both sea and land so frozen for the greatest part of the tyme as they are not penetrable, no plant or vegetable thing appearing out of the earth . . .' He returned to Ireland with most of his family. However, having spent nearly thirty thousand pounds on the settlement, he was not prepared to abandon it. It struggled on for some years but never grew as had been hoped. Calvert spent the last years of his life obtaining concessions further south in Maryland, where Baltimore is now the capital, aspiring to a place where religious tolerance for Catholics would be assured. He died in 1632 before he had the chance to settle there.

Henry Cary was another prominent courtier. He was well bred and educated, having attended Exeter College, Oxford, with distinction. After serving in the Low Countries he joined the Court on being appointed a 'gentleman of the bed chamber'. Knighted in 1616, he was made a privy counsellor a year later. He became Viscount Falkland in 1620 and was elected an M.P. Two years later, he was appointed lord deputy of Ireland by favour of the Duke of Buckingham.

Ireland, not unusually, was experiencing 'troubles' and, according to the Dictionary of National Biography, Falkland was not up to the task. 'In office he showed himself both bigoted in his opinions and timid carrying out a policy, which continually dallied with extremes: though conscientious, he was easily offended, and he lamentably failed to conduct himself with credit when confronted with unusual difficulties.' Eventually, he was relieved of his duties in 1629, but continued in the king's good favour.

It was while a privy councillor that Falkland became interested in colonisation. He sat on the committee that reviewed Richard's book in 1619 and was one of only three who signed both the report and the later letter to the archbishops, the other two being Calvert and the

Earl of Arundel. He bought a narrow strip of land from Sir William Vaughan known as South Falkland in 1620 and later a massive section from the Newfoundland Company known as North Falkland that included the north-west quarter of the extensive Trinity Bay, so favoured by Richard.

Falkland appointed Richard as his adviser in 1621 but on what terms is not known. Little is known about the small settlement that was established at Fermeuse in 1623 under Sir Francis Tanfield, a cousin of Lady Falkland. Before that, Richard had written two 'loving invitations to His Majesties Subject', that detailed descriptions on how plantations based on cod-fishing should be organised. The first, specific to Falkland's holdings, was printed by Felix Kingston separately from Richard's book in 1622. It gave factual accounts of South Falkland and Trinity Bay with details of harbours, the land and natural resources, climate and sea defences. He showed how ships and men could be employed in the cod fishing industry by the proposed plantation and he suggested conditions under which intending 'adventurers' might join Lord Falkland. It ended by referring to the charge for victualling a ship of 100-tons with a crew of forty. This list detailed quantities and costs of sixty six items, costing £420 in total, which are to be found with more detail in a second 'loving invitation'. In a long letter dated December 24 1622, Richard gave Lord Falkland further extremely detailed advice on all aspects for his plantation, anticipating that a start would be made in the following spring. He dealt with the financial considerations as with all the practical details for mounting an expedition from both London and Ireland.[m5] Richard, hoping to be appointed governor of Falkland's colony, must have been disappointed when Sir Francis Tanfield was given the post.

Little information remains about this colony that was started at Fermeuse in 1623. Richard evidently paid it two visits but his suggestions and criticisms were received with resentment, according to a letter to Falkland dated 27 February 1626[m6], just six months after Lord Falkland had knighted him at Dublin Castle. Exeter was suffering from the plague, many ships had been taken by pirates in the autumn and the English expedition to Cadiz had been a disaster. Richard was depressed and moaned at length to Falkland on several counts, not the least about his lack of reward from the State. By implication Falkland had been less than generous.

Falkland ignored the hint, and within six months, Richard wrote to Buckingham seeking employment in the navy. From then on, the colony faded quietly into oblivion. Other failed attempts to establish settlements included one at St John's by a William Payne and some London merchants, and another at Placenta Bay by William Vaughan. Only slowly did a resident population become established through informal settlement.

It was not for want of trying by Richard, but bleak weather, foreign wars, lack of readily exploitable natural resources, other than cod, and disinterest by English governments held back the development of Newfoundland for many more decades.

Quodlibets

Robert Hayman was born in Totnes, Devon. His father was a merchant and an M.P. After graduating from Exeter College Oxford in 1596, Robert became a student in Lincolns Inn. He also studied in Portiers. While at Oxford he gained a reputation as a poet and among his circle of friends was William Vaughan, founder of the colony at Renewse in 1616.. Very little is known of his early career, but he claimed to be familiar with the Elizabethan court.

Robert's sister married John Barker, a Bristol merchant who was Master of that city's Society of Merchant Adventurers that was involved in Guy's Newfoundland colony at Cupids. When a second settlement was started at Bristol Hope in1618, Robert was possibly the first Governor to be appointed. He spent many of the next ten summers, and at least one winter in Harbour Grace overseeing the new settlement, not unsuccessfully. His ample hours of spare time he used writing poetry and translating works by Rabelais and others. After relinquishing his governership he spent some time in England before sailing to Guiana in 1628 where he died of fever a year later.

His "Epigrams and other small parcels, both moral and divine" were all "composed and done at Harbour Grace, in Britaniolo, anciently called Newfoundland." And were "Printed by Elizabeth All-de for Roger Michell, and are to be sold at the sign of the Bulls Head in Pauls Churchyard. 1628."

Here are a few samples from his pen:

1.27. The Worlds Whirlegigge.

Plenty breeds Pride, Pride Envy, Envy Warre:
Warre Poverty, Poverty humble care;
Humility breeds Peace, and peace breeds Plenty;
Thus round this World doth rowle alternately.

1.117 A Skellonical continued rhyme in praise of my Newfoundland.

Although in cloathes, company, buildings faire;
With England, New-found-land, cannot compare,
Did some know what contentment I found there,
Always enough, most times somewhat to spare,
With little panes, less toyle, and lesser care,
Exempt from taxings, ill newes, lawing, feare,
If cleane, and warme, no matter what you weare,
Healthy, and wealthy, if men carefull are,
With much-much more, then I will now declare,
[I say] if some men knew what this were,
[I doe beleeve] they'd live no othere where.

2.89 To Sir Richard Whitborne, Knight, my deare friend, Sometime Lieutenant to Doctor Vaughan for his plantation in Newfound-Land, who hath published a worthy booke of that most hopeful Country.

Who preaching well, doth doe, and live as well,
His doing makes his preaching to excell,
For your wise, well-pend Booke this land's your debtor:
Doe as you write, you'le be belee'd tthe'better.

21

Home is the Sailor

'For now, after more then forty yeeres spent in the foresaid courses, there remains little other fruit unto mee, saving the peace of a good conscience, which gives me this testimony, that I have ever been a loyall Subiect to my Prince, and a true lover of my Countrey, and was never as yet in all my time beholding to any Doctors counsell, or Apothecaries drugs, for the preservation of my health.'

Richard Whitbourne – The Preface

Richard lived another fifteen years after writing his book. We have seen that the fruit for the first five years rotted on the bough, when his high hopes for colonising Newfoundland were frustrated. For his last ten years the clues are meagre.

Early in 1625, Richard still had no satisfaction for all the time, trouble and money, spent in promoting his much-loved Newfoundland. He asked nine of his friends and acquaintances to write a reference to the king commending his record. Three were baronets, three knights and three squires. It was all to no avail, for the king died that March.[1]

This reference came to light when it was used to accompany the lengthy letter by Richard to the Duke of Buckingham in his capacity of Lord High Admiral in November 1626.[m7] With perhaps overdue deference to his grace, Richard sets out his grievances. He hopes that the duke will reward him for his past services to the State. Written in Richard's own hand, it serves as a curriculum vitae, listing Richard's experiences and skills, hoping that the duke can find employment for him – and much more besides.[m7]

A year later England, already two years into a disastrous war against Spain, was about to take on France as well for no good reasons. Charles I may have been full of good intentions and grandiose plans but Parliament refused to finance them. The navy was in near terminal decay after forty years of neglect following the Armada. The land forces – hardly worth the title of an army – were a rag-tag rabble of sick, lame, lazy and untrained men, ill-equipped and poorly paid. England was in no state to take on such powerful enemies. And yet Buckingham was planning an expedition to La Rochelle in support of the Protestant Huguenot enclave opposing Catholic France.

We hear next of Richard from aboard *Bonaventure*, a naval ship under command of Sir John Chudleigh. He was the brother of Sir George Chudleigh, one of the signatories to Richard's reference mentioned above. On 11 October 1627, Richard wrote a letter from aboard *Bonaventure* to his friend Hugh Peachey, an employee of the Admiralty.[m8] At 66, Richard's writing was still firm, neat and readable. He said that he had joined the ship, lying at Tilbury, at the earnest request of Chudleigh. Given the rank of lieutenant, his brief was to hasten the squadron's passage round the Downs en route for Portsmouth. It is clear from other correspondence that the fleet had been hastily provisioned and his ship was short of crew. Of sixty men, pressed by the Cinque Ports, all but ten absconded. Even Chudleigh had to wait till he reached Plymouth before receiving his commission.

Bonaventure was due to sail from Tilbury on 6 October but contrary winds and adverse tides lost her three days. She did not arrive off Margate until 14 October and did not leave Dover until the night of 16 October. She joined Buckingham's forces at Plymouth on the 18 October.[2] The plan was for an expeditionary force of 6,000 to cross the channel and join forces with the Huguenots of La Rochelle. On arrival at the offshore Ile de Rhé, few of the Huguenots wished to join the Duke, whose forces then encamped in and around the fortress of St Martin's. There they waited while the French closed in. Before starvation forced the English to surrender they escaped across marshland to embark in the relieving ships, suffering very heavy casualties on the way. The force returned to England 'with no little dishonour to our nation, excessive charge to our treasury and great slaughter of our men', as one commentator put it. It is not known if Richard stayed on to witness this operation. The following year Buckingham was assassinated in Portsmouth while preparing a further expedition for the relief of La Rochelle.

A week or so before embarking on *Bonaventure*, Richard had completed a reversion order on his tenement in Exmouth, which he leased from the Lord of the Manor of Littleham, in favour of one Elizabeth Whitrow and after her death, her son Thomas.[3] Elizabeth Whitrow (1591–c.1666) was the daughter of William Whitcombe, a ships' master who lived in Littleham.

There are eleven entries in the shipping records between 1591 and 1620 in which William is quoted as master. Of these he was twice listed as master of *Gift of God* and once master of *Endeavour*. Richard held an interest in both ships at some time. Another master, Tristram Whetcombe, could have been Elizabeth's uncle or grandfather. Elizabeth married Thomas Cooke (1584 to c.1626) and they had a son, also Thomas, born in 1619. It may be that Elizabeth kept house for Richard after his wife Joan died in 1619.

Richard's future looked uncertain by September 1627 and he was happy to let the now widowed Elizabeth live in his Exmouth house and inherit it on his death. On 31 December 1627, three months after Richard had signed the order, Elizabeth married Benedict Whitrow in Littleham. Benedict had been twice married and widowed. He too was a mariner and, according to the 1619 survey of South Devon Mariners and Ships, owned the 14-year-old *Patience* of Exmouth [34 tons] which was then in Newfoundland. He also had a third share in the 60-ton *Constance* of Lympstone. They had one son, Samuel (c.1628 to 1650). When Benedict died in 1633, he left ten shillings to the church of Littleham. This could have helped the churchwardens that year to find one shilling for the cost of 'a warrant at Houmington for Elezebeth Whittrow for not cominge to churche'. Poor woman. To be so chastised at the age of 72 seems decidedly uncharitable.

Richard was unlikely to have lived in Exmouth after that. He owned several properties in Dawlish and Teignmouth or he might have gone to live with his daughter, Katherine Hele, who had married the incumbent of St John the Baptist parish of Bishopsteignton. If then a widow, she may have been living at or near Coombe Farm although the fact that, two hundred years later, both a William and a Thomas Hele occupied land adjacent or close to Coombe Farm, is probably coincidental. There is no further mention of Richard before his death in 1634 or 1635 although he could have continued activities as a merchant and made voyages across the channel.

A 'memorand' of the Littleham Parish register recorded 'that upon the 5 day of January this year (1634) was cast away upon the coast of France the good Ship called *Dieu Grace*, by meanes of which wrack were drowned of this parish Osmond Fawster, Bennet Crosse, Leonard Frisson and Jo Hussy, together with a French boy. And of the parish of Withycombe, Richard Cheyny & Alexander Hodder.'[4] The presumption must be that these six sailors drowned and, if their bodies were recovered, they were buried in France while the rest of the crew survived and were repatriated in due course.

One victim, Richard Cheyny of Withycombe Raleigh, was aged 30, or thereabouts, in 1619. He is listed in the Duke of Buckingham's Survey of the mariners and ships of South Devon, which was dated 28 February 1619. This data would have been collected the previous summer and is unique to Devon for that period. It is more detailed than similar surveys. It lists 3,653 mariners by name, age, parish and occupation, also 247 ships, including forty-five of twenty tons or more in the Exe Estuary customs area. Details on ownership, tonnage, age, ordnance carried and present voyage are given. No less than nineteen were on fishing voyages to Newfoundland at the time of the survey, including *Due Grace*, of Exmouth, the age of which was given as thirty years.[5] There are no less than thirty-three known voyages of *Due Grace* between 1582 and 1620 including ten to Newfoundland, seemingly by a single ship. It is possible that the self-same ship ended life on the French coast in 1634, at the grand old age of fifty-two. If so, she must have been soundly built and have had one or more complete refits during her lifetime. If all her time at sea had been in temperate waters she would not have suffered from tropical ship worms (*Teredo navalis*) which bored into the hulls of wooden ships with devastating consequences at that time.

A possible scenario would be that Richard, aged seventy-three, was aboard *Due Grace* at the time and was rescued, dying some months later while still in France. No more details of the shipwreck have come to light from either English or French sources. Richard's death is registered, however, with the Prerogative Court of Canterbury: 'Whitebourne Richard [batchelor] – died beyond the seas c.1649 – no place – administration granted to Edward Drake.'[6] Although the date is badly displaced, and he was both a knight and a widower, this is assuredly our Richard since there is an entry in the Bishop's transcripts of the West Teignmouth Parish Register for August 1635 for the burial of Sir Richard Whitbourne in the churchyard of St James-the-less. This entry does not appear in the original register and seems to have been added later to the Bishop's Transcript. It has not been possible to identify Edward Drake from the known genealogy of the Drake group of families, but it is likely to be the Edward Drake who wrote a personal reference on 13 July 1626 from Ashe House, Musbury[7]: '. . . that my Lord (Buckingham) hath not a man to command a ship of more experience and a man that is well acquainted with all the ports of Christendom . . .'

Richard's death is confirmed by an entry in the Littleham Manorial Court records dated 1 September 1635 as follows: 'That Sir Richard Whidborne Knight held of the lord of this manor one tenement with appurtenances in Exmouth and one messuage or stable there for the term of his life by copy of Court Roll according the customs of the said manor and paid since the last court [held] and there happened due to the Lord on his death'.

'That Elizabeth Whitrow sometimes Cooke claims the premises after his death and for life the Reversion to Thomas her son by a copy from Sir Richard Baker dated 26 September 3 Charles [1627] by the rent of 25s[hillings] yearly and other the first and serving due at accustomed and showed her Copy.' [8]

It is sad to think that Richard probably died in a strange country, without friends or relatives around him: maybe not even shipmates.

It seems appropriate to end this book with an extract from Richard's writings. The one I have chosen is from the 'Second Motive and Inducement of The Discourse.'

I have called it:

In Praise of The New Found Land

I am filled with an ardent desire to have her called Sister-land.
For as great *Brittaine* hath ever beene a cherishing Nurse and
    Mother
to other forren sonnes and daughters,
feeding them with the milke of her planty,
And fatting them at her breasts,
when they have beene even starved at their own.
Even so hath this worthy Sister-land, from time to time,

given free and liberall entertainment to all that desire her
  blessings,
and chiefly (above all other Nations) to the English.
What receive we from the hands of our owne Countrey,
Which in most bounteous manner wee have not had, or may
  have, at hers?

Nay, what can the world yeeld to the sustentation of man,
which is not in her to be gotten?
Desire you wholesome ayre? (the very food of life) It is there.
Shall any Land powre[pour] in abundant heapes of
  nourishments and necessaries before you?
There you have them.
What Seas so abounding with fish?
What shores so replenished with fresh and sweet waters?
The wants of other Kingdomes are not felt here:
And those provisions which many other Countries want,
Are from thence supplied.

. . . What sweetnesse other Countries have suckt from thence
  by trade thither,
In buying fish, and other commodities from our Nation:
. . . Trumpets lowd enough to make *England* fal more and
  more in love with such a Sister-land.
I am loth to weary thee (good Reader) in acquainting thee thus
To those famous, faire and profitable Rivers,
And likewise to those delightfull, large and inestimable
  Woods,
And also to those inticing Hills, and delightfull Vallies; there
  to hawk and hunt,
Where there is neither savage people,
Nor ravenous beastes to hinder their sports.
They are such, that in so small a piece of paper as now my love
  salutes thee with,
I cannot fully set them downe as they deserve.

Perhaps not Wordsworth or Keats, yet delightfully said by the untutored son of a 16th century Devonshire yeoman-farmer.

A Discourse of Newfoundland

Containing a briefe relation of that Countrie
And the comodities thereof

Together with the advantages and benefits w^{ch}
will arise to his Ma^{ie} & his Kingdomes by
setling an orderlie plantation there
and with what easie meanes and verie litle
charge the same may be effected

Dedicated to the kings most excellent Matie

By Captaine Richard Whitborne
Of Exmouth in Devonshire

NOTES.

Richard Whitbourne's Draft Manuscript for his Preface and Discourse is held by the British Library under 'MSS Additional 22564.' In the Mss: title page (above) Richard spelt his name without a 'u.'

With the draft title page, the doument consists of twenty folios bound together, each slightly smaller than Quarto size plus one 'slip'. Folios are numbered at top right. The slip is on top of folio No 5. It is cut from a previous abandoned Preface draft; on the back of the slip are the first few lines |(almost identically worded) of the Preface. These are not reproduced here.

A pencil note on the fly-leaf states that the Mss was purchased at S. W. Vingers sale, 3rd August 1858. Lot No. 220 or 270.

The writing is in Richard's neat 'secretary' hand and in brown ink.

The Mss: ends abruptly, at the bottom of a page, indicating that one or more folios are missing. Otherwise it is in good condition, all but a few words being easily read. The style is often rather 'long-winded and the spelling and abbreviations used are unfamiliar to twenty-first century readers. To make it more readable the following alterations have been made:

1. All spelling and syntax is modernised: For instance, 'hath' becomes 'has' and 'liveth' becomes 'lives.'

2. Special abbreviations used by Richard are mostly transcribed in full. A special 'p' is used for 'per' and 'pro', as in *p*son for 'person'; also superscriptions as 'w^ch' and M^tie for 'which' and 'Majesty' . He uses 'and' or & as the pleasure takes him. I do likewise. Where he uses 'ec' for etcetera, I use 'etc.'

3. He usually writes numbers as '.145.' In the printed book this becomes '145.' That I use. For '50^li I use '£50.' Likewise proper names of people and places, beginning with a capital letter followed by unusually large script are shown in italics. So 'Spain' becomes '*Spain*', as in the printed book.

4. Occasionally a word or part of a word is omitted to improve the sense: it is shown: '[un]to'. An added word is <u>underlined</u>.

5. There are many sections crossed out in the Preface. These are struck through, thus: ~~In the Discourse~~. In the Discourse only occasionally is a word crossed out. These are ignored as they add nothing to the understanding of the text.

6. The last word of a page is written by itself on the last line, right aligned. The word is repeated on the following page. I show page breaks thus {lastword-5/6} or {again-6/6}, using the folio numbering.

7. In other ways I try to follow as he writes: and/& CAPS/caps: etc/ec.

Whitbourne's Draft Preface

Although I well know that it is a hard matter to persuade people to adventure into strange Countries, specially to remain there ~~as an colony~~, though the conditions thereof be [n]ever so beneficial and advantageous for them: Yet I cannot be out of all hope, that when it shall be taken into consideration what infinite riches and advantage other nations, and in particular the Spaniards & Portuguese have gotten to themselves by their many plantations not only in *America*, but also in *Barbary, Guinea, Binnie* and other parts. And when it shall plainly appear by the following discourse that the Country of *Newfoundland*, as it is truly described, is little inferior to any other for the commodities thereof, and lies as it were with open arms toward England offering itself to be embraced and inhabited by us. I say, I cannot be out of hope, but that my countrymen will be induced, either by the thriving example of others or by the strength of reason, to hearken & to put their helping hands to that which will, in all likelihood, [will] yield them a plentiful reward of their labours, and tend undoubtedly both to the glory of God, the service of his Majesty, and the general profit of his kingdom.

But before I enter into the discourse itself of the Country itself, I hold it is fit to make known the means and degrees whereby I attained unto the experience & knowledge I have thereof.

And first for my own poor estate and condition it is well known that my breeding and course of life {hath-2/3} has been such, as I have spent most of my days in travel, and especially merchandising & sea voyages. I have been in *France, Spain, Italy, Portugal, Savoy, Denmark, Norway, Poland, the Canary* and *Seris islands* (~~and what divers crosses in divers of these countries~~) And for Newfoundland I may truly say it is almost as familiar to me as mine own country.

In the year .88. I served under the then Lord Admiral as Captain of a ship of mine own, set forth at my own charge, against the *Spanish Armada*. And upon the dissolution of the fleet, coming to take my leave of his Lordship, he was pleased to give me particular letters of recommendation to the Deputy Lieutenant of the County of *Devon* for s??? a contribution towards the defraying of my said ship, which was afterwards performed upon further warrant from the lords of the Counsell. And although I have suffered often & great losses by pirates & sea rovers, yet in this point I have tasted of God's exceeding mercy that never any no ship wherein I was at any time miscarried or came to other mischance by casualty or the sea while I was in her.

So as I may well say that my life hath been a mixture of crosses, and comforts, wherein nevertheless they have not been so equally balanced, but that the one has overweighed the other. For now, after more than 40. years spent in the aforesaid courses there remains so little other fruit unto me, saving than the peace of a good conscience, which gives me this testimony that I have ever been a loyal subject to my Prince, no way offensive to my neighbours and a true lover of my Country. And it {will be-3/3} will be unto me a contentment above all others if I may be so happy to become the instrument of any public good thereof. But to come to my voyage speak of some few of my voyages I have made to *Newfoundland* which make most of the present purpose.

My first voyage thither was about 40. years since in a worthy ship of the burden of 300. tons set forth by one Mr *Cotton* of *Southampton*. We were bound for to the Grand Bay (which lies on the north side of the land) purposing to trade there with the savage people, for whom we carried sundry commodities, and to kill Whales, and make train oil, as the [*Biscainers*] Basque do there yearly in great abundance. But this our intended voyage was overthrown by the indiscretions of our Captain, and the faint-heartedness of some Gentlemen of our company, whereupon we set sail from thence, and bore with Trinity harbour, where we killed great store of fish, deer, bears, beavers, seals, otters, and such like, with abundance of sea fowl, and so returning for England, we arrived safe at Southampton.

In my second voyage there happened little worthy of the relation. In my third voyage which was about 36 years since.

In a voyage I made thither about 36. years since, I had the command of a worthy ship of 200. tons, set forth by one Mr *Crooke* of Southampton. At that time *Sir Humfrey Gilbert* a Devonshire Kt.

came thither & brought with him a large Patent from the late Queen *Elizabeth*, and in her name took possession of that Country in the {harbor-3/4} harbour of *St Johns*, whereof I was an eye witness. But he had not the good hap himself to bring home tidings of the execution of his Commission. For as he sailed from thence towards Virginia, by reason of the unhappy direction in his course, the greatest ship he had struck upon shelves on the coast of *Canada*, and was there lost. And he himself being then in a very small Pinnace of twenty tons returning for England in the company of his Vice-Admiral, ne Capt: Hayes, was in a great storm at sea overwhelmed, and so perished.

~~My fourth voyage to that country was~~ Another voyage I made thither about 34. years past, ~~in which I~~ wherein also I had the command of a ship & company. At that time one *Sir Bernard Drake* (of Devonshire also), came thither with a Commission and having divers good ships under his command he there took many Portuguese vessels laden with fish, and brought them into England.

Omitting to speak of many other voyages I made thither during the late Queen's reign, I will descend to later times.

In the year *1612*. I made another voyage [un]to *Newfoundland*, at which time that famous Arch-Pirate *Peter Easton* was there. He had with him ten sails of ships, well furnished and very rich. I was kept eleven weeks under his command, and had from him many golden promises, and much wealth offered to be put into my hands (as it is well known) his entreaties then being that I would come for England to some friends of his, & solicit {them-4/4}

them for his offer, only I promised him to release a certain ship which he had taken belonging to one Captain of Foy which being delivered to me I caused to be laden with Fish & brought her home the same, yet I had never thanks for my labour. And so leaving Easton I came for England.   (inserted slip)

them to be humble petitioners to his Majesty for his pardon. But having no warrant to touch such goods, I gave him thanks for his offer, ~~and so left him Yet~~ only I came for England and gave notice of his intention, letting pass a voyage I intended for *Naples*, and so lost both my labour and my charge. For before my arrival, there was a pardon granted and sent him from *Ireland*. But Easton hovering with those ships, and riches upon the coast of *Barbary* (as he had promised he would) with a longing desire and full expectation to be called home, lost that hope through too much delaying of time by him that carried the pardon; Whereupon he sailed into the *Straights of Gibraltar*, and was afterwards entertained by the Duke of Savoy with whom he now lives very rich.

I was also there in the year *1614*. when ~~that worthy sea Captain~~ Sir Henry Manwaring was upon that coast with six good ships strongly provided. He caused me to spend much time in his company, ~~using me very kindly~~ often conferring with me touching *Newfoundland* and the fitness & ~~urgent nesstie~~ convenience of settling a plantation there. ~~What his speaches were, himself in person & in better termes than I, is able to deliver.~~

In the year *1615*. I returned again to *Newfoundland* carrying with me a commission out of the Court of Admiralty under the great seal thereof, authorising me to empanel juries , and make inquiries upon oath of sundry abuses & disorders committed amongst fishermen yearly upon that coast, and of the fittest means to redress the same, with some other points {having-5/6} having a more particular relation, to the office of the Lord Admiral. What was then done by virtue of that commission (which was wholly executed at my charge and upon my purse) has been at large by me already certified into the Court of Admiralty. Nevertheless seeing the same has there slept ever since, and has not produced those good effects, which were expected and hoped for, I will in some convenient place of this Discourse set down a brief collection of part of my endeavours ~~spent~~ in that service, not doubting that it will be as available for the furtherance of our intended design as any other reason I shall ~~set????~~ deliver.

In the year *1616*. I had a ship at Newfoundland ~~in a fishing voyage~~, which ship returning laden from thence, being bound for *Lisbon*, was met withal by a French Pirate of Rochell, who rifled her, to the overthrow and loss of the voyage in more than the sum £860. and although I caused due proof to be made thereof at *Lisbon* before the *Lord Ross* then his Majesty's extraordinary Ambassador to the King of Spain, and represented the same in this country as appertained. Yet for this great loss I could never get any recompense from the French.

This year I myself went from England to *Villa-nova* in *Portugal* in a small bark, ~~purposing~~ and from thence ~~to yoo~~ by land unto *Lisbon*, to meet with my said ship. This bark also, laden with figs, was in her return homewards taken by a Turkish man-of-war, and carried away with all the goods in her, ~~being of good value.~~

Shortly after my ~~arrival~~ return from {*Lisbonne-6/6*} *Lisbon* I was sent for by a Gentleman, who about a year before had undertaken to settle people in *Newfoundland*. He acquainted me with his ~~proceedings &~~ Designs and after some conference touching the same we so concluded that he gave me a ~~???orderly~~ conveyance under his hand and seal for term of my life with full power to govern within his circuit upon that coast. Whereupon (being desirous to advance that work) in an: *1618*. I sailed thither in a ship of my own , which was victualled by that Gentleman myself and some others. We likewise then set forth another ship for a fishing voyage, which also carried some victuals for those people which had been formerly sent to inhabit there. But this ship was intercepted by an English erring Captain (that went forth at first with *Sir Walter Raleigh*) who took the Master of her, the Boatswain, and two other of the best men, with much victuals, (the rest of the company for fear running into the woods) and so left the Ship as a prize, whereby our intended fishing voyage of both ships was quite overthrown, and the plantation hindered for that time.

~~But~~ I cannot deny that of all those Gentlemen & others of sort & quality who have seen *Newfoundland* not only as eye witnesses but tasted also, and were relievers by the plentiful commodities thereof, no one has hitherto graced the same with any public relation nor proscribed any means how a plantation might be settled there. The consideration whereof has moved me, though of all others the least able to undertake the same, as well to discharge my conscience which has often prompted me thereunto, as hoping thereby to stir up the hearts of many of his Majesty's good and religious subjects duly to weigh the piety, honour & benefit that will {arise-6/7} arise from such a plantation, and how fitly, and conveniently by his Majesty's permission a Colony may be spared and sent thither, considering how his Majesties Kingdoms do abound and overflow with people.

~~And least any man should think me so ignorant or simple, as to go~~
~~about to persuade a thing already done I here confess that I know well~~
~~that his Majesty has many years since granted a Patent for a~~

~~plantation there. But on the one side it wanted at the first a solid~~
~~foundation, so the undertakers in their projects have not proceeded~~
~~upon true grounds, nor held fit courses therein, and the efforts have~~
~~been miserable thereunto. For notwithstanding the continuance of~~
~~time, their labours & the expense of great sums of money for bringing~~
~~the work to some perfection (wherein certainly they deserve great~~
~~commendation) Yet nothing has been hitherto performed worthy the~~
~~name of a plantation, yes, it seems to me that it does rather go back~~
~~than otherwise. And questionless, excepted it be assisted and~~
~~strengthened with new helpers and greater powers, it will of itself in~~
~~short time fall to the ground. But this is no fit place to speak~~
~~more particularly thereof. My aim in this book is to persuade a~~
~~real proceeding to a plantation in *Newfoundland*: whether this Patent~~
~~shall be made the instrument thereof, or whether any new course shall~~
~~be thought of, so it be done. I have my desire & the reward of my~~
~~labour.~~

And so I descend to the particular relation of the country.

Discourse of Newfoundland

With the inducements and means
of settling a plantation there.

Newfoundland is an Island, bordering by west upon the continent of America, (from which it is divided by the sea as England is from France) and lies between 46. and 53. Degrees north latitude. It is as spacious as Ireland, and lies near the course that ships usually hold in their return from the west Indies and half the way between Ireland and *Virginia*.

I shall not need to commend the wholesome temperature of the country, seeing the greatest part thereof lies about three degrees nearer the south than any part of *England* does. And that it has been approved by some of our Nation that have lived these many years, that even in winter it is pleasant and as healthful as *England* is. And although the example of one summer be no certain rule for other years, this much I can truly affirm, that in the year *1615*. of the many thousands of English French Portuguese and others that were then upon that coast among whom I sailed too and fro more than *100*. leagues, I neither saw nor heard of any man or boy of either of either of these Nations that died there during the whole voyage or was so much as sick.

The natural Inhabitants as they are but few in number, so are they a rude and savage people, having neither knowledge of God nor living under any kind of civil government. In their habit, customs {manners-7/8} and manners, they resemble the Indians of the continent from whence they come. They live altogether in the north and west parts of the country, which is seldom or never frequented by the English. But the [biscainers] <u>Basque</u> and French who resort thither for the whale fishing report them to be ingenious and tractable people (being well used) ready to assist them with great labour and patience in the killing, cutting and boiling of whales & making train oil, without expectation of other reward than a little bread, or some such small hire. Only they take a felicity to stealing knives hatchets and such like implements, when they have fit opportunity.

All along the coast of this Country, there are many spacious and excellent Bays, some of them stretching into the land and toward another more than 20. leagues. On the east side of the country, are the Bays of Trinity and Conception which each stretch themselves towards the south-west: *Tor* Bay and *Capelin* Bay, lying also on the East stretch towards the west: The Bay of Trepassey, St Mary, Borrell, and Plaisance, on the south part of the land, extend their arms toward the North. The Great Bay of St Peters lying to the south-west and east southerly from the great river of Canada being about 20.. leagues distance from the same stretches towards the East. And here notice that the bottoms of these bays doe meet together within the compass of a small circuit. From the Bay of St. Peters round about the west side of the land you come to the Grand Bay which {lyeth-8/8} in the North, and so from thence till you come back to Trinity Bay, are abundance of large and excellent Bays, which are the less known because not frequented by the English who seldom fish to the northward of Trinity Bay. And it is to the observed that round about the coast, and in the Bays, there are many small Islands, both fair and fruitful. Neither does any one part of the world afford greater store of good harbours, more free from dangers or more commodious than are there built by the admirable workmanship of God. I will only instance [in] one or two of the chiefest.

Trinity harbour lies near in 49. degrees, being very commodiously seated to receive shipping in any weather both to anchor in, and from thence to set sail toward either the east, west or south. It hath three arms or rivers, long and large enough for many hundred sail of ships to moor fast [in] near a mile from the harbour's mouth. Close adjoining to the rivers side, & within the harbour is much plain champion land, sufficient winter & summer to maintain great store of ordinary cattle, besides hogs and goats.

Trepassey in like manner is as commodious a harbour lying in a very temperate climate almost in 46. degrees. And it is both fair and pleasant and a wholesome coast, free from rocks & shelves, for of all other harbours, it lies most conveniently to receive our shipping passing to and from *Virginia* and the *Bermuda Island*.

But I will not insist upon further particularities, seeing our men that yearly trade to this coast know it to be as safe, as any other whatsoever.

{The Soile} The soil of this country is so fat and fruitful, as in divers places the summer naturally produces great plenty of green peas and fitches, faire round full and wholesome, as our fitches are in England. Strawberries red and white, raspberries, gooseberries, and many other delicate berries which I cannot name.

There are also many other fruits which may serve for food as pears, cherries, Filberds[1] etc. And of these berries & fruits the store is so great, that the Mariners of my company have oftentimes at once gathered more than half a hogshead would hold, of which divers times eating their fill, I never heard any man whose health was thereby any ways impaired.

There are also herbs for Salads and broth, as Parsley Alexander, Sorrell etc. And flowers, as the red and damask rose, with other kinds, most beautiful, and delightful both to sight and smelling.

And questionless, the country is stored with many physical herbs and roots, albeit their virtues are not known because not sought after. Yet within these few years many of our nation finding themselves ill have bruised some of the herbs, and strained the juice into some beer wine or aqua-vita, and by gods assistance after a few drinking it has restored them to their former health. The like virtue it has to cure a wound or any swelling, either by washing the grieved places, or by applying the herbs plaster-wise which I have seen by often experience.

This being the natural fruitfulness of the earth, producing such varieties of things fit for food without the labour of man I might in reason hence infer, that if the same were manured and husbanded as our grounds are, it would be apt to bear corn, and no less fertile than the English soil. But I need not confine myself to probabilities, seeing our men, that have wintered there divers years, who for a trial & experiment thereof did sow some small {quantie-9/9}quantity of corn found the increase to be great and the grain very good. And to my

---

[1]Hazel nuts.

knowledge, cabbage Carrots, Turnips, Lettuce, and suchlike prove very well there.

In the woods and divers other parts of the country, there is great store of deer, hares, foxes, squirrels, beavers, wolves, and bears, with other sorts of beasts serving as well for necessity, as for profit and delight. Neither let me seem ridiculous, if I annexe a matter of novelty rather than weight into this discourse. In the year *1615* it is well known to *48.* persons of my company, and divers others, that three several times the wolves and beasts of the Country came down where they were fishing, near the sea-side, howling & making a noise, so that at each time my mastiff dog went unto them: And one fawning and playing with another, they went together into the woods where he stayed with them every of these times 9. or 10.days, and did return unto us without any hurt. Whereof I am no ways superstitious yet it is something strange to me, to see the wild beasts being followed by a Dog, to grow to a familiarity with him, not withstanding their natures are repugnant: Surely the people by discrete gentle usage may be brought to society, being already inclined thereunto.

But to return to our purpose, and to speak something of the great plenty of fowls of that country, as well land-fowls as water-fowls, the variety of both kinds is infinite. For land-fowl besides great numbers of small birds flying up and down, some without name, some not worthy to be named, there are hawks great and small, Partridges, Thrush and Trussels[2] there are also birds of prey as Ravens, Gripes[3] Crows ec: For water-fowl, there is certainly as good and as much variety as in any part of the world, Goose, ducks, Pigeons, Gulls, Penguins & many other sorts.

[This] These {**Pengouin-9/10**} Penguins are as big as Geese, but fly not, but they multiply so much within a certain flat Island, that men drive them up upon a board into their boats, by hundreds at a time, as if god had made the innocency of so poor a creature, to become an admirable instrument for the sustenance of man. There are also Goodwit, Curlews and certain kinds of fowl called Oxen and Kine[4] with such like, which breed greatly upon rocks and Floes in the Sea.

The fresh waters and springs of this Country (which are many in

[2]American thrush-like bird (Cell).
[3]Vultures (Cell).
[4]Local name for waders, such as Dunlin (Cell).

number and [withal] very pleasant and delightful) are so sweet delicate & wholesome that no country in the world has better.

Fuel for fire is so plentiful here that there is never like to be wont of that commodity. In the like manner there is great abundance of trees fit to be employed in other serviceable uses. There are fir & Spruce trees, sound, good, and fit to mast ships [withal], and as commodious for boards, or building, as the spruce and fir trees of *Norway*. And out of these come abundance of Turpentine. No Country can show Pine and Birch trees of such height & greatness, as those are here. And doubtless if our men find time, and would be industrious to search further and more thoroughly into the Country, there might be found many other commodities of good worth. Amongst the which I may not omit, there is much probability of finding mines.

The rivers also and harbours are generally full of delicate fish as Salmons, Peals[5], Eels, Herring, mackerel, Flounders, Launce[6], Capelin, Cod and Trout the fairest, fattest & sweetest that I have seen in any part of the world. The like for Lobsters Crayfish Muscles hens[7], & other varieties of shell-fish. And observe how, that in those places there is usually store of the spawn, & fry of several sorts of fishes. {10/10}

The sea likewise all along the coast of this Country doe plentifully abound in other sorts of profitable fish, as Whales, Spanish Mackerel, Dorrell-Poles,[8] herringhogg[9] Porpoises, Otters, Seals, and such like royal fish.

But chief commodity of *Newfoundland* yet known, and which has grown to a settled & constant trade, which will be much bettered by an orderly plantation there, as shall be declared, is the Cod fishing upon that coast, by which both our nation, and many other Countries are enriched. And if I should here set down a valuation of that fish which the French Basque & Portuguese, fetch yearly from that coast, and the Bank (which lies 25 leagues of the south cape of *Newfoundland*, where the French use to fish winter and summer, usually making two voyages a year thither, to which places are yearly

[5]Small species of Salmon (Cell).
[6]Fish of the genus *Ammodytes* (Cell).
[7]Kind of bivalve shellfish (Cell).
[8]Species of deep water flounder called 'dory & pole'? (Cell).
[9]Hog-fish, *percina caprodes* (Cell).

sent from those countries more than *400.* sail of ships,) it would seem wonderful and incredible. Yeas, some men are of the opinion that the people of France, Spain and Italy could not so well live, if the benefit of the fishing upon this coast, & his Majesty's other dominions were taken from them. But it will be sufficient that I give an estimate of our own trade thither, and the wealth & commodities wee reap thereby, without any curious search into other men's profits.

In that year, 1615, when I was at Newfoundland with the Commission before mentioned, which was an occasion of my taking more particular observations, there were in that coast of his Majesty's Subjects 250 Sail of ships great & small. The burden & tonnage of them all one with another (as near as I could guess) allowing to every ship *60.* tons (For as some of them contained less, so many of them held more) amounted to more than *15000.* Tons. For {everie-10/11} every *60.* Tons (according to the usual manning of ships for those voyages, agreeing with the note I then took) there are to be set down 20 men and Boys, by which computation in these 250 sails, there were no less then *5000.* persons. Now every one of these ships, so near as I could take notice, had about *120000.* fish, and five tons of train oil one with another. So that the total of the fish in these *250.* sail, when it is brought into England, France or Spain, and sold after the rate of [4li]£4 for every *1000.* of fish (which is not fully a penny a fish, and if it yield less it is ill sold) amounts in money to *120000.* pounds.

Now as I have said before, allowing to every ship of *60.* tons, at least *5.* tons of train oil, the total of that <u>amounts</u> to 1250 Tons, which being undervalued at £12.[li] so as the whole value thereof in money amounts to the sum of *£15000.*[li] [whereunto] <u>which added</u> to the fish, it will appear that the total value of the fish & train (oil) of those *250.* [sail of ship] might yield to his Majesty's Subjects better than the sum of *£135000.*[li] omitting to reckon the over prizes which are made & gotten by the sale there-from in foreign Countries, being much more, from what is made at home.

And this certainly in my understanding is a point worthy <u>of</u> consideration, that so great wealth should yearly be raised by one sole commodity of that Country, yes, by one only sort of fish & not upon the whole trade of fishing, which must surely yield greater riches. And this also to be gathered & brought home by the Sole labour & industry of men without exchange or exportation of our coin or native commodities, or other adventure than of necessary {provisions-11/11} provisions for the fishing, as salt, nets, leads, hooks, lines & the like, and of victuals, as bread, beer, beef, pork, etc, in competent measure, according to the number & proportion of the men employed in those voyages.

By this little which has been thus briefly spoken, of the situation, temperature, safeness of the coast, natural fertility, commodities, & riches of *Newfoundland* it does already plainly appear, that it is a Country not only habitable & lying open ready to receive the first comers, but also for the goodness thereof worthy to be embraced & made the habitation of Christians. What the reasons, motives, & inducements are, either of goods profit or advantages, which may justly invite his Majesty, and all his good subjects, to take some speedy & real course, for settling a plantation there, I will endeavour in this plane shortly to deliver.

First, it is most certain that by a plantation, & by that means only, the poor misbelieving Inhabitants of that country may be reduced from Barbarism to the knowledge of God & light of his truth, and to a civil and regular kind of life and government. This is a thing so apparent that I need not enforce it any further, or labour to stir up the charity of good Christians to give their furtherance towards a Work so pious, every man knowing that even we ourselves were once blind as they in the knowledge & worship of our Creator, and as rude and savage in our life and manners. Only that much I will add, that it is not a thing impossible, but that by means of these slender {beginnings-11/12} beginnings which may be made in *Newfoundland*, all the regions adjoining may in time be converted to the true Worship of God.

Secondly, the uniting of a Country so beneficial already, and so promising, unto his Crown without either bloodshed, charge, or usurpation, must need be a perpetual honour to his Majesty in all succeeding ages and not so only, but also a great benefit & advantage to the State, by a new access of dominion. And what Prince or State can enlarge their territories by [more easy] easier and more just means than this. The English have been the first discoverers of this Country and a Subject of this State has long since taken possession thereof to the use of the royal Crown, which possession hath been therein continued by several Patents & Commissions, so that of right it appertains unto his Majesty & yet it is not peopled with his Majesty & subjects. I know well as I have said that his Majesty has granted a

Patent for a plantation there, but hitherto it hath produced no efforts deserving that name. This plantation as it hath divers considerations of a higher nature than some others which were held abroad, so to make it effectual, it would be managed by the special directions of his Majesty's & his Council & not left to the care of private men.

Neither seems it improbable to me, but that his Majesty may in time annexe unto his Crown, a great part of the continent of *America* bordering upon *Newfoundland*, the same lying near to his Majesty's Kingdom than any other Country of those our known parts of the world, and for the most part under the same elevation of the Pole with us, and not above *600.* leagues distance from here. {**But-12/12**}

But if this design of a plantation be not entertained & thoroughly prosecuted, may it not be justly doubted that some other Prince will step in & undertake the same, which if it so fall out his Majesty shall not only lose all those advantages & benefits which himself and his subjects would reap by their own plantation but also the actual possession of those that usurp his Majesty's right, will be a hindrance to his Majesty either to remove them or to plant by them without hazarding a breach of the peace. And it may be well feared that such a plantation growing to have strength, his Majesty's subjects shall be (if not prohibited) yet at the least hindered [of] from their free trading in the fishing, or constrained to take their fish of the plantation & at their prices, which would be a notable disservice to his Majesty & the utter overthrow of his subjects' trade thither. But in setting down the advantages wee shall have by a settled plantation of his Majesty's subjects, I shall sufficiently discover what our losses will be if wee suffer ourselves to be prevented by others.

By a Plantation of his Majesty's subjects in *Newfoundland* that Country may be made a place of great use and advantage for this state in any action that may engage us by way of attempt or defence in regard of those parts of the world.

For the first, this Country lies so near the course which the Spanish ships that come from *Mexico, Havana, Brazil,* and other places of the West Indies hold in their return from thence, that they usually sail within *100.* leagues of the south part thereof. And divers Portuguese ships have come thither and laden fish from the English, and sailed from hence with it to *Brazil*, where they have made good markets.

In the year 1615 while I was in the country {**three-12/13**} three ships from the West Indies, stopped there, to refresh themselves with water, wood, fish & fowl, and so have divers other ships done at other times. The Dutch likewise (who little frequent this fishing) have often[times] come thither purposely to buy fish, which they afterwards transported into other parts, making good profit thereof. We have already spoken of the great numbers of French & Portuguese shipping that usually trade to this coast every year and the places adjoining. So that what [in] the likelihood may be in the event of a plantation to be made here if either Spain or France should break league with his Majesty or his Royal progeny, I leave to the consideration of deeper judgements.

And certainly as his Majesty's subjects sailing to and from *Virginia* and the *Bermuda Island* might in any extremity, (having spent a mast or yard, or when any leak is sprung) be relieved and at other times refresh themselves in their voyage, if a plantation were settled near about Trepassy: So upon occasion of any attempt or other injuries which might be offered those more remote plantations, they might from thence receive help and succour.

Neither in my opinion ought it to be one of the least motives to this plantation the hope of making further discoveries from thence into the main continent of *America* and of finding out new trades, and per adventure the supposed Northwest passage. For if it can be proved or if there be any possibility or probability that there be such a passage on the north side of *America* towards *Japan* and *China*, which in the opinion of some men {is to-13/13}is to lie near the height of 64. degrees, the fittest place from whence to proceed to that discovery is in my opinion *Newfoundland*. For I would have those that henceforth attempt to search that strait or passage, to set forth somewhat earlier than heretofore they have done, and to sail directly to some convenient harbour in *Newfoundland* (of which I think Trinity Harbour to be the fittest) there to refresh themselves well with such provision as shall be needful, and so put out from thence about the [20th] end of May (if it be once set in a fair westerly wind) and to sail along the north part of *Newfoundland* and the coast which is called *Cambaleu* continuing that course unto 64. which is about 15. degrees from Trinity harbour, and may be sailed in less than six days with a fair westerly wind which commonly makes for a clear coast all along to the North both from fog and ice also, both of which are violent hindrances to men that undertake those voyages. For coming to seek out those straights or passages with a largely easterly, southerly, or Northerly winds, which bring on that coast the fog and ice, and coming so late in the summer they have thereby lost the advantage & benefit of time for finding out so happy a business.

Besides all this it would be a great ease to the rest of his Majesty's subjects, if some part of our super-abounding multitudes, were transported into *Newfoundland*. For besides the great numbers of idle persons that live here, spending their time in drinking & other excesses (of which number are many of our *Newfoundland* men during the winter) and wastefully consuming the blessings of God which are given for necessity not luxury, to the {**dishono**ʳ –13/14}dishonour of God, decay of their health & estates and beggary of their wives and families who suffer the wants of their Superfluities. I say, besides those there are many thousands of poor people of both sexes who might be spared out of England and Scotland, who living here penuriously and in great want, if they could be persuaded to remove their dwelling into *Newfoundland* might not only free themselves of their present miseries, but also by their industry in time enrich themselves, and deserve well of the state by their employment there.

Neither are the people of these his Majesty's kingdoms any way inferior to other nations in courage either to undertake or maintain, but they are often less industrious and diligent. And with grief it [is to be spoken] <u>must be said</u> that by our sluggishness some of our neighbours have won from us the ancient honour of the kingdom, and that reputation by which we were held the Masters of Navigation, & Commanders of the Seas. And in the trade of fishing they are most remarkable, of which if their audit were published to the world, it would certainly be found to be one of the best Agents they have both for their strength and wealth.

But that which is like to be the present benefit of a plantation, and which in my opinion, will weigh most toward the furtherance of this work, by reason of our trade to *Newfoundland* which will fall out in [divers respects] <u>various ways</u>.

For whereas every ship of the burden of *100.* tons employed there in a fishing voyage, doth usually carry in her 36 men and boys, much of this company might very well be spared if there were a plantation. For such a ship will sail to *Newfoundland*, and from thence to the straights of *Gibraltar* or other part of Christendom with *20.* men. And by this means the Merchant should not only save the victuals of those men (which yet were something, every man's allowance for such a voyage being a hogshead of beer & 100. of bread besides beef other provisions): but also those parts of the ship which are taken up and pestered with so many unnecessary persons, their victuals trunks & such like trumpery, might be filled with fish and other profitable commodities.

Again whereas they who now frequent this fishing trade begin commonly to provide and dress their ships in the Months of *December* and *January,* and are ready to set forth towards the end of *February* (which is commonly the foulest time of the year) hoping to arrive first in harbour whereby they obtain the name of Admiral of the harbour for the year, and have the choice places to make their fish on. But if there were a plantation, no ship should need to set sail before 25th of March. For if they might be sure at their coming to find convenient places & other necessaries ready for their use & occasions, the other point which is but an emulation of honour would soon vanish. And from this would arise a double benefit, first the cutting of the superfluous expense of one month's victuals now consumed to no purpose. Secondly, the prevention of sundry dangers into which they now run. For by this too hasty setting forth, and bearing an over-pressed sail in so desperate a manner (as no true understanding seamen do the like) the ship running on full sail even in the thickest fog & darkest night, when they cannot discern the length of three ships before them, {the yce-14/15} the ice also threatening much peril, and most of their company then asleep, I say by these ill courses, they are often[times] so beaten with rough & stormy weather, sometimes forced back with loss of man men and goods, and sometimes ships, goods & men, all cast away upon the sudden, of which we have had too often woeful experience. And I myself amongst other of my losses had one ship lost in this kind.

Moreover it often falls out that the ships being safely arrived there, (if they be not of the first comers) they are *often 20.* days providing boards & timber to fit their boats for fishing, and necessary rooms to salt and dry their fish in, whereby the voyages are greatly hindered and prolonged, and greater plenty quantities of victual spent; whereas by means of a plantation, the fishing pinnaces, stages & houses \would be orderly kept & in readiness against the ships' arrival there, whereby a mean place to [mark]make fish on, would be more commodious than the best is now that men so chargeably & desperately run for every year. And every ships company might then fall to fishing the very next day after their arrival.

And whereas they usually let their fish stand in the place where it is dried, packed upon heaps uncovered in all the heat & rains that fall, until it be shipped, which is commonly about two months, whereby great abundance of good fish is there yearly spoiled & cast away, houses might be built, at times of leisure by those of the plantation near about the drying places, for preservation of the fish.

Furthermore, whereas we trade thither now in the summer only, making but one voyage a year, we might then make [divers]several voyages, and trade thither in the winter more safely & with less danger than we {doe-15/15}do at that time of year to *Bordeaux* in France. Neither should we want commodities. For those of the plantation besides their search of hidden commodities which our men by reason of their short stay cannot look after, would spend their time in fishing [of]for cod, mackerel & herring, in cutting masts, and seasoning boards and timber for buildings, preparing these commodities to be transported into *Spain* or *Portugal* where they will yield good money, and may be sold [cheaper] more cheaply by our men than by the Hollander, who fetch the same from *Norway*, *Sweden* & other places, buying them at dear rates, & yet making good profit thereof. And our men likewise wintering there might take of the beasts of the country yielding furs, when they are in season & in their perfection. And in process of time they may also settle a traffic with the Savages for their furs, Beavers, Seal-skins, & what also is of worth among them.

So all these things considered it is out of all question that if an orderly plantation were settled in Newfoundland the trade would be much bettered, and every ship receive an increase of gain some 100%,[10] some 200%, some more, according to the proportion of their burdens & greatness.

Yet if this be not sufficient I will hereunto add, that by means of a plantation the whole fishing trade may be drawn into the hands of his Majesty's subjects only, and whether then it will be bettered, let every man judge. And here I do not intend that other nations should be prohibited the full privilege of fishing which for many years they have

[10]Difficult to say what sign was intended here.

equally enjoyed with us, or that we should assume it unto ourselves alone by strong hand, or constrain those that come thither to take their fish of us at our prices: this is my only meaning; that whereas at [this] present the French, <u>Basque</u>, and Portuguese, send yearly to that Country many {**saile of-15/16**}sail of ships, as I have already declared, our men by sailing with fewer places than now they [use to] do, by multiplying their voyages, & spending less time in the same, and carrying better fish (all which as I have already declared might be done if there were a plantation) would be able not only to furnish *France,* *Spain* and *Italy* <u>with</u>[of] this commodity, by continually carrying fresh supplies thither, but also to sell far [better] cheape<u>r</u> than any of those nations can possibly fetch the same from there with their own shipping & labour: and which of them will then adventure there when he knows his return will be a certain loss?

This trade to Newfoundland being thus enlarged both in bulk & benefit, the number of adventurers will also questionless increase. The Kingdom shall be thereby more plentifully stored with wealthy men, and our Western parts (whose chief trade this fishing is) greatly enriched.

Shipping also (the walls and Bulwarks of this Kingdome) will be hereby not only maintained but also increased both in numbers and burden, which would be a great advantage to his Majesty, and a notable addition of strength unto the Kingdom. For his Majesty may from thence call home on all occasions & upon very short warning hundreds of good serviceable ships (for I doubt not but in short time they will be increased to four or five hundred of sail) which I believe could not be done from the East Indies or other remote trades, or perhaps from places nearer home where our ships are subject to the arrest & stay of other Princes, were our necessities never so pressing & urgent.

But ships without Mariners are but as a Carcase without life, and wanting them we should want a principal limb & member of our commonwealth. These also are here every year bred & increased. And from hence his Majesty might command thousands {**of-16/16**} of lusty strong and serviceable seamen, to be employed in his Majesty's royal navy or fleets or otherwise.

From this nursery of seamen, our ships sailing to other foreign Countries, specially that go the East India voyage (which bring home commonly fewer sailors than they carry forth) are and will be much better & cheaper manned, than otherwise they could.

Many poor artifiers and others will be hereby in greater numbers set to work, as Bakers, Brewers, Coopers, Shipwrights, Smiths, Net-makers, ropemakers, line-makers, hookmakers, pulley-makers, & many other trades, who with their families would have the best part of their livelihood and maintenance, from these voyages. Add unto these the families or servants of <u>various</u> [divers] owners of ships & others that go there, which are hereby well maintained.

And by the increase and bettering of this trade, an augmentation of his Majesty's revenue in his customs must of necessity follow.

Our ordinance also (which of late years has been tooming[11], transported & sold into foreign Countries, partly for want of fit ships to place it in) might by this means be kept at home, and serve to furnish our own ships.

And certainly if this trade & a plantation were well settled by us, it would prove more commodious and beneficial than any other we have elsewhere. For it brings in great wealth (as has been said) and yet carries away nothing but a little victuals, which would be consumed by so many idle persons, in less than half that time, and the Kingdom should receive no benefit by them.

Neither in my opinion ought it to be one of the least motives {to-16/17} to this plantation, the settling of some order and government among the fishermen & the reformation of sundry abuses by them committed, part of which I will here briefly insert according to the several presentaments of Juries delivered unto me in the year *1615*. (at which time as has been said I was Commissioner for the Lord Admiral upon that coast) by *170*. Masters and officers of English ships in sundry harbours of that Country.

1 First, they did all acknowledge under their hands and seals (as they have done the rest of the presentments) that there is no difference of days observed amongst the fishermen, every man presuming to go to sea, and to fish with hook and line, upon the Sabbath day, as usually upon the week days.
2 Secondly that divers of our nation do take into their ships very

---

[11]Possibly misread. Toom, v, 2. To empty out. SOED.

great stones to press their dry fish withal in their ships which being done, they cast those stones into the harbours where ships use to ride at anchor, which will utterly spoil the roads & harbours, to the endangering of the ships, yes and men's lives too, if it be not reformed.

3 That there are many men who unlawfully convey away other men's fishing boats from the harbours and places where they were left, and some cut out the marks of them, and rip and carry away the pieces of them, to the great prejudice of the true owners of such boats.

4 That there are some men who arriving first into a harbour do rip and pull down stages left standing there for the splitting and salting of fish and others they set on fire, which is a great hindrance to the voyage of such men as are not with the first in harbour for that they must spend much time for preparing new stages.

5 There are also some who arriving first in harbour, take away men's salt that they have left there the year {before-17/17} before and also rip and spoil their train vats and tear down flakes whereon men yearly dry their fish, to the great hurt & hindrance of many others that come after them.

6 Some men likewise steal away the bait out of other men's nets by night, and also out of their fishing boats by the ship's side, whereby the fishing from whom it is so taken, is overthrown for the next day.

7 They acknowledge that some men take up more room than they need, or is fitting, to dry their fish, whereby other men are often[times] greatly hindered.

8 They found that divers of his Majesty's subjects have come to that coast in vessels not appertaining nor employed by any of his Majesty's subjects, who they conceived worthy of reformation.

9 Lastly it appeared unto them that divers were hired for these voyages, when they come there, who, not withstanding that they were still in health, would not work, or were so lazy and idle that heir work was to little purpose.

These are part of the abuses and disorders which necessarily require reformation: some other things there are which [tending to] <u>assist</u> the advancement of trade, order and quietness amongst the fishermen, which must be settled by government there: but neither of them can be done but by means of a plantation. So that there is after a sort necessity, as well as honour or profit, inviting us into this plantation.

Much more might be said to this purpose: but it is above my reach to invent or enlarge matters beyond my observations. Yet this much I may truly say, that the fishing on the coast of *Newfoundland* is the best and surest trade that great Britain has, and therefore {deserves-17/18} deserves to be mst cherished. For trading thither and returning, we little fear the Turks bondage & circumcision, nor the Popish inquisition, nor the Spanish embargement, nor such contagious heats as those find that trade near the line, nor the dangers and hurt of the art-worm[12], whereunto our ships that trade to the most parts southwards are subject, nor the many hazards & inconveniencies to which all other of our tradings generally are subject.

And this plantation will be in all respects more beneficial by far than any of those we hold aboard elsewhere, so may the same be effectually proceeded <u>with</u> in much more safety and with far less charge.

For first of all touching the transportation of men victuals & other necessaries from here [un]to *Newfoundland*, it will be by cheapest & most easy way that can be, for there will be no occasion to hire any ships expressly for that voyage, as is usually done to other of our plantations from where, having unloaded, they return with few or no commodities. But our ships that go yearly [a] fishing to the coast of that Country go there not half laden and many of them empty, so that what[so]ever shall be thought fit & necessary to be transported from here towards the furtherance and setting forward of that plantation, may be carried there for a very little charge, and without trouble or hindrance to the voyage.

And for the providing and furnishing of the plantation with victuals and provisions for their livelihood, the chief want at the beginning of the plantation will be corn, the Country itself yielding plenty of fowl, fish, & fruits as was before spoken of. And if need be they may sail in less than 5. days with a fair wind from *Newfoundland* to the Islands {of-18/18} of *Flowers* and *Azores*, abounding in Wheat beeves, sheep, goats, hogs, hens, Potatoes, muskmillion[13], onions, and

---

[12]'ship-worm' or teredo navalis.
[13]Musk-melon.

many other fruits, which they may have there at cheap rates. But if all should fail our countrymen may be supplied from home with as little inconvenience & prejudice, as other plantations have been until the Country shall be by their pains and industry made fit to bear corn.

Now for the settling of people there I conceive it will be done after two manners. The first will be of those that shall themselves go either alone, or together with their families voluntarily go there in their persons. To those it is fit that there should be good conditions made both for allowing them land & other convenient privileges. The other sort of people will be such as shall be left there as servants by the merchants. To give these encouragement to remain there, every such servant who shall reside there in the winter, shall have a single share allowed him of such fish as is taken by the labour of the whole company in the summer, in the like manner as if he returned in the ship to make sale thereof. And this single share will be sufficient to defray every such servant without putting his master to any further charge.

For the employment of our man in the absence of the shipping it will be double, either in the preparing of commodities to be transported, as fish (both Cod, mackerel and herring) Masts for ships, timber for building, deal boards, furs, and skins of beasts & the like, or else in labouring {Cxxxxy for-18/19} for advancement of the plantation & trade, by the cleansing of land, building of houses both for their own habitation for the use of the fishermen, boiling of salt, preserving of the stage, fishing pinnaces or boats & other necessaries which the fishermen shall leave there and making new of all sorts, & seeking out the more commodious places to fish in: So that although thousands of our people should at once go there, yet there would be present employment for them all; no man shall need to live idle for want of work, and indeed I would not have any man left there which should not be fit or would not employ themselves to some of the works aforesaid.

And as *Newfoundland* is nearer to us by *500.* leagues than *Virginia* and far from the plantations of the King of *Spain*, which peradventure might make this business the more difficult: so those of this plantation will have one comfort & encouragement above all others, in that they shall not be left desolate in a remote country to shift for themselves, but after six months past, they shall again see great numbers of their countrymen & have company for the rest of the year.

Neither are there here whole nations of Savages to oppose & resist our men planting, as it has fallen out in other places. Those that are, live in the North & west part of the Country (as has been said) where our men trade not, for that to settle a plantation there would be little available for us. Yet if it should be attempted, considering that the Savages want those arms weapons offensive & defensive which we have & the right art & use of them, it is probable that it might be performed without much difficult. But on the East and South side of the Country where the English fish altogether and {w^ch - 19/19} which is the fittest place for a plantation, there is not the least sign or appearance, that ever there was any habitation of the Savages, or that they ever came into those parts, of which I could give some reasons if it were not a thing so well known as it is to all people that have seen the Country.

And as they shall stand in no fear to receive hurt from the Savage, So may they be easily secured against the injuries of Pirates (who sometimes come there, and not only take from the fisherman victuals, & other provisions & munitions, but also carry away many serviceable mariners into Barbary & other parts) by maintaining yearly two good ships of war of 200 tons a piece, & two Pinnaces of *40.* tons apiece upon that coast, the which ships may easily be defrayed, so be that every ship or vessel fishing on that coast shall contribute there[un]to, the value of half a good days fishing in the whole voyage, which will be abundantly recompensed unto them in regard that they may then fish continually without interruption or danger, which now often[times] they dare not do. For which course we have the example of our neighbours the Hollanders, who generally in all their trades, but most especially in their fishing upon his Majesty's coasts, are attended with men of war, which are defrayed by a contribution of those men in whose defence they are deployed. And by this means the merchants receive far greater benefit than if they should themselves set forth in warlike manner. For besides the security they have, and the saving the charge which such provisions would require, they have much more room in their ships for their commodities. And in these ships thus sent to guard the fleets which are {called-19/20}called wafters, are bred many serviceable & able seamen, not only mariners, but also good soldiers & commanders.

Now because my desire is that not only Merchants or such as live near the sea-side, but also all others should give their furtherance to this plantation, either by adventuring their moneys or sending men there, I think it fit to show how such persons may adventure. To such as should here object that those who live far from the sea, whether Gents or others, and are not experienced in affairs of this nature, cannot so conveniently adventure there I answer that none of his Majesty's subjects dwell further than *100.* miles from the sea-side, which is no great journey, that by the same reason that commodities brought from foreign parts & landed on our coasts & haven towns are dispersed through all places of this Kingdom and so wonted, our men living in any of those places may be with as little difficulty adventure into other countries. That we have the example of various [divers both] Gents and others of *Italy, Spain, Germany, Savoy* the *Low Countries* & other places, that come yearly more than *300.* Miles to the City of *Seville* purposely to sail to the west Indies, And lastly that any man may safely adventure without trouble to his own person, so that he provide himself of a trusty servant and one that will be diligent to manage his business, and one whose friends and means as well as his credit or honesty may bind him to make just accounts.

But to return to our purpose, Those that shall {have-20/20} have a desire to send people to the *Newfound-land* or adventure otherwise towards the furtherance of this plantation, must as I conceive either buy or hire ships for the passing of people, victuals, & provision in the spring of the year, and for the returning of fish & other commodities from there, as shall be procured by the labour of those men sent.

In this case if I might be believed, I would advise this course to be held by those that shall adventure either separately by themselves, or jointly with others, viz To buy two ships the one of *100.* or *150.* ton, and the other of *30.* or *40.* ton, the smaller vessel to be sent before as a Pinnace to prepare & fit a place where the greater ship might follow as to the intended place of habitation. The reason why I could wish that ships should be bought, is because that then they may send their ships from there to any port beyond the sea, where they think good, to vend their fish and other commodities, and being there sail from one port to another for making their employments. For by the hire of ships there to load fish & train oil, and transport it into *Spain Portugal France & Italy* the Merchant does often suffer great loss. For by the contracts which are commonly made under hand and seal (which we call charter-parties) it is expressed in how many days the owner of the ship is to make the same ready and how many days his ship shall stay at *Newfoundland* & then to what port he must sail, although the place where he arrives be never so much overlaid with the like commodities, commodities which he is to re-load, be there much dearer, than at some other place not far from there, which has been a great loss to many Merchants, & caused cavils between those that have laden & those that have let ships to hire in that manner. So that in my judgement the buying of ships to follow that service is the best & most profitable course that can be taken therein.

And here[un]to I must add one thing more, that such as will adventure as aforesaid, must acquaint themselves with a fit man to be Master in such ship who understands the order of a fishing voyage. And such a man will not only procure good fishermen to go with him but will also acquaint you with every particular thing for the voyage and also guide & direct those people which shall be so sent with him for the time of fishing.

If after all this I should be demanded what places are fittest to be first peopled, I conceive that the harbours of *Trinity* & *Trepassey* are the two chiefest. For as *Trinity* harbour lies near the *Bay of Flowers* which the savages for times frequent, by which means an intercourse might be got with them: So *Trepassey* lies very advantageously for us in several [divers] respects, as has been shown. And the bottom of these two bays meet together, within a small distance. Not far from *Trepassey*, something to the northwards of 46 degrees & a half lies the harbour of *Renouse* which is a place easy to be defended there being at a low ebb not *18.* foot water firm sand, yet in danger to be spoiled by the stones & ballast which our men throw in the same. There is a great store of good champion {land-21/}.

References and Notes

Dates

All dates are according to (old style) Julian calendar used in England until 17xx, excepting year is assumed to have commenced 1st January, not 25th March. To equate to modern Gregorian calendar, add ten days.

Abbreviations

APC.	Acts of the Privy Council.
BL.	British Library.
CSP	Calendar of State Papers.
CDNB	Canadian Diction of National Biography.
Cell.	Gillian Cell. Editor *Newfoundland Discovered*. Hakuyt Society. 1981.
DCRS	Devon & Cornwall Record Society.
DNB.	Dictionary of National Biography.
DRO.	Devon Record Office.
Enc. Brit.	Encyclopaedia Britannica.
PRO	Public Records Office.
TDA	Transactions of the Devonshire Association
WCSL	West Country Studies Library.

Prime Source Manuscripts

m1 Mar:? 1616/17.
Account of my goods taken by pirates from my   PRO.SP/14/90
Flyboat, the *Seraphine* and damage sustained thereby.

m2 c. Summer 1619.
Draft of Richard Whitborne's Preface and Discourse: BL Addit 22564
in his handwriting.

m3 c. Xmas 1619
Memorial to king James I summarising the Discourse.   Harrow School
Photocopy not available. Transcription by B. Lascelles:
Archives.
In Eng: Hist: Revie: Jan 1903.

m4 c. Xmas 1619.
Letter to Sir George Carew, Governor of Guernsey, etc,
with abstracts of some material points in my Discourse   Lambeth Pal:
of Newfoundland presented to the King. Signed twice.   Lib: Mss.454.

m5 24 Dec: 1622.
Letter to Lord Falkland, Lord Lieutenant of Ireland: BL. Sloane
from London. Signed Ric Whitborne Reproduced:.   MS 3827.ff.15
in Cell; pp 220-221.

m6 27 Feb: 1625/6
Letter to Lord Falkland. Written from Exmouth; not   BL. Sloane
RW handwriting.:Signed Ric Whitbourne Reproduced   MS 3827.ff.67
in Cell pp 237-241

m7 10 Nov: 1626
Letter of Petition to Duke of Buckingham London: PRO CO
signed Ric. 1/4.16 Whitbourne. Also Certificate to   No 16&: 16.1
king by 8 notables

m8 11 Oct: 1627
Letter to Hugh Peachey from aboard the *Boanventure*:   PRO: S.P.16/8
signed Ric Whitbourne.

m9 22 Sep: 1597
Will of John Whidborne, father of (Sir) Richard   PRO: PCC. WILLS.
Whitbourne.   PROB. 11/90

Chapter Notes and References
Chapter 1. Fair Child.

1. DNB.1900. Whitbourne, Sir Richard. In the 'on-line' edition of 2004, this has been corrected – at last.
2. 'The Worthies of Devon', John Prince , 1810 and T Risdon 'Survey of the County of Devon ' 1811 were published by Rees & Curtin of Plymouth. Both contain the story that is quoted.
3. Memorials of Exmouth.' Rev William Everett, 1885. page 106.
4. Statutes & Constitutional Documents, 1558-1625. Ed: G. W. Prothero, 1913. pp: 185,186.
5. Notes by John Reid, of Teignmouth Museum. Jan: 1989.
6. DRO. 57/11/11.Bishopsteignton. c.1675. An indenture: Mortgage. Richard. Whitbourne. (Will dated 1677). Gives details of Coombe acreages.
7. 'The English Yeoman.' Mildred Campbell, 1942. p 200,201.
8. Wicked Monk of Lidwell. For comprehensive account, see 'Dawlish.Its ancient history.' Rev. R Cornelius, 1954. (booklet). The legend seems to be based on a true incident in 1329. The chapel ruins endure on the farm possessed for over 200 years by Whidborne family, being sold after World War 2.
9. 'Devon's Bee Keeping Past.' Robert Ogden in Devon Historian, Oct: 1994.

Chapter 2. Learning a Trade

1. 'Synopis Chronographical of Devonshire. 1598.' John Hooker. TDA. Vol47. 1915.
2. 'A View of Devonshire in 1630.' Thomas Westcote. 1811. pp: 55,56
'Bread for the Poor' Adam Moore, 1663 p.17
3. Elizabeth. Cap XX.11. (1559)
4. Two valuable works consulted:
'The Evolution of the Fishing Village.' Ha ld Fox. 2001. [Late medieval times, S Devon coast.]
'Local Markets & Regional Trade in Medieval Exeter.' M. Kowalski. 1993.
5. This, and much of the rest of the chapter is based on an unpublished thesis by J.L. Wiggs (Mrs Joan Thomas) 'The sea-borne trade of Southampton in the second half of the 16th century.' Southampton University, 1955.
6. Southampton Court Leet Records.' Ed: Hearnshaw. Southampton Records Society: at least sixteen instances of John Crooke, in his later life, up before the Court on various misdemeanours charges.
7. Cell page 111.
8. Cell page 112. (1623 edition)

Other works consulted included:
'The Art of Navigation in England in Elizabethan & early Stuart times.' D.W. Waters, 1978.
A number of other publications by the Southampton Record Society concerned with our period.

Chapter 3. Beginnings of Empire

1. 'Train' oil, variously spelt, was obtained by boiling the blubber of whales or seals, or from the liver of fish, notably cod. Used to make soap, in oil lamps, etc, in 15/16th century. The word train probably comes from Dutch meaning 'drop' or 'leak' for rendered oil.

2. Version abstracted from: 'Principal Navigations by Richard Hakluyt.' Hakluyt Society. Extra Vol. VI. 1903–05.

Works consulted include:
'Hakluyt's Voyages – A selection by Richard David.' 1981. (for Edward Hayes' Report.)
'The Voyages and Colonizing Enterprises of Sir Humphrey Gilbert.' D B Quinn. 1948.
'The Life of Sir Humphrey Gilbert.' W G Gosling. 1911.

Chapter 4. Rumblings of War

1. see: 'The Defeat of John Hawkins.' Rayner Unwin 1960. A very full account of his third Slaving Voyage.
2. PRO. SP/2/179 of 20 June 1585.
3. Dictionary of Canadian Biography, under DRAKE, SIR BERNARD. Compiled by David B Quinn with full references.
4. Although probably not buried there, Musbury's St Michael's Church has a fine monument to three generations of Drakes and their wives. All kneeing, Sir Bernard is the central figure. This is illustrated in 'The Book of the Axe', G P R Pulman, 1875, pp; 745, 746 & full text on p. 734.n. Pulman says Sir Bernard was buried in Musbury church: if so he would have been re-interred.
5. 'Sir Francis Drake's West Indian Voyage 1585-86.' Hakluyt Society, 1981. Ed: M F Keeler.

Chapter 5. Against the Spanish Armada

1. APC. Vol:16. New Series. 1 April 1588.
2. 'State Papers relating to the defeat of the Spanish Armada: Anno 1588.' Ed: J K Laughton. 1895. Vol II. Page 323 on.
3. 'Maritime Trade of Exeter in Mediaeval Times.' H M Whitley. TDA.1912. pp 544-546. Appendix No 3.
   K.R. Customs. Exon Port. 1588.
4. Laughton: Vol I: p.126. Letter Drake to Council dated 30 March 1588.
5. 'The Armada Lord Lieutenant:' John Roberts. TDA 1970. From 1586, for nearly forty years, William Bourchier, Earl of Bath, was Lord Lieutenant of Devon. He seems to have been very ineffectual and there are few records of any details of his tenure in high office.

Chapter 6. Crossing the Pond

1. For details of the great quantity of stores required for long sea voyages, see:
   (a) RW's list for a 100 tonner, for Newfoundland voyage: Cell pp: 173-175.
   (b) John Scantlebury's 'The Success: A Postscript, Journal R.I. Cornwall. 1997. List of stores, etc, loaded for 60 tonner's maiden voyage to Naples.
2. 'Early-Stuart Mariners and Shipping, 1619-35.' Ed: and introduction by Todd Gray. 1990. Full details, all maritime surveys of the period for Devon & Cornwall.
3. 'The Maritime History of Devon., M. Oppenheim,1968. page 59.
4. 'John Rashleigh & the building of his New Carvell, the Success.' J Scantlebury. Journal R.I.Cornwall, 1996.
5. Cell: pp. 130,131.
6. Cell: p 131. 25th March equivalent to April 4th, modern calendar.

7. Cell: pp: 191,192. This is in 'A Conclusion to the former Discourse',.1623 edition.

Other works consulted included:
'The Great Explorer – The European Discovery of America.' S E Morison. 1986.
'The Three-masted Ship and Atlantic Voyages' Ian Friel, in 'Raleigh in Exeter.' Ed: Joyce Youings, 1985.
'Ships and Navigation in Atlantic Canada in the 16th Century.' Peter Pope. (see web-site: www.matthew.co.uk.)

Chapter 7. Bountiful Sea

1. 'A Briefe Discourse of the New-Found-Land.' John Mason. 1620. Re-printed in Cell. This quotation in Cell p. 94.
2. 'A History of Newfoundland.' D W Prowse, 1895. Parkhurst, quoted on page 60, writes in a letter to Haklyut, dated 13th November 1578.
3. Cell p 185. Richard wrote that it was only the prospect of exceptional profits that induced the French to spend many bitter winter months cooped up in a cold ship at sea, short of wood to burn , food and water.
4. 'The Journal of James Yonge 1647-1721.' Ed: F N L Poynter, 1963. Abstracted from pp: 56-58.

Other works consulted: 'The Cod Fisheries.' Harold Innes, 1954.
Three books by Mark Kurlansky, (1) 'Cod', 1997 (2) The Basque History of the World', 2000 &
(3) 'Salt', 2002. Only small parts of these interesting books are relevant.
'English Enterprise in Newfoundland.' Gillian Cell, 1969.

Chapter 8. The Years Between

1. Letter from Christine Thorn, Teighmouth & Shaldon Museum & Historial Society, dated 5 November 2003.
2. 'The West Country Merchants in Newfoundland.' Lecture to Newfoundland Historic Society, 10 dec: 1968
3. Same Reference as Note 5 of Chapter 1.
4. '120. Letters testimonial for Mariners' J. F. Chanter, in Devon & Cornwall Notes & Queries, 1924, p:113.
5. Cell pp: 156,157.
6. TDA. 109. pp73-116. 1977: 'Epidemics in Devon, 1538-1837.' Neville C. Oswald. (very comprehensive.)
7. Cell. p.116.
8. 'The Spanish Armada.' Colin Martin & Geoffrey Parker. 1988. p.253.
9. The Journal of James Yonge 1647-1721.' Ed: F N L Poynter, 1963. pp. 58,59.

Chapter 9. Peter Easton. Arch-Pirate

1. 'Purchas, His Pilgrims.' 1625. Vol iv. P.1882.
2. Cell. p113.
   Other than those concerning Richard, references to specific sources are too numerous to include here, but those consulted included:
   CSP. Ireland 1606-1608 ; CSP Ireland 1608–1610; CSP Ireland 1611-1614; Including the Introductions.

CSP Venetian. 1619-1621; CSP Venetian 1622-1613. Including Introductions.
'A Nation of Pirates.' Clive Senior, 1976.
Two articles in unrecorded issues of Newfoundland Quarterly by John S
Mitchell. 1) 'A letter about Peter Easton.' 2) 'Peter Easton's Pardons. A
Clarification.'

Chapter 10. First Court of Admiralty

1. The earliest known text of the Laws of Oleron, in 14th century handwriting, is
   contained in the 'Liber Memorandum' of the Corporation of the City of London
   and titled 'La Charte d'Olerrun des Juggements de la Mier.' These laws have
   much in common with the 'Wisby' sea laws of the North Sea and Baltic as well as
   the 'Rhodian' and 'Consulate' laws.
2. Deodands: Lit: A thing given by God. Legal; Chattel of dead person forfeited to
   the Crown.
3. The first part of this chapter was written in 1988, using the Encyclopaedia
   Britannica for underlying detail. This has now been replaced by the New
   Encyclopaedia Britannica. Not only is the page numbering different, but so is the
   content..
4. A History of Newfoundland.' D. W. Prowse, 1895. p.99.n2.
5. Cell pp. 158-161, 218. & pp 239-240.
6. See; Agenda Paper 1962-47 of the Historic Sites and Monuments Board of
   Canada: 'First Court of the Admiralty, Trinity, Newfoundland.' This gives full
   details & arguments on Whitbourne's Court and its legal status, including Helen
   J Crumps' belittling comments on him.
7. CSP. Col: 1574-1660. Vol 1. No. 39 . Dec? 1618. (No.40. Company's reply.)
8. CSP. Col: 1/54.
9. APC. Col 1. 22-23.
10. Proceedings & Debates of Parliament re: North America. L F Stock. P25, etc.

Chapter 11. Greatly Wronged by Pirates

1. 'Of the Beginnings, Practices, & Suppression of Pirates.' Sir Henry Mainwaring.
   1618.
2. Ibid.
3. Cell. pp.113, 114.
4. Cell. p.114n.
5. Cal: CSP. Dom: 1611–1618. p.455. S/P. 14/90/155.
6. CSP DOM.Dom.Add, 1625–1649, p.217.
7. Cell. p.238.

Chapter 12. Full Powers to Govern

1. 'Dictionary of Canadian Biography.' Under 'Vaughan, Sir William.' By Gillian
   Cell.
2. Cell, p.115.
3. Cell, p.135.
4. Cell, pp. 209, 210. Also see Cell pp151-153.
5. Cell, p.135.

Chapter 13. The English Nunnery at Lisbon.

1. The Story of the English Bridgettines of Syon Abbey.' John Rory Fletcher.1933. [Short and readable, but now hard to come by. This little known story needs retelling, but is far too long for more than the briefest of summaries here.]
2. 'The Anatomy of the English Nunnery at Lisbon in Portugall.' Thomas Robinson, London 1622. Published by Authority. [Robinson pulls no punches.]
3. The pictures were reproduced in an exclusive book published in 1993 by and for the Roxburge Club. Called 'Syon Abbey. The Library of the Briggettine Nuns and heir Peregrinations after the Reformation', it consisted of an essay by Christopher de Hamel and the manuscript that was to have accompanied the paintings. Only 200 copies of this book were printed.
4. The play ('that perfect piece of literary political art.') was reproduced, with its related history, and analysed in scholarly detail in a recent (1997) book, 'A Game at Chess' edited by T H Howard-Hill. Middleton draws on three main sources for his historical detail; one is Robinson's 'Anatomy.'
5. *ibid.* Appendix 1. No; '7. John Hollis, Lord Haughton to the Earl of Somerset, Wednesday 11 August 1624.'
6. *ibid.* Appendix 1. No: '30. Inscribed in copy of Second Quarto, 1625.'

Chapter 14. Discourse and Discovery

1. See preamble to [m4,] Letter to Lord Carew; ' right Honorble, Most Humblie showeth an Abstract of some material points that are in my discovery of New-land which was presented to his Majesty at Hyntingdon the 17th day of October 1619 . . .'
2. '1603', Christopher Lee, 2003. Page 138.
3. 'A History of the English Speaking People.' Winston Churchill,1956. Vol II. P. 136. (Actual date of audience not found).
4. Names of those to serve were: The Earl of Arundell, LordCarew, Lord Digbie, The Treasurer and the Controller of his Majesties Holusehold, Mr Secretary Naunton, Me Secretary Calvert, Master of the Wards.
5. APC.(Col). Vol I. :p.429. Star Chamber. (Note. The Star Chamber was used conveniently as a meeting place for the Privy Council, although normally kept for the 'Court of the Star Chamber.')
6. APC (Col). Vol 1. p575. Whitehall. Those present were: : Lord Chancellor, Lord Seale, Earl of Arundell, Lord Digbie, Mr Secretary Naunton, Mr Secretary Calvert, Master of the Rolles, Master of the Wards. Mr Comptroller.

Chapter 15. At the Sign of the Golden Cock.

1. Statutes & Constitutional Documents, 1558-1625. Ed: G. W. Prothero. p.188. Injunction: LI.
2. Ibid. pp. 169-172.
3. 'A Transcript of the Registers of the Company of Stationers 1554-1640.' Aber.Vol IV. p.40.
4. 'A Short Title Catalogue Of Books, 1475-1640' K F Pantzer, 1991. Vol III.
5. Cell pp:204-206. N.H. was probably a settler at Ferryland. [p3 l 23]
6. Web-site is: www.mun.co/rels/hollmann/relsoc/texts/whitbourne [p4 l 6]

Other Works consulted include:
'Stationers Company.' Cyprian Blayden, 1960.
'Printing in London.' P. M. Handover, 1960.

'A History of Printing in Britain.' Colin Claio, 1965.
'A Dictionary of the Booksellers and Printers. 1641–1667. Henry Plomer, 1907. p.109.
Enclopeadia Britannica. Article under 'Publishing.'

Chapter 16. A Brief for Richard

1. Cell. p.101. Also: PRO.P.C. 2/30. PC213; pp.578.
2. Cell: pp. 104,105.
3. Cell: pp.103,104.
4. Cell: pp102,103.
5. TDA. Vol.27. 1895: Article: ' Devonshire Briefs,' T. N. Brushfield. Page 675: 'The estimated damage, according to the heading of the Brief, was £11,000; but Dr. Lake states it was computed at £11,030 6s. 10d., and this amount was raised.'
   'Exmouth & Neighbourhood.' (Edward Edwards), (1868).S.Drayton & Sons. pp322-324.

Other works consulted: 'Church Briefs.' 1896. W. A. Brewes.
'West Country Harbour – Teignmouth 1690-1975.' 1976. Prof: Harold Trump.

Chapter 17. Of Wolves, Water Dogs, Flies & Flightless.

1. Cell. p.193.
2. 'The Newfoundland Wolf.' John E Maunder. (Newfounfland Museum Notes No.8)
3. In Portuguese: 'caes de Aqua.' By the 1960s, their numbers were down to thirty. Since then a breeding programme at the nature park of Ria Formosa, Algarve, has ensured the breed's survival.
4. Cell. pp.192, 193
5. The Journal of James Yonge 1647–1721.' Ed: F N L Poynter, 1963. p. 60.
6. 'Haklyut's Voyages.' Richard David. 1981. p.270.
7. Cell. p.122.

Chapter 18. Something of a Strange Creature

1. I have fond nothing on Hawkridge's background or beginnings. He may have been apprenticed to Richard in 1610. Later he was a persistent explorer for the Northwest Passage – in 1612, 1615 & 1616, 1619 & 1625, when he captained the expedition. A Skilled navigator, he was later held captive by Algerian pirates.
2. Cell pp. 194, 195.
3. 'The Mermaid & Mitre Taverns in Old London.' Ken Rogers, 1928.
4. 'Purchas, his Pilgims.' Vol 3. London 1627. Hudson's log pp: 567-603.
5. Cell. p.35, 36.
6. Maritime Monthly (Newfoundland), November 1874. Article: 'A trio of Forgotten Worthies.'
7. 'Mermaids and Mastodons. ' Richard Carrington, 1957.
8. 'A Short History of Nearly Everything.' Bill Bryson, 2003.

Other works consulted include:
'Sea Enchantress.' Gwen Benwell & Authur Waugh, 1961.
Sea of Slaughter.' Farley Mowat, 1984.

Chapter 19. An Ingenious & Tractable People

1. The pre-history opening of the chapter is derived from the well-produced and informative web-site 'www.heritage.bf.ca/aboriginal/. Other sections of the same site deal comprehensively with the whole spectrum of the Province's heritage. There are twenty-five well-illustrated pages devoted to the Beothuk people alone.
2. Cell.p.117.
3. Cell.p.
4. Cell.p.118.
5. Cell.p.137
6. The standard authority for the Beothuk people is: 'A History and Ethnology of the Beothuks.' Ingeborg Marshall, 1996.
7. Cell.p.198
8. Cell.p.154.
9. Cell.p.154.
10. Cell.p.153
11. I have difficulty with Richard's statement that the natives went naked all the year round. Marshall suggests that 'naked' did not mean 'stark naked' in his day so much as scantily dressed, perhaps with only a loin cloth. When Fernado De Magallanes (Magellan) reached Tierra del Fuego on his way round the world in 1520, he found the natives walking around naked in latitude 54^0 S.
12. Cell. p.192. See Chapter 1 regarding 'signing' of sheep.
13. Cell. p.194.
14. Cell. p.162.
15. Cell. p.125.
16. Cell. pp .118, 119
    [Two rogue numbers to be eliminated [6] on p.3 l 46 & 7 p3, l 48]

Chapter 20. Planting and Withering

1. Second Series, No 160. Still available from the Hakluyt Society.
2. Ref: Draft Discourse· [m2] pages 197-198.
3. Ref: Draft Discourse [m2] pages 189-190.
4. Cell. p.134.
5. See DNB. Under 'CALVERT, George.' The French ambassador was Tilliçre. [ACCENT – grave]
6. Cell. p. 198.
7. Royal Charter for Avalon. PRO. C.O. 1/2 , 23. 1623.

Chapter 21. Home is the Sailor

1. P.R.O. CO 1/4.16.1. 'This is a true copy of one sent earlier to H. jM. Jamaes I.' (Cal.S.P. 1574-1660) The signatories were: Edward Seymour Bt: Edward Gyles Kt: John Drake Esq: Francis Fulford Kt: Edward Prideaux Bt:. Robert Duke Esq: George Chudleigh Bt: Arthur Maynwaringe Kt: Tho: Vaughan Esq:
2. This voyage is well covered by letters to and from *Bonaventure*, recorded in PRO. S.P 16/80/.
3. DRO. Littleham Manorial Documents.346/M268-2693. There is no reason to doubt the claim made by Elizabeth Whitrow after Richard's death.
4. As for 3. I have not found any record of Richard's Littleham properties. He would need storerooms for cargos and all manner of spares for his ships. As a farmer's son, it would be natural for him to keep a horse or two for when he wished to ride to Exeter , London, etc.

5. 'Early-Stuart Mariners and Shipping. 1619–35', Ed: Todd Gray.
6. See British Record Society CC Wills – xii 193/242.-afministrations 1649–1654. '
   <u>Folio 134</u>. 'Whitebourne Richard [batchelor] died beyond the seas c.1649 – no place – administration granted to Edward Drake.
   Folio 56 – Richard Whitebourne [Batchelor] died beyond the seas.– administation granted to Bishopsteignton c.1650.'
   See also PRO. PROB. 6/24. PCC.Folio 51. Dated 1651. Entry in latin, faulty, unreadable.
   Folio 134? Richard Whitbourne? Esquire. 1650. Latin, not understood.
7. P.R.O. SP 16/31,71. Addressed 'To my Worthy Friend Edward Nicholas Esquire Secretary to my Lord Dukes grace these.
8. DRO Manorial documents 346M/M268-269, Littleham, 1 September 1635.

Index